BASIC ENGINEERING
PROCESSES

THE TECHNICAL COLLEGE SERIES

General Editor

E. G. Sterland, J.P., M.A., B.SC.(ENG.), C.ENG., F.I.MECH.E., F.R.AE.S.
Principal, Rolls-Royce Technical College, Bristol

INTRODUCTION TO WORKSHOP TECHNOLOGY
M. H. A. Kempster
C.ENG., M.I.MECH.E., A.F.R.AE.S., M.I.PROD.E.

CERTIFICATE MATHEMATICS, Vol. 1
N. Abbott
B.SC.(TECH.), A.F.I.M.A.

APPLIED MECHANICS
CERTIFICATE MECHANICAL ENGINEERING SCIENCE
J. D. Walker
B.SC.(ENG.), C.ENG., F.I.MECH.E.

BASIC
ENGINEERING
PROCESSES

S. CRAWFORD
C.Eng., M.I.Prod.E.

Manager, Training Workshop,
Rolls-Royce Technical College, Bristol

THE ENGLISH UNIVERSITIES PRESS LTD

ISBN 0 340 06331 9 (boards edition)
ISBN 0 340 06336 X (paperback edition)

First printed 1964
Reprinted 1965, 1969
Second edition 1972

The English Universities Press Ltd
St Paul's House   Warwick Lane   London EC4P 4AH

Printed in Great Britain by
Elliott Bros and Yeoman Ltd, Speke, Liverpool

GENERAL EDITOR'S FOREWORD

THE Technical College Series covers a wide range of technician and craft courses, and includes books designed to cover subjects in National Certificate and Diploma courses and City and Guilds Technician and Craft syllabuses. This important sector of technical education has been the subject of very considerable changes over the past few years. The more recent of these have been the result of the establishment of the Training Boards, under the Industrial Training Act. Although the Boards have no direct responsibility for education, their activities in ensuring proper training in industry have had a marked influence on the complementary courses which Technical Colleges must provide. For example, the introduction of the module system of training for craftsmen by the Engineering Industry Training Board led directly to the City and Guilds 500 series of courses.

The Haslegrave Committee on Technician Courses and Examinations reported late in 1969, and made recommendations for far-reaching administrative changes, which will undoubtedly eventually result in new syllabuses and examination requirements.

It should, perhaps, be emphasised that these changes are being made not for their own sake, but to meet the needs of industry and the young men and women who are seeking to equip themselves for a career in industry. And industry and technology are changing at an unprecedented rate, so that technical education must be more concerned with fundamental principles than with techniques.

Many of the books in the Technical College Series are now standard works, having stood the test of time over a long period of years. Such books are reviewed from time to time and new editions published to keep them up to date, both in respect of new technological developments and changing examination requirements. For instance, these books have had to be rewritten in the metric system, using SI units. To keep pace with the rapid changes taking place both in courses and in technology, new works are constantly being added to the list. The Publishers are fully aware of the part that well-written up-to-date textbooks can play in supplementing teaching, and it is their intentions that the Technical College Series shall continue to make a substantial contribution to the development of technical education.

E. G. STERLAND

v

PREFACE

THE increasing demands for more and better trained technologists, technicians, and craftsmen has created a problem of national importance which is reflected in the emphasis now being placed on the need for the integration of theoretical and practical training.

The Industrial Training Act is aimed at increasing the quality and quantity of training in British Industry. In the engineering industry, advances in this respect are most likely to come from improved basic training facilities, provided by Firms, Local Education Authorities, in Government Training Centres, and by the Boards to be set up under the Act. This book will provide a thorough background of information for students undergoing such training.

Having had first-hand experience of the problems associated with the training of young engineers, the author of *Basic Engineering Processes* is firmly convinced that a sound general knowledge of such processes is the most adequate foundation upon which the subsequent specialised engineering career can be built.

The aim of this book, therefore, is to help the mechanical engineering apprentice or student to acquire such essential background knowledge of the basic processes, and to provide a text-book which will supplement his practical training, stimulate added interest and increase understanding of that practice.

Under the guidance of the technical college lecturer or workshop instructor this book should prove useful as a text-book for students working for the following examinations:—

City and Guilds of London Institute:—

Engineering Craft Studies Course;

Mechanical Engineering Technicians' Course;

and also for the National Certificates in Mechanical Engineering.

The author acknowledges with gratitude the help he has received from the engineering firms mentioned below who have supplied information and drawings—

The Birmingham Aluminium Casting Co. Ltd.

The British Oxygen Co. Ltd.

The British Standards Institution

The Butler Machine Tool Co. Ltd.

The Churchill Machine Tool Co. Ltd.

Clarkson Engineers Ltd.

The L. S. Starrett Co.

Finally the author records his grateful thanks to his many colleagues at the Rolls-Royce Technical College for their generous assistance, advice, and encouragement.

S. CRAWFORD

CONTENTS

Abrasive wheels:—structure, grain, bond, specification, factors affecting choice of wheel. Regulations. Basic operations:—movements of wheel and work. Plain external, universal. Mounting wheels, balancing, truing and dressing, loading, glazing. Internal machine. Centreless machine:—methods of feeding, advantages, work blades. Surface grinders:—horizontal spindle with reciprocating table, horizontal spindle with rotating table, vertical spindle machine.

Details of construction, clapper box function and setting. Quick return mechanism, stroke adjustment, cutting speed. Work holding. Tools and tool holding.

Types of machines:—Pillar, turret, radial, sensitive. Drill types:—straight shank, taper shank. Standard twist drill. Drill sockets, sleeves, drill removal. Core drills, centre drills. Reamers:—machine, hand.

Basic stages in sand casting. Pattern making. Sand moulds:—open, closed, green, dry. Types of moulding sand:—facing, parting, moulding. Two part mould (solid casting):—pattern, turnover board, drag, cope, vents, feed gate, pouring metal, gates and risers. Two part mould (hollow casting):—split pattern, loose piece, sand core. Casting defects.

Basic methods. Gravity process:—dies, advantages, collapsible cores, Pressure die casting:—hot chamber, cold chamber, advantages and disadvantages, die material, venting.

Principle of process, flask moulding, manufacture of die, wax pattern, runner, investment, mould, wax removal, casting, fettling, inspection. Investment shell moulding.

Definition. "Grain-flow". Effects of forging. Examples of grain-flow. Methods of forging:—Hand forging, drop forging, machine forging. Hand forging equipment:—forge, anvil, vice, swage block. Tools:—hammers, tongs, cold sets, hardies, hot sets, gouge, fullers, flatter. Operations:—Upsetting, drawing down, setting down, bending, punching and drifting, hot cutting, welding.

Elements of measurement. Standards:—yard, metre. End standards of length. Micrometer calliper. Inside micrometer. Micrometer depth gauge. Vernier scales:—vernier calliper, height gauge, depth gauge, bevel protractor. Dial indicators. Gauge blocks. Sine bar. Limits and fits:—definition, classes of fit. B.S. 4500. Limit gauges:—design, fixed gauges, adjustable gauges. Screw thread measurement:—thread elements, screw thread limit gauges, adjustable screw thread gauges.

HAND FORMING PROCESSES

The twentieth century, with its ever-increasing emphasis on mechanisation, automation, and specialisation, can be truly defined as the machine age. In the engineering industry, as in many other industries, increased efforts are being made towards the elimination of hand labour and the use of hand-operated tools.

Despite this, however, it is equally true that hand tools are still essential in many branches of engineering, and all young people who aspire to become mechanical or production engineers are still advised to gain knowledge and experience in the correct and skilful manipulation of the main types of hand tools.

Those who accept this advice will soon discover that to become proficient in this sphere is a much more demanding task than merely operating a machine tool, and secondly, that there is no real substitute for practical experience.

The first three chapters of this volume on Hand Forming Processes deal briefly with Basic Bench Fitting, Sheet Metal, and Metal Joining, but the reader must appreciate that the type of work included under each of these sub-headings might vary from one workshop to another, depending on the type of products being manufactured and whether the factory is laid out for small batches or for mass production. Many of the basic principles will apply to all types of production.

1

CHAPTER ONE

BASIC BENCH FITTING

The work of the bench fitter is carried out at his bench with the aid of hand-operated tools and a small bench or pillar-type drilling machine. His work might include the making of individual parts from plate or bar material by the removal of metal, marking-out, drilling, tapping, and assembly, for example making special tools, templates, gauges, jigs and fixtures. Alternatively the fitter may be primarily engaged in the adjustment and assembly of details manufactured in the machine shop.

The tools most commonly used by the bench fitter can be broadly divided into two main groups:—

(i) Tools used for the removal of metal: these cutting tools would include files, hacksaws, hammer and chisel, scrapers, reamers, dies, and taps.

(ii) Tools used for checking and measuring the accuracy of the parts: steel rules, callipers, try-square, protractor, micrometer, straight-edge, and surface plate.

In addition to the equipment mentioned in (i) and (ii) the fittter needs his bench and vice.

The Fitter's Bench

A typical fitter's bench is shown in Fig. 1. It must be of rigid construction, the legs made from at least 100×100 mm timber and adequately supported by bracing cross members. The top is made of heavy hardwood of not less than 65–75 mm thick, covered with thin gauge galvanised-steel sheet, and this is folded over the front edge for about 65 mm to minimise wear. The standard height is 800 mm, and width 760 mm, the length varying depending on the number of vices to be mounted. The maximum span between the main supports should not exceed 1500 mm.

The bench should be positioned so that the maximum benefit can be derived from natural light, although artificial lighting is usually provided. A shelf or rack at the back will provide storage space for small tools; a drawer is also provided for the fitter's personal tools.

Fig. 2 shows an all-metal portable vice bench consisting of a malleable iron table supported by three tubular wrought-iron legs carried on a malleable iron base plate.

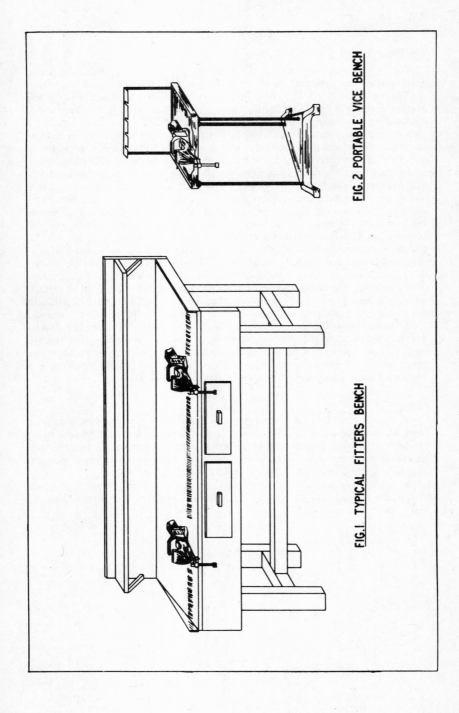

FIG.1 TYPICAL FITTERS BENCH

FIG.2 PORTABLE VICE BENCH

The Fitter's Vice (Quick-grip type)

Fig. 3 shows a section through a parallel jaw type vice fitted with the quick-release mechanism, one of the best types for general engineering work.

The body or fixed half is a hollow saddle-shaped casting. The upper portion forms the fixed jaw, while three lugs protruding from the base carry the holding-down bolts which pass through the bench top and are secured by nuts on the lower side. The sliding jaw is a hollow inverted channel-section casting which slides into the body, and is shaped to form a jaw at its outer end, this section corresponding to the fixed jaw on the body. The main screw of buttress-thread form is located in the sliding jaw and engages with a half-nut housed in the body of the vice. The plain portion of the main screw has a collar which locates against the sliding jaw, a retaining plate holds the screw in position, and also carries a 'trigger' which controls the movement of the half-nut. The half-nut has a tongue which projects downwards, and the rocking bar attached to the trigger engages in a slot in the tongue. When the trigger is pressed in towards the main screw the rocking bar turns and dis-engages the half-nut from the main screw. The sliding jaw may then be pushed in or pulled out to give the required gap necessary to hold a particular piece of work. When the trigger is released the spring returns the half-nut to engage with the screw. The vice is then tightened to the required pressure by operating the handle; the latter should be tightened by hand and not with a hammer.

Whenever possible the work should be held in the centre of the jaw-plates. The quick-operating mechanism can only be used when there is no pressure on the screw. The body and sliding jaw are usually made of cast iron, the other parts of steel. Vices built to withstand the most arduous conditions have a body and sliding jaw of high-tensile malleable iron or steel.

Jaw-Plates

Standard jaw-plates in both body and sliding jaw are made or hardened steel, and the contact face is serrated to give additional grip. To prevent these serrations marking and damaging the work, a pair of simple jaw-pieces made from soft sheet material can be fitted over the jaw-plates. Fibre jaw-pieces can also be obtained to fit over the standard jaws.

Special jaw-plates or shaped clamps are used for holding work which is unsuitably shaped for gripping with standard jaw-plates, e.g. threaded parts, tubes, etc.

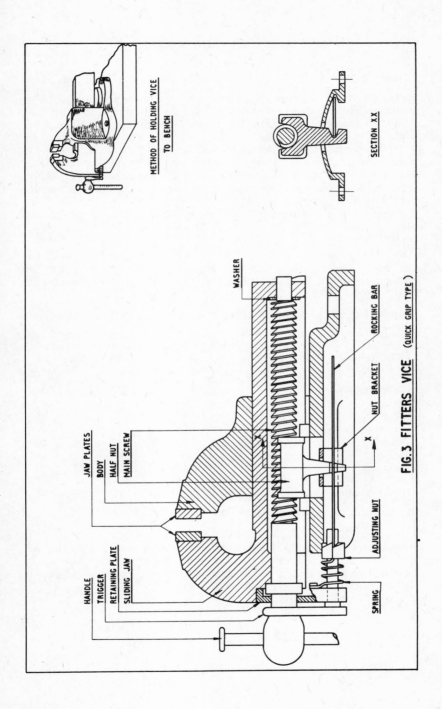

METHOD OF HOLDING VICE TO BENCH

SECTION XX

WASHER

ROCKING BAR

JAW PLATES
BODY
HALF NUT
MAIN SCREW

HANDLE
TRIGGER
RETAINING PLATE
SLIDING JAW

NUT BRACKET

ADJUSTING NUT

SPRING

x

FIG.3 FITTERS VICE (QUICK GRIP TYPE)

The File

The file is the cutting tool which the fitter uses most frequently, but he requires much practice if he wishes to become really proficient in its use.

Fig. 4 shows the main parts of a file and includes body, shoulder, point, tang.

Files are made from high-carbon steel, and after the teeth are cut it is hardened and tempered, leaving the cutting portion brittle. The tang which fits into a wooden handle is softer than the body. Files are graded or classified according to their length, type, spacing of the teeth, and the shape of the cross-section.

Lengths of file vary from 100–500 mm, but those in general use are from 100–300 mm.

Teeth are classified in two ways:—

(a) The cut or spacing, which is defined as the number of teeth per 25 mm and this will govern the coarseness or fineness of cutting. The standard grades are: Rough, Bastard, Second Cut, Smooth, and Dead Smooth. See Figs. 5 and 6.

The pitch $\left[\dfrac{25}{\text{spacing}}\right]$ varies with the length of the file, e.g. the pitch of a 300 mm second-cut file is not the same as the pitch of a 150 mm second cut; the shorter the file the finer the pitch. (The rough grade not specified in British Standards).

The following table will give approximate values for other grades:—

Length of File (mm)		100	150	200	250	300
Bastard	Cuts	40	32	26	24	21
Second Cut	per	42	38	32	28	26
Smooth		60	50	44	42	40
Dead Smooth	25 mm	88	84	80	76	72

(b) Single Cut or Double Cut

Single cut files have teeth cut parallel to each other at an angle of about 45° to the file edge. Fig. 5. Double cut have an additional set of teeth cut across the first at an angle of 70–80° from the opposite edge. Fig. 6. Both types are used on general work but most flat sides are double cut.

MAIN PARTS OF A FILE

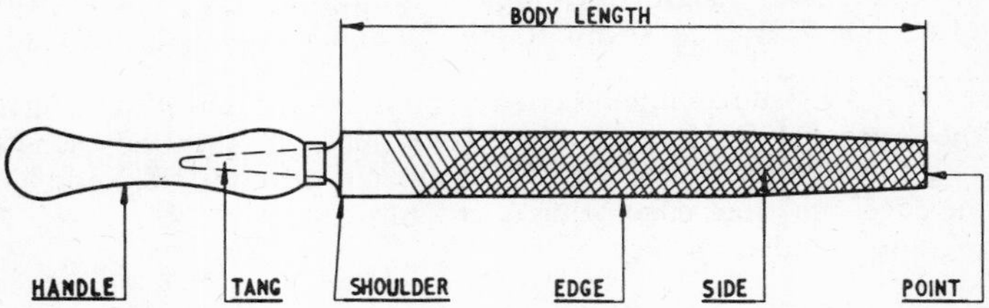

BODY LENGTH

HANDLE   TANG   SHOULDER   EDGE   SIDE   POINT

FIG 4

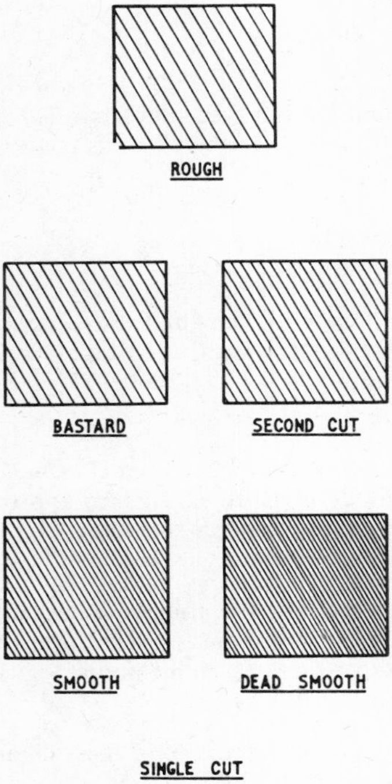

ROUGH   ROUGH

BASTARD   SECOND CUT   BASTARD   SECOND CUT

SMOOTH   DEAD SMOOTH   SMOOTH   DEAD SMOOTH

SINGLE CUT   DOUBLE CUT

FIG 5   ## FIG 6

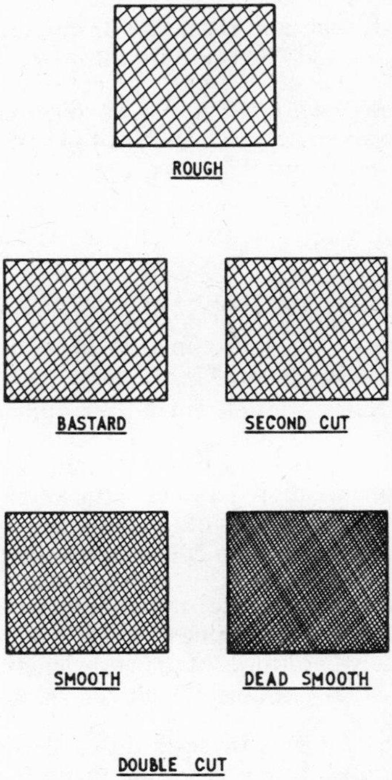

Cross-section and names of files   B.S. 498

Flat File   A file of rectangular cross-section, parallel for approximately two-thirds of the body length, then tapering towards the point in width and thickness. Fig. 7. Both sides are double cut and both edges single cut.

Hand File   A file of rectangular cross-section, parallel in width throughout, in thickness parallel for approximately two-thirds of the body length, then tapering towards the point. Fig. 8. Double cut on both sides and single cut on one edge, the other edge being uncut and known as 'Safe-edge'. Prevents cutting into an adjacent face.

Square File   A file of square cross-section, parallel for approimately two-thirds of the body length, then tapering towards the point. Fig. 9. Double cut on all sides.

Round File   A file of round cross-section, parallel for approximately two-thirds of the body length, then tapering towards the point. Fig. 10.
     Rough and Bastard under 150 mm—single cut.
     Rough and Bastard 150 mm and over—double cut.
     Second Cut and Smooth—single cut.

Half-round File   A file having one flat and one curved side, parallel for approximately two-thirds of the body length, then tapering towards the point in width and thickness. Fig. 11.
     Flat side—double cut in all grades.
     Curved side—Rough and Bastard—double cut.
                Second Cut and Smooth—single cut.

Three-square or Triangular File   A file of equilateral triangular cross-section, parallel for approximately two-thirds of the body length, then tapering towards the point. Fig. 12.
     Sides—double cut. Edges—uncut.

Warding File   A file of rectangular cross-section (similar to flat files but of thinner section) parallel in thickness throughout, in width parallel for approximately two-thirds of the body length, then tapering towards the point. Fig. 13.
     Sides—double cut. Edges—single cut.

Knife File   A file of uniform wedge cross-section, the thinner edge being straight and the thicker edge being parallel to the thinner edge for approximately two-thirds of the body length, then tapering towards the point. Fig. 14.
     Sides—double cut. Edges—single cut.

Special Files   In addition to the common types of engineer's files already described, other types are made for special applications:—
     Precision files, more accurately made than the standard types, used for precision tool making.
     Needle files or Swiss files, small fine-cut files of various cross-sections, used for instrument work and in the watch-making industry.

CROSS SECTION AND NAMES OF FILES

FIG 7   FLAT FILE

FIG 8   HAND FILE

FIG 9   SQUARE FILE

FIG 10   ROUND FILE

FIG 11   HALF ROUND FILE

FIG 12   THREE SQUARE FILE

FIG 13   WARDING FILE

FIG 14   KNIFE FILE

FIG 15   FILE CARD

Milled-Tooth Files Files made from a hard alloy steel, in two types, hand and half-round.

1. Standard Cut, nine teeth per 25 mm. Used when filing lead, white metal, and aluminium.
2. Fine Cut, thirteen teeth per 25 mm. Used for filing mild steel, copper, phosphor bronze, and brass.
3. Extra fine, seventeen teeth per 25 mm. Used for filing cast iron, stainless steel, and high carbon steel.
4. Superfine, thirty-four teeth per 25 mm. Used for producing fine finishes on hard materials.

1–3 can be obtained in 200, 250, 300, 350 and 400 mm lengths, 4 in lengths of 200 and 250 mm only.

Pinning

When filing soft metals there is a tendency for the file teeth to become clogged or pinned with small particles of metal. If these are not removed they will reduce the efficiency of cutting and also scratch the surface of the work.

These pins should be removed by means of a file card shown in Fig. 15 or by means of a strip of thin metal. Coating the file with chalk will help to minimise pinning when filing ductile metals.

File Handle

A tanged file should never be used unless it is fitted with a handle. This should be fixed firmly on the tang of the file and should have a ball end. Fig. 4.

Method of Holding File (Cross-Filing)

The method of holding the file is most important. The feet are placed apart with the left foot in advance of the right. The handle of the file is gripped with the right hand with the thumb on the top. The point of the file is gripped with the left hand, the ball of the thumb on top and fingers gripping underneath; this allows heavy weight to be applied to remove metal quickly. When a small amount of material has to be removed, lighter pressure is necessary and the fingers of the left hand are placed on top at the point end.

Little difficulty will be found in removing metal with the file as it is pushed across the work; no pressure is exerted on the return stroke. The difficult part of filing is to ensure that the file does not rock or seesaw over the work; the aim therefore is to keep the file as flat as possible when pushing it across the work. As the file is moved across it should also be moved sideways to obtain a shearing action, either from left to right, or from right to left as shown in Fig. 16. This method is referred to as cross-filing.

Draw-Filing   Fig. 17

To produce a fine finish on a narrow surface draw-filing is employed. The file is place across the work and is then pushed or pulled along the surface. A smooth flat file should be used for this purpose.

FILE MOVEMENTS

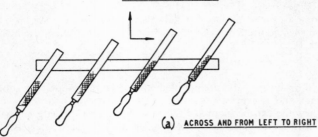

(a) ACROSS AND FROM LEFT TO RIGHT

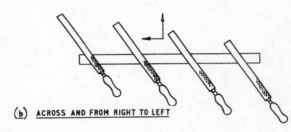

(b) ACROSS AND FROM RIGHT TO LEFT

FIG.16 CROSS FILING

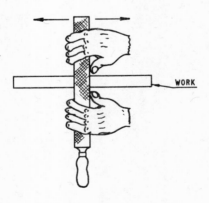

WORK

FIG.17 DRAW-FILING

Testing Filed Surface

When testing a narrow surface for flatness a straight-edge may be used. To test a large surface use a surface plate. To test for squareness use a solid try-square. See Fig. 52, p. 31.

Care of Files

Files should be always carefully handled, and when not in use they should be kept in a rack and not thrown together in a drawer or cupboard. The cutting life of a new file can be increased by using it first on soft materials, such as copper or brass, and when partly worn using it on harder materials.

The Hacksaw   B.S. 1919:1967

A hand hacksaw is used by the fitter for cutting off metal, and for making thin under-cuts or recesses prior to filing or chipping operations.

The frame can be either fixed or adjustable, the latter being the most useful, and accommodating blades of 250 and 300 mm lengths. At each end of the frame a square-section slide supports a small pin on which the blade is located. The wing nut at the front end is used for tensioning the blade. Fig. 18 illustrates a standard hacksaw with adjustable frame.

Fig. 20 shows a tubular frame adjustable hacksaw with the 'pistol-grip' type handle.

The blades are made of low tungsten steel, or of high-speed steel, approximately 0·6 mm thick and 13 mm wide, and in lengths of 250–300 mm. The blades are available in three conditions:—

(a) 'All hard'; hardened throughout and very rigid, which is an aid to accurate sawing.

(b) 'Flexible'; hardened on the teeth only, far less brittle than (a).

(c) 'Spring-back'; the blade hardened uniformly along the length of the toothed edge, the remainder of the blade being spring tempered.

The teeth are set, that is, alternately bent slightly outwards so that they make a cut slightly wider than blade thickness, thereby providing the necessary clearance.

Blades are available with 14, 18, 24, and 32 teeth per 25 mm and the pitch of the teeth is an important factor when selecting a blade for a particular application.

e.g.   14 teeth per 25 mm—suitable for large solid sections of soft material, e.g. mild steel, aluminium, brass, and copper.

18 teeth per 25 mm—most suitable for general use. Small solid sections of mild steel, aluminium, brass, and copper. Large solid sections of hard materials, e.g. alloy steel, heat-treated and stainless steel, heavy angles, and cast iron.

24 teeth per 25 mm—small solid sections of hard materials, e.g. alloy steel, heat-treated and stainless steels. Sections between 3 mm and 6 mm thick.

32 teeth per 25 mm—sections less than 3 mm, thin tubing, sheet, and light angles.

Tooth size selected must be such that at least three consecutive teeth will always be in contact with the material being cut.

Cutting Speed

Use a long steady stroke at the approximate rate of 50 strokes per minute for low tungsten steel blades, and 60 strokes per minute for high-speed steel blades.

Points to be observed when using a hacksaw

1. Fit the blade with the teeth pointing away from the handle.
2. Tension the blade by taking up the slack and applying three full turns only.
3. Secure the work rigidly, and hold it in such a position that the cutting can commence on a flat surface with as many teeth in contact as possible.
4. Start the cut carefully, either using the thumb as a guide, or by notching the work with a file.
5. Use the full length of the blade and saw at the correct speed.
6. When possible, hold the work in such a manner that the cut can be made in the vertical plane.

Tension Files   Fig. 19

The tension file is made from high-tensile steel wire with teeth cut around its circumference and extending over its length. The diamter at each end is increased to form ball-ended projections. Special clips are provided to fit the locating pins of the hacksaw frame; they are also drilled and slotted to suit the ball ends of the tension file.

Tension files are obtainable in lengths of 200, 230 and 250 mm and are used to cut out irregular shapes in thin-gauge materials. Thicker sections of material which have been chain drilled can be cut out with this versatile tool.

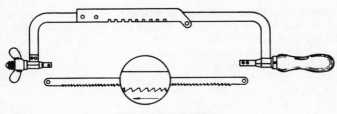

DIRECTION OF BLADE TEETH

FIG.18 HACKSAW (STANDARD ADJUSTABLE FRAME)

(a)   TENSION FILE

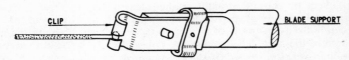

CLIP   BLADE SUPPORT

(b)   ATTACHMENT TO HACKSAW FRAME

FIG.19 TENSION FILE AND CLIPS

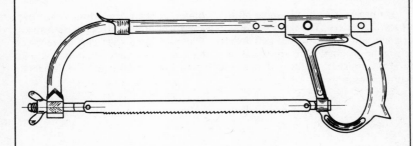

FIG. 20 HACKSAW (TUBULAR ADJUSTABLE FRAME WITH PISTOL GRIP)

Hand Hammers B.S. 876:1964

The bench fitter frequently uses different types of hand hammers for fitting operations requiring force, e.g. driving pins or shafts into their mating holes, driving pulleys, couplings, or collars on the mating shaft, peening over the end of rivets, striking other tools such as centre punches, chisels, or drifts.

The three types of hammer most generally used by the fitter are (a) Ball Pein, (b) Cross Pein, and (c) Straight Pein, shown in Fig. 21.

All three are of a standard shape at the striking face end but can be readily identified by the shape of the opposite end known as the pein and from this they derive their names.

All hammer heads should be manufactured from wrought steel (specification En. 9 in B.S. 970) in the form of a forging or stamping. The striking face and the pein should be hardened and tempered, but the centre section into which the handle fits is left soft. Particulars of form, nominal dimensions, and weights are also specified in the British Standard 876.

Ball pein hammers vary in weight from as light as 100 g up to 1·5 kg. The two other types mentioned range from 100 g up to 1 kg.

The handles must also be made to specified shape and size from well-seasoned, tough, and straight grained ash or hickory, free from knots or defects. These are shaped to fit the eye in the hammer head and must be securely fixed by means of a hardwood wedge, which should lie along the length of the head. The handles are waisted below the head to give a certain amount of spring and then thickened out to form a comfortable grip. The handle should be firmly held in the right hand by that portion called the 'grip'. See Fig. 22. An effective blow is impossible if the handle is held near to the head.

Soft Hammers Fig. 23

Hammers with heads made of lead, copper, rubber, or rawhide are known as soft hammers. The head is usually in the form of a cast tube with a recess at each end to locate the soft inserts. The rawhide inserts can be renewed when the original pair are worn or damaged. This type of hammer is used to strike finished surfaces that would be marked or damaged if a hardened hammer were used.

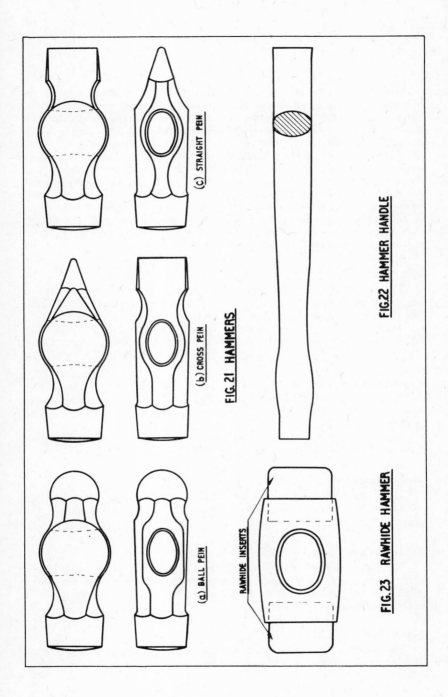

(a) BALL PEIN

(b) CROSS PEIN

(c) STRAIGHT PEIN

FIG. 21 HAMMERS

FIG.22 HAMMER HANDLE

RAWHIDE INSERTS

FIG.23 RAWHIDE HAMMER

Chisels

Much of the metal cutting formerly carried out by the fitter with the aid of a hammer and various shaped chisels is now performed on machine tools, but even in a modern engineering works it is sometimes expedient to do a limited amount of hand chipping. This is particularly true on certain types of repair and maintenance work.

Chisels are made from octagon-shaped steel bar, the cutting end being forged to the desired shape. High-carbon steel chisels are hardened and tempered at the cutting edge. Chisels made from alloy steel are hardened but need no tempering. The cutting-point angle ground on the chisel will vary from 30–70°; the value selected is determined by the nature of the metal to be chipped. See table for approximate cutting angles, p. 20.

Chisels vary in length, section, and shape according to their application; the most common types include:—

Flat Chisel　Fig. 24

The flat chisel is used for chipping large surfaces and for general cutting purposes, e.g. cutting thin sheet, and cutting internal shapes which have been previously chain drilled. See Fig. 30(a) and 30(b).

The largest flat chisel is approximately 250 mm long by 25 mm wide, other sizes varying in length and width down to 5 mm wide by 100 mm long. The cutting edge is slightly rounded to prevent the corners digging in.

Cross-Cut Chisel　Fig. 25

The cross-cut chisel is used for chipping channels in large surfaces prior to using the flat chisel, and also for cutting key-ways in shafts and their mating components. See Fig. 30(c).

The width of the cutting edge is 3–10 mm, the blade tapering back slightly from the front to provide the necessary clearance in the slot being cut.

Half-Round Chisel　Fig. 26

The half-round chisel is used mainly for cutting oil channels in bearings or bushes, and roughing out small concave surfaces. See Fig. 30(d). The cutting edge is formed by a single bevel.

Diamond-Point Chisel　Fig. 27

The diamond-point chisel is chiefly used for cutting vee-shaped grooves, chipping through flat plate, and chipping in sharp corners. See Fig. 30(e). The single bevel which is ground on the end of the square section forms a diamond-shaped cutting edge.

Side Chisel　Fig. 28

The side chisel is a most useful tool for chipping rectangular-shaped slots after the main bulk of metal has been removed by drilling. See Fig. 30(f).

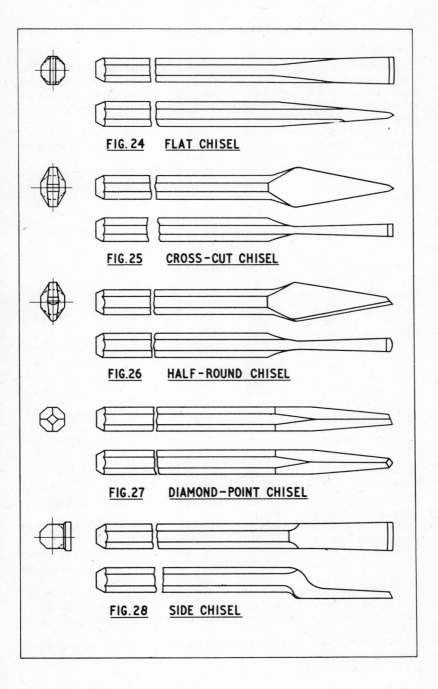

FIG. 24   FLAT CHISEL

FIG. 25   CROSS-CUT CHISEL

FIG.26   HALF-ROUND CHISEL

FIG.27   DIAMOND-POINT CHISEL

FIG.28   SIDE CHISEL

Rake and Clearance Angles

Fig. 29(a) shows the approximate position of a flat chisel when cutting, indicating clearance, rake, and angle of inclination. The latter will depend largely on the nature of the material being cut. If the angle is too great the cutting edge will penetrate the metal too deep, preventing the formation of a chip. If the angle is too small no cutting action is possible.

The accepted value of the clearance angle is about $10°$; therefore the rake will depend upon the cutting-point angle and the angle of inclination of the chisel, and is illustrated in Fig. 29(b).

In the example the rake angle can be easily calculated:—

$$\text{Rake angle} = 90° - (\text{Point angle} + \text{Clearance angle})$$
$$= 90° - (65° + 10°) = 90° - 75°$$
$$= 15°$$

$$\text{Angle of Inclination} = 10° + \frac{65°}{2} = 10° + 32\tfrac{1}{2}° = 42\tfrac{1}{2}°$$

Table showing point angle, angle of inclination, and rake angle suitable for various materials when clearance angle is $10°$

Material to be cut	Point angle	Angle of Inclination	Rake angle
Aluminium	$35°$	$27\tfrac{1}{2}°$	$45°$
Brass	$40°$	$30°$	$40°$
Mild steel	$55°$	$37\tfrac{1}{2}°$	$25°$
Cast iron	$60°$	$40°$	$20°$
Cast steel	$65°$	$42\tfrac{1}{2}°$	$15°$

Safety points when using a chisel

Chipping should not continue to the edge of a surface, particularly if the metal is of a crystalline nature.

When approaching the edge the work should be reversed and the chipping commenced from that side.

When approaching the end of a cut the chip should be removed by a series of light hammer blows on the chisel head, this precaution preventing chips flying across the shop.

Due to repeated hammer blows, the head of the chisel will burr over and tend to split at the edge. These burrs should be removed regularly by grinding the head back to its normal shape; failure to do this could cause both hand and serious eye injury.

Wise fitters wear protective eye-shields when carrying out a chipping operation.

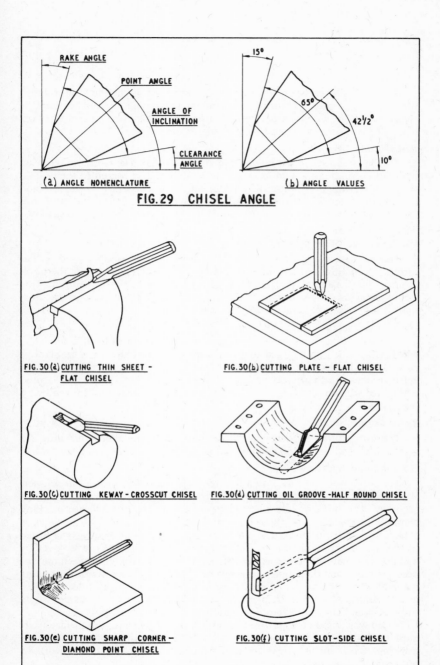

RAKE ANGLE

POINT ANGLE

ANGLE OF INCLINATION

CLEARANCE ANGLE

(a) ANGLE NOMENCLATURE

15°

65°

42½°

10°

(b) ANGLE VALUES

FIG.29 CHISEL ANGLE

FIG.30 (a) CUTTING THIN SHEET – FLAT CHISEL

FIG.30(b) CUTTING PLATE – FLAT CHISEL

FIG.30(c) CUTTING KEWAY – CROSSCUT CHISEL

FIG.30(d) CUTTING OIL GROOVE – HALF ROUND CHISEL

FIG.30(e) CUTTING SHARP CORNER – DIAMOND POINT CHISEL

FIG.30(f) CUTTING SLOT – SIDE CHISEL

Scrapers

Scrapers of several different shapes and sizes are used by the fitter to finish the surface of a piece of work to a degree of accuracy unobtainable with the chisel or the file. Furthermore he may also use a scraper to correct errors in machined components caused by warping or distortion.

Flat Scraper   Fig. 31

The flat scraper is often made from an old flat file. The teeth are removed by surface grinding the two faces, the point end is then forged to the desired shape. After rough grinding the cutting edge is re-hardened by heating and quenching. After final grinding the scraper is carefully sharpened on the oilstone. Flat scrapers are used to remove the high spots from flat bearing or locating surfaces.

Hook Scraper   Fig. 32

The hook or draw scraper is an alternative type of scraper used on flat surfaces. The standard flat scraper cuts on a forward stroke, while the hook scraper cuts the metal as it is being drawn towards the fitter using it. This technique of scraping known as 'draw' scraping is used extensively on machine-tool fitting, e.g. slides and guideways.

Half-Round Scraper   Fig. 33

The half-round scraper is often produced from an old half-round file, which is softened and forged to the shape shown in diagram. The blade is curved and is also hollow ground. After hardening and final grinding the cutting edges are sharpened on a fine oilstone. This type of scraper is used mainly for scraping bearings and bushes, chamfering holes, and for removing burrs.

Three-Corner Scraper   Fig. 34

The three-corner scraper is used chiefly by the toolmaker, who finds it a most useful tool for gauge making and other types of precision fitting work.

Scraping Flat Surfaces   Fig. 35

The surface of the work is first lightly scraped all over with a flat scraper. Its flatness is then checked against a surface plate (see Fig. 53) of proved accuracy. The surface plate is wiped clean, and lightly coated with marking compound (engineer's marking blue) and the scraped surface of the work is rubbed to and fro upon it. The contact or high spots will be clearly revealed by the marking compound adhering to them. These high spots are removed by additional scraping, and the work is re-checked on the surface plate. It may be necessary to repeat these operations several times, each successive scrape being made at 90° to the previous one to prevent the formation of hollows and to give a pattern which is more pleasing to the eye. Finally when flat the whole surface should show an even distribution of small contact spots.

When working on the surface of a large heavy workpiece, the surface plate must be brought to the work. After lightly coating the surface plate with marking compound it is inverted and rubbed over the face of the work to reveal the high spots.

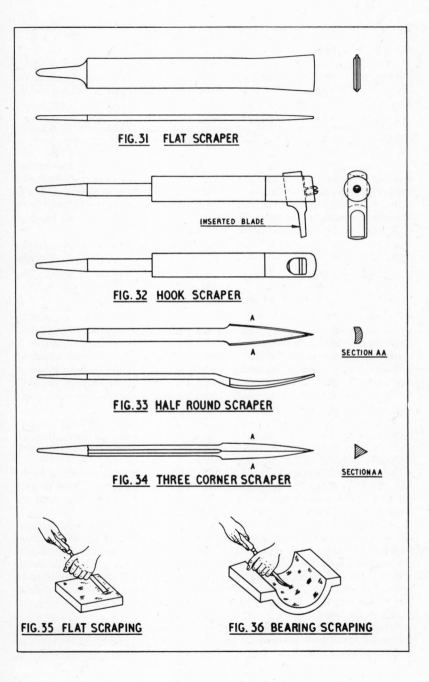

FIG. 31 FLAT SCRAPER

INSERTED BLADE

FIG. 32 HOOK SCRAPER

A

A

SECTION AA

FIG. 33 HALF ROUND SCRAPER

A

A

SECTION AA

FIG. 34 THREE CORNER SCRAPER

FIG. 35 FLAT SCRAPING

FIG. 36 BEARING SCRAPING

Scraping Bearings

Most frequently the bearing is made in two halves, and these are lined with anti-friction metal such as phosphor bronze, brass, or gun-metal. The lower halves are fitted in the bearing pedestals, and the journals of the mating shaft are coated with marking compound. The shaft is carefully lowered into position, and is rotated in the half bearings.

After removal of the shaft, contact spots are revealed where the marking medium has adhered and these are removed with a half-round scraper, as shown in Fig. 36.

The operations of trying the shaft in position, and scraping away the high spots are repeated until all the lower half bearings show even distribution of small contact spots. When this has been achieved, the top halves of the bearings are located over the shaft, and the holding bolts tightened sufficiently to allow rotation of the shaft. These top halves are removed and the high spots scraped until even distribution of markings is obtained.

When the top halves are finally bolted down a slight amount of tightness should be felt on revolving the shaft to allow for bedding down while running in.

Drills and Reamers   Refer to chapter on drilling pp. 224–233

Hand Screwing Taps   B.S. 949:1969

A hand tap as shown in Fig. 37 is the tool used by the fitter for cutting internal threads of various forms, the tap being screwed into a hole slightly larger in diameter than the minor (core) diameter of the mating screw.

Hand taps are made of high-carbon steel suitably hardened and tempered, or alternatively made of hardened high-speed steel. Taps in both types of material are classified as either Cut Thread or as Ground Thread.

Cut-thread taps are those in which the threads on the body of the tap are fully formed before hardening.

Ground-thread taps are those in which the threading operation is performed by grinding the threads on the hardened blanks. This method of manufacture eliminates the possibility of distortion due to heat treatment, and gives a thread of far greater precision.

A standard set of hand taps consists of three as shown in Fig. 38: (a) Taper tap; (b) Second tap; (c) Bottoming tap. The latter is often referred to as a Plug tap, and this causes confusion with American terms; therefore the nomenclature adopted by B.S. 949 should be adhered to.

The taper tap has a chamfer or tapered lead for a length of 8–10 threads; this allows the tap to enter the hole, and be maintained in an axial cutting position; it also provides a progressive series of cutting edges which gradually cut a full thread. The second tap has a tapered lead for a length of about 4 threads, and is used to follow the taper tap. If the hole being tapped is an open or through hole the second tap is quite suitable for finishing the thread. The bottoming tap has a very short tapered lead and is used to finish the thread in a blind hole.

Several flutes are cut along the body of the tap to perform the following functions: (a) to form efficient cutting edges; (b) to curl and break the chips so that they occupy minimum space; (c) to form grooves to accommodate the

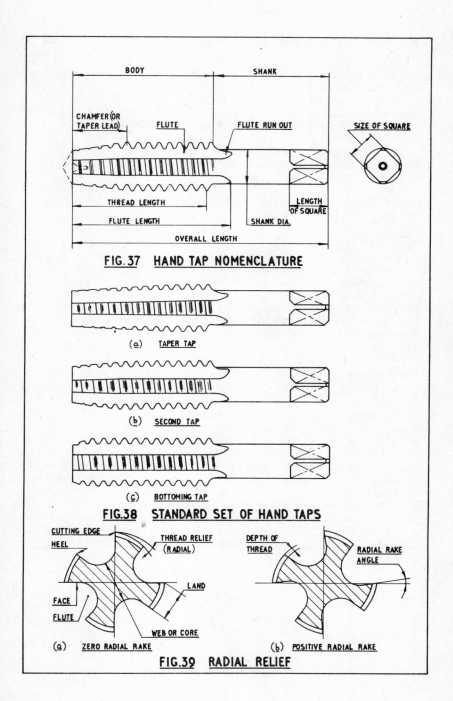

FIG.37 HAND TAP NOMENCLATURE

FIG.38 STANDARD SET OF HAND TAPS

FIG.39 RADIAL RELIEF

B

chips; (d) to allow the cutting lubricant to reach the cutting edges. Straight fluted taps above 13 mm diameter usually have four flutes, below this range often three flutes, and very small sizes only two flutes.

Taps, in common with all cutting tools, must have some form of relief or clearance to ensure proper cutting action and to reduce friction. The relief can be provided either axially in the form of back taper relief or radially by thread relief.

Back taper relief consists of a gradual decrease in thread diameter along the body of the tap towards the shank end, the amount of reduction may be only 0·002–0·005 mm per 25 mm.

The most common form of radial relief is known as eccentric relief which extends the full width of the tap lands from cutting edge to heel as shown in Fig. 39.

Serial-Type Taps

Serial-type taps are similar to hand taps in general dimensions and fluting, but they differ fundamentally in operation. Each tap of the series is arranged to cut a definite percentage of the thread form. A standard set of serial-taps comprise No. 1 and 2 taps used for roughing and No. 3 tap for finishing. The No. 1 tap cuts a very shallow thread, this is enlarged by No. 2, and finally No. 3 cuts the full-form thread of the required dimensions. These taps are recommended for heavy duties such as tapping long blind holes in tough materials.

Tap-Wrench   Figs. 40 and 41

As its name implies the tap-wrench is required to provide a convenient method of revolving the tap in the drilled hole. The wrench is located on the square end of the tap, and the two handles are gripped and rotated by the fitter, equal pressure being applied by both hands. Care must be taken to ensure the tap is kept square, i.e. at 90° to the face being tapped. After starting the tap, it should be checked with a small try-square as shown in Fig. 42. If adjustment is required it can be made by altering the pressure on the wrench handles in order to guide the tap in the appropriate direction.

After the tap has been correctly positioned cutting may proceed, but after every half turn the tap should be reversed slightly to clear the threads, and periodically the tap should be reversed several turns to cut off the chips and to prevent binding. For most materials apart from cast iron a cutting oil should be used to lubricate the taps and to improve the finish of the threads being cut.

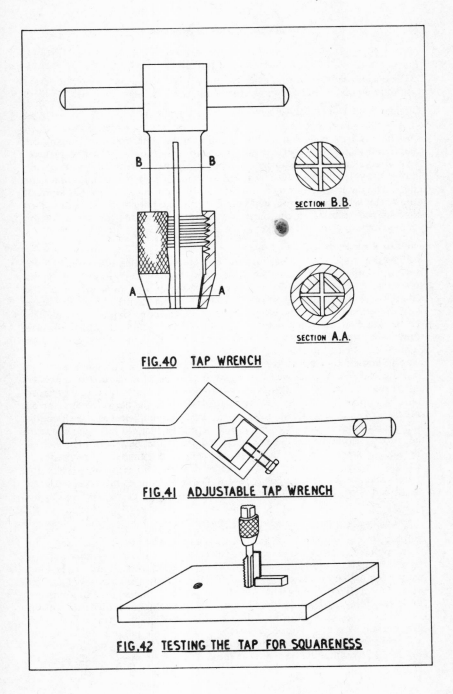

SECTION B.B.

SECTION A.A.

FIG.40   TAP WRENCH

FIG.41   ADJUSTABLE TAP WRENCH

FIG.42   TESTING THE TAP FOR SQUARENESS

The Stock and Dies

The tool used for cutting external threads is called a die, several different types are available and the most commonly used include:—

Circular Split Die (Often referred to as 'Button' Die)

Fig. 43 shows a plain adjustable die, a circular disc of hardened high-speed steel having a threaded hole through the centre. The first two threads are chamfered to form a tapered lead for centralizing the die on the workpiece. Several equi-spaced holes drilled parallel to the axis of thread and breaking into it provide the cutting edges and sufficient space to accommodate the chips. The die is split through one side and this permits a limited amount of adjustment when setting the die to cut either an easy- or tight-fit thread. Two cone-shaped recesses in the periphery serve as locations for the adjusting screws carried in the die stock.

Die Stock for Split Die   Fig. 44

The die stock is a circular housing having two handles. The counter bore is slightly larger in diameter than the die, and its depth corresponds to the die thickness. A clearance hole allows the bar being screwed to pass through the stock. Three adjusting screws are so arranged that the centre screw will engage with the split in the die, the other two locate in the cone-shaped recesses. The die is placed in the stock with the chamfered face exposed, and the centre screw is tightened to open out the die. The two remaining screws are then tightened to help grip the die firmly.

The end of the bar to be threaded is chamfered and this will assist in locating the die. When commencing to cut the thread, care is required to ensure that the face of the die is square with the work being cut. Equal pressure must be applied to both handles of the stock. Once the cut has been started satisfactorily the die is fed downwards, but frequently reversing direction similar to the technique used in tapping. After the first cut has been taken to the length required, the die is unscrewed from the bar, and the work is checked for size; if the thread is tight the centre adjusting screw of the stock is slightly released and this will close the die, the two retaining screws are re-tightened, and a second cut is taken. These operations are repeated until the thread is cut to the required size.

Loose Dies   Fig. 45

Loose dies are rectangular blocks made of the same material and manu-factured in a similar way to the split dies, but finally, instead of being split at one point, the block is parted completely, giving a die in two halves. Both halves are marked indicating size and position in the stock. They are located in the rectangular recess of the die stock (Fig. 46) by means of a vee-shaped groove cut in the half dies which fit the vee-slides in the stock. An adjusting screw controls the depth of cut. Loose dies are frequently used for cutting threads over 13 mm diameter; their design enables the thread to be cut progressively, starting with a very shallow cut, and gradually adjusting the dies and taking subsequent cuts until the final thread is produced. An additional advantage is the fact that these dies can be opened sufficiently to

FIG. 43 CIRCULAR SPLIT DIE

FIG. 44 DIE STOCK FOR CIRCULAR SPLIT DIE

FIG. 45 LOOSE DIES

FIG. 46 DIE STOCK FOR LOOSE DIES

(a) SQUARE DIE NUT   (b) HEXAGON DIE NUT

FIG. 47 SOLID DIE NUTS

pass over the unscrewed bar and then be adjusted to commence the cut, thereby eliminating the problem of starting off the thread square with the axis of the bar, always a difficulty if starting to cut from the end of a bar.

Die Nuts   Figs. 47(a) and 47(b)

The solid die nut made from square or hexagonal material is of similar design to the split die but without any facility for adjustment. Normally a standard spanner is used to rotate the die nut. Apart from cutting gas threads the die nut is not frequently used to cut threads from the solid bar, but is very useful for renovating threads which may have been knocked or damaged.

Basic Measuring Tools

The tools previously mentioned are used by the bench fitter for holding or for cutting the work; additional tools are required to check the accuracy of dimensions and form. The most commonly used tools under this heading would include:—

The Steel Rule   Fig. 48

The steel rule can be defined as a graduated strip of metal used to determine any required dimension within the scope of the graduations.

Steel rules are obtainable in a wide variety of lengths and widths, with many alternative types of graduations, including English measurements, Metric, and Metric and English graduations.

Fig. 48 illustrates a typical metric rule obtainable in both 150 mm and 300 mm lengths and in several widths. The lower edge is graduated in $1 \cdot 0$ mm divisions, every tenth division designated by a number, while the upper edge is graduated in $0 \cdot 5$ mm divisions, with every ten millimetres indicated by numbers.

The engineer's rule is made from tempered steel, either plain carbon or stainless steel, the latter possessing the great advantage that it will not stain or corrode.

The degree of accuracy possible with rule measurement is usually regarded as within $0 \cdot 1$ mm of actual size. For marking-out operations a rule of suitable length is held in a rule stand as shown in Fig. 65 and this provides a convenient type of vertical scale.

Callipers

Callipers are used for measuring distances between or over surfaces, or for comparing distances or sizes with existing standards, e.g. plug gauges or slip gauges.

Outside Callipers

Fig. 49(a) shows the firm-joint type of outside calliper; two curved legs are secured at the fulcrum by means of a pair of washers and a rivet or bolt. The opening between the two legs is maintained by friction at the joint. When setting the calliper or checking a dimension, the legs are set to the approximate

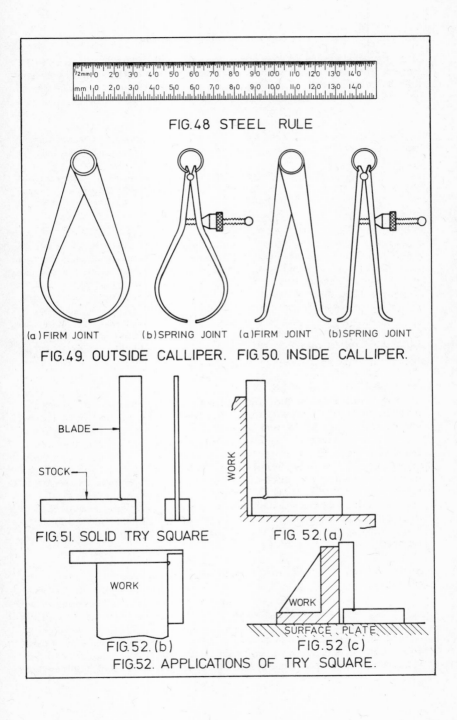

FIG. 48 STEEL RULE

(a) FIRM JOINT   (b) SPRING JOINT   (a) FIRM JOINT   (b) SPRING JOINT

FIG. 49. OUTSIDE CALLIPER.   FIG. 50. INSIDE CALLIPER.

BLADE

STOCK

FIG. 51. SOLID TRY SQUARE

WORK

FIG. 52. (a)

WORK

FIG. 52. (b)

WORK

SURFACE PLATE

FIG. 52 (c)

FIG. 52. APPLICATIONS OF TRY SQUARE.

opening, and one leg is then firmly tapped against a solid object until the correct 'feel' or contact is obtained. Fig. 49(b) shows the spring-joint type of outside calliper; the joint is free, but a spring provides the required tension, and adjustments are made by means of the nut working on a screw. This nut may be solid or of the special quick-acting type, making the spring-joint calliper quicker and easier to set and operate.

When setting or checking a dimension with callipers, the contact should not be too heavy otherwise the legs may spring and a false reading would be obtained.

The actual size between the legs can be read on a steel rule; alternatively the size may be set or checked by means of a standard plug gauge, slip gauge, or component of known dimension.

Inside Callipers

Used mainly for checking internal surfaces, e.g. measuring diameters of holes and widths of slots. Fig. 50(a) shows the firm-joint inside calliper, and Fig. 50(b) the spring-joint type. The adjustment of these callipers is carried out in the same way as that outlined for the outside calliper.

The inside calliper can be set with the aid of an outside micrometer, a ring or gap gauge, or a pre-set outside calliper.

Both outside and inside callipers are specified according to the length of the legs measured from the joint to the contact points. Spring joints are obtainable in sizes ranging from 75 up to 300 mm, while firm joints are made in much larger sizes.

Solid Try-Square   B.S. 939: 1962

The solid try-square shown in Fig. 51 is a precision tool used to test the accuracy of two surfaces which must be at right angles to each other. It consists of a thin blade and a stock accurately set at 90° to each other. The blade is hardened but the stock can be soft. The expensive types have both hardened blade and stock.

The British Standard specifies three grades of accuracy—reference grade, inspection grade, and workshop grade; each must conform to the limits contained in B.S. 939.

Fig. 52 shows three typical applications: (a) testing with the outside edge of stock and blade; (b) testing with the inside edges; (c) testing work piece in conjunction with a surface plate, the stock should be kept at right angles to the work.

Surface Plates   B.S. 817: 1957

The surface plate shown in Fig. 53 is a precision piece of equipment used as a reference or master surface against which the surface of a component is checked for flatness. It is also used extensively for marking-out and inspection purposes.

The surface plate is made from good quality close-grained cast iron or from alloy cast-iron, adequately ribbed on the underside to ensure rigidity, and prevents deflection when a concentrated load is applied at the centre of the plate.

The British Standard 817 specifies two grades of accuracy for plain cast-iron surface plates:—

Grade 'A' surface plates; these are the most accurate, the upper face being finished by scraping or by a grinding process which furnishes a similar type of surface to that obtained by scraping, the error in flatness must not exceed 0·005 mm over any area 300 mm square.

Grade 'B' surface plates are finished by grinding or planing; the error in flatness must not exceed 0·02 mm over any area 300 mm square. This grade is normally provided for workshop use.

Both grades have the four edges finished straight, parallel, and square to each other and the top face. Plates up to and including 300 × 75 mm are not required to have handles but are provided with suitable hand-grips, plates of ₀350 × 250 mm up to 450 × 300 mm must have at least one detachable handle at each end, while plates up to 900 × 600 mm must have two detachable handles at each end. Above this size provision must be made for lifting by other than manual means.

Plates are provided with three supporting feet, the small and medium-size plates locating directly on a bench, the larger sizes are located on a cast-iron stand which is adequately braced.

Before using a surface plate to test the flatness of a component the plate must be wiped clean; a thin even coating of engineer's blue or other marking compound is applied to its surface. The face to be tested is also wiped clean, and must be free of burrs; it is then lightly rubbed to and fro over the surface plate. The contact or high spots will be revealed by the marking compound adhering to them; these are removed by scraping. Fig. 35.

Straight-Edges   B.S. 863: 1939, B.S. 818: 1963

Straight-edges are used to check the flatness of surfaces and for testing alignment of machines. The simplest form shown in Fig. 54(a) is a rectangular-section steel strip made in various standard lengths, the depth and thickness being dependent on the length. The British Standard 863 specifies two grades of accuracy:—

Grade 'A' steel straight-edges, which must be made from high-quality steel and be hardened on the working faces. Close limits are laid down for straightness, parallelism, and squareness.

Grade 'B' steel straight-edges may be supplied in the hardened or un-hardened condition; the latter must be made from cast steel. The limits specified for this grade are approximately double those required for Grade 'A'. Both grades are bevelled to give a thin edge on the working face. In use the straight-edge is placed against the work and small errors in flatness can be readily detected by the appearance of light between them; a gap of 0·005 mm can be readily discerned in this way.

Fig. 54(b) shows the more elaborate type of straight-edge, a rigid ribbed cast-iron casting, accurately machined and ground on the working face to the required limits of accuracy.

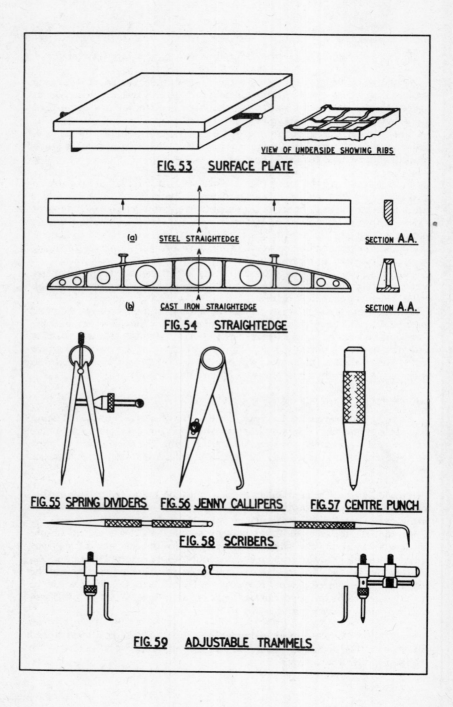

FIG. 53   SURFACE PLATE

VIEW OF UNDERSIDE SHOWING RIBS

(a) STEEL STRAIGHTEDGE

SECTION A.A.

(b) CAST IRON STRAIGHTEDGE

SECTION A.A.

FIG. 54   STRAIGHTEDGE

FIG. 55 SPRING DIVIDERS   FIG. 56 JENNY CALLIPERS   FIG. 57 CENTRE PUNCH

FIG. 58   SCRIBERS

FIG. 59   ADJUSTABLE TRAMMELS

Marking-Out

Marking-out or setting-out operations are an essential part of a bench fitter's work. Briefly it involves the marking or scribing of lines on the workpiece to indicate shape required, position of holes and slots, and to provide an approximate guide for cutting the metal in subsequent operations.

Marking-out is also associated with machine-shop work, particularly when only a small quantity of any one component is required. The casting or forging when received for machining will incorporate machining allowances, therefore it will need to be marked out to indicate the position and extent of the necessary machining. When dealing with large quantities, special jigs or fixtures are supplied for locating the work and guiding the tools, and these eliminate the need for marking-out.

The marking-out operations for both fitting and machining will involve the use of some of the equipment already dealt with, e.g. surface plate or marking-out table, steel rule, try-square, and also the following additional tools and equipment.

Dividers

A tool used for measuring the distance between points, for transferring a length directly from a steel rule, and for scribing circles and arcs. A useful form of divider is shown in Fig. 55. The points of the two legs are hardened and tempered to prevent wear.

Jenny Callipers Fig. 56

The jenny or odd-leg callipers are used to scribe arcs and to scribe lines parallel to the edge of the work. When setting the jenny calliper to a steel rule, the curved leg is set against the end face of the rule and the scriber leg is adjusted to the required length.

Centre Punch

A centre punch as shown in Fig. 57 is used for making small indentations or dots along the marked-out lines on the work; these provide a guide to the fitter or machinist should the original lines become obliterated. They are also used to mark the centre point of hole positions, and also to provide a centre dot for locating one leg of the dividers when scribing arcs or circles.

Centre punches are made from cast steel suitably hardened and tempered at the point; this is usually ground to an included angle of 60° or 90°.

The size of the dots made by the punch should be kept as small as possible.

Scribers

A typical engineer's scriber is shown in Fig. 58. Made from tool steel hardened and tempered at the point, and knurled on the body to provide a firm grip. Used for scribing straight lines with the aid of a steel rule, try-square, or straight-edge.

Adjustable Trammels Fig. 59

The adjustable trammel is used to measure the distance between points too great to be reached by means of dividers. Two adjustable points are carried on a cross beam, and these can be set to the required length with the aid of a steel rule. The points when set to the approximate length can be finally set with the fine adjusting screw carried on the beam.

Scribing Block

The scribing block or surface gauge is shown in Fig. 60 and consists of a central steel pillar supported on a cast-iron or hardened-steel base. The pillar carries an adjustable scriber point. This tool is used in conjunction with a surface plate or a marking-out table for scribing centre and other lines which have to be parallel to a common base.

The universal surface gauge is shown in Fig. 61, a tool which can be used for a wide variety of purposes in both bench and machine-tool work.

Vee-Blocks Fig. 62

Vee-blocks are made in pairs from good-quality cast iron or of steel, hardened and ground. The vee-shaped grooves are accurately ground parallel and square with the outside faces. The two square slots provide a location for the clamps. This item of equipment is used frequently for supporting cylindrical components in marking-out and machining operations.

Angle-plate

A fixed angle-plate as shown in Fig. 63 is used for holding work at right angles to the marking-out table. The work is held with bolts and clamps or by means of a toolmaker's clamp. Fig. 64.

The adjustable-type swivel angle-plate is often used when marking-out angular work.

Toolmaker's Clamps

The toolmaker's clamp shown in Fig. 64 is a convenient item of equipment for quickly clamping a workpiece to the angle-plate for marking-out and light drilling operations.

Marking-Out Table

A typical marking-out table is shown in Fig. 65. Alternative methods of locating the workpiece are also illustrated.

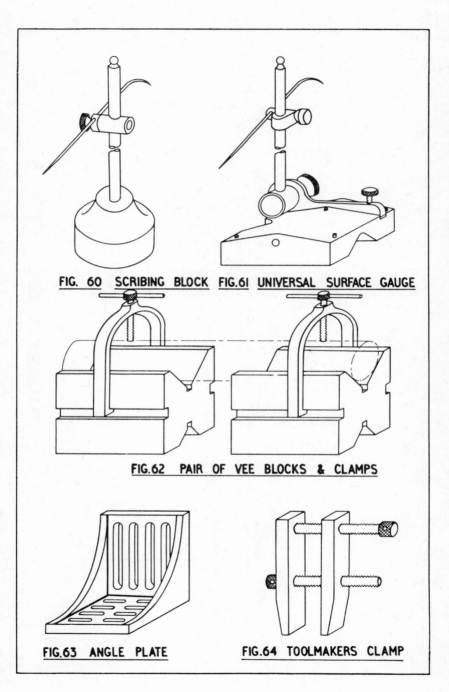

FIG. 60 SCRIBING BLOCK FIG.61 UNIVERSAL SURFACE GAUGE

FIG.62 PAIR OF VEE BLOCKS & CLAMPS

FIG.63 ANGLE PLATE

FIG.64 TOOLMAKERS CLAMP

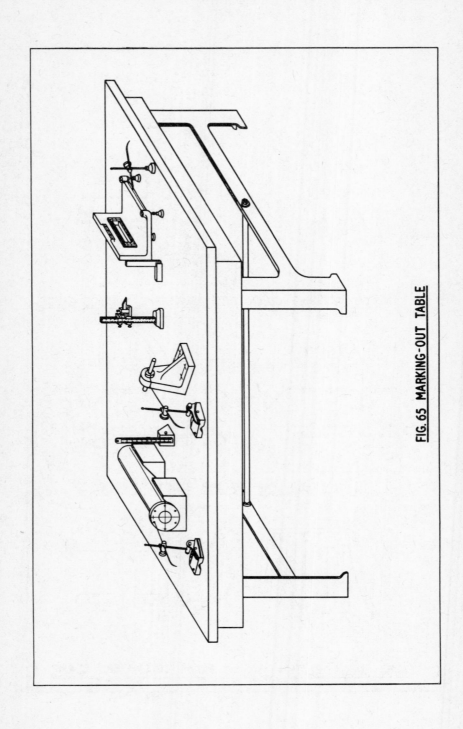

FIG. 65 MARKING-OUT TABLE

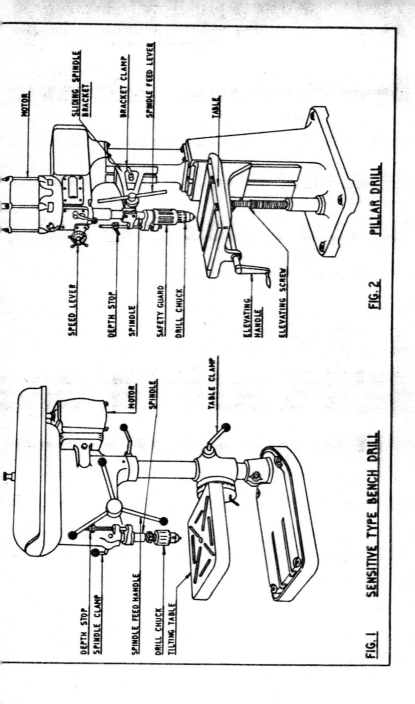

SENSITIVE TYPE BENCH DRILL

MOTOR

SPINDLE

TABLE CLAMP

DEPTH STOP

SPINDLE CLAMP

SPINDLE FEED HANDLE

DRILL CHUCK

TILTING TABLE

FIG. 1

PILLAR DRILL

MOTOR

SLIDING SPINDLE BRACKET

BRACKET CLAMP

SPINDLE FEED LEVER

TABLE

SPEED LEVER

DEPTH STOP

SPINDLE

SAFETY GUARD

DRILL CHUCK

ELEVATING HANDLE

ELEVATING SCREW

FIG. 2

Examples of Marking-Out

1. Fig. 66(a) shows a typical clamp plate as used on machine tools for work holding. See Fig. 39(a). Chapter Six, p. 169.

This mild-steel clamp is machined to length, width, and thickness prior to marking-out.

When marking-out, it is important to work from accurate datum faces, or if this is impossible the datums must be established by marking them on the work. In this example the faces 'A' and 'B', already machined flat and square, can be used as datums. To ensure that the marking-out lines are sharp and easily visible the plate can be coated with copper-sulphate solution or with one of the proprietary marking compounds. Referring to Fig. 66(b) it can be seen that the plate is located on face 'A' and using either a vernier height gauge (Fig. 10, Chapter Fourteen) or a rule stand and surface gauge the centre line, width of slot, and intersections of the angular faces with face 'C' are marked, the latter two lines being continued across the edges of the plate.

The plate is then placed on face 'B' (Fig. 66(c), and using the same equipment the centres of the radii, and intersections of the angular faces with faces 'A' and 'D' are marked; these again being continued across the plate edges. Lightly mark the centres of the radii with a centre punch, scribe the circles with a pair of dividers, then with a straight-edge and a scriber mark the angular faces as shown in Fig. 66(d).

2. Fig. 67(a) shows a small casting which is to be marked-out before machining operations, and this involves a different technique to that used in the previous example.

The casting is received from the foundry with excess material on the base and boss faces, and the machinist requires centre lines indicating the positions of the holes and the extent of the machining necessary on the faces. Datum faces are established by marking and care must be taken to ensure that these maintain the overall symmetry of the casting, i.e. hole in the centre of boss, etc. If the casting is of cast iron it would be painted in the appropriate places with whitewash to simplify marking and give clear lines.

Initially the casting is set up on three support jacks as shown in Fig. 67(b) and the centre of the boss and edges of the base are set in the horizontal plane. In this position the centre line of the boss can be marked all around the casting; in addition the centres of the holes in the base are marked, using a surface gauge and rule stand. The casting is then positioned as shown in Fig. 67(c), the boss centre line and the front face being set in the vertical planes.

Using a surface gauge the boss centre is marked, then dropping the surface gauge the required amount the base face can be marked, indicating the amount of metal to be removed by machining.

Setting the casting relative to the previously marked lines, as shown in Fig. 67(d), the thickness of the boss faces and the hole centres can be marked. As in the previous example the hole circles are marked with a centre punch and dividers.

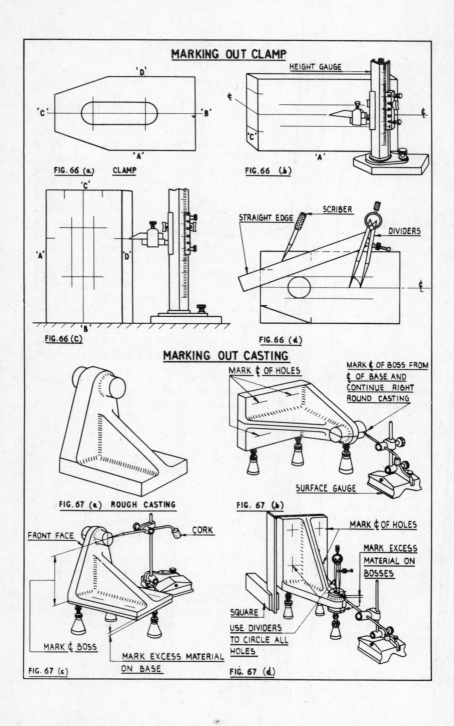

MARKING OUT CLAMP

FIG. 66 (a)   CLAMP

'D'   'C'   'B'   'A'

HEIGHT GAUGE

FIG. 66 (b)

'C'   'A'   'D'   'B'

FIG. 66 (C)

STRAIGHT EDGE   SCRIBER   DIVIDERS

FIG. 66 (d)

MARKING OUT CASTING

FIG. 67 (a)   ROUGH CASTING

MARK ₵ OF HOLES

MARK ₵ OF BOSS FROM ₵ OF BASE AND CONTINUE RIGHT ROUND CASTING

SURFACE GAUGE

FIG. 67 (b)

FRONT FACE   CORK

MARK ₵ BOSS   MARK EXCESS MATERIAL ON BASE

FIG. 67 (c)

MARK ₵ OF HOLES

MARK EXCESS MATERIAL ON BOSSES

SQUARE

USE DIVIDERS TO CIRCLE ALL HOLES

FIG. 67 (d)

CHAPTER TWO

SHEET METAL WORK

Sheet metal work can be broadly divided into two main groups:—

1. Hand work, i.e. the production of components in a wide variety of shapes and sizes from metal sheet with the aid of hand and bench tools and a few simple machines. In this type of work the emphasis is on skill in the manipulation of the sheet metal and appropriate tools, and not on rapid mass production.

2. Machine work, i.e. the rapid quantity production of components made from metal sheet with the aid of power-driven presses and complex dies or press-tools. The mass production of domestic appliances and motor-car-body parts are typical examples of this type of sheet metal work.

As the first section of this volume is concerned with hand processes reference will only be made to the first of the two groups of sheet metal work.

Basic Sheet Metal Tools and Equipment

Some of the tools and items of equipment used by the bench fitter are also used by the sheet metal worker including the bench, vice, marking-out tools, and common measuring tools. Certain additional tools are used exclusively by the sheet metal worker, including the following:—

Cutting Tools

Hand Shears (Snips)

Hand shears of various shapes and lengths are the most common type of cutting tools used for sheet metal.

Straight Snips

Fig. 1 shows the standard-pattern straight snips, normally used for straight cuts, or a large outside radius, and for notching sheet when making corners and seams. The size of the snips is related to the thickness and toughness of the metal to be be cut. The standard lengths vary from 150–400 mm; the heavier the gauge or toughness of sheet, the longer the length of snips selected.

Bent Snips

Fig. 2 shows the standard-pattern bent snips, curved on the cutting blades, used for cutting circles or irregular shapes, and internal diameters. Made in the same range of lengths as the straight snips.

Universal or Gilbow Shears

Fig. 3 shows the universal or gilbow shears, which as the name suggests can be used for cutting along straight or curved lines in all directions. The shape and position of the handle enables the operator to see the marking-out lines as cutting proceeds, and his hand is well clear of the sheet being cut. This type of shear may be left- or right-handed; the hand is defined by the relative position of the upper and lower blade.

Scotch Shears

Fig. 4 shows the scotch shears used for cutting heavy-gauge materials, available in lengths from 250–600 mm.

Bench Shears

In addition to the range of hand shears a sheet metal shop is usually equipped with various types of mechanical shears which provide a quicker method of cutting sheet metal, especially those of thicker gauges.

Fig. 5 shows the standard type of hand-lever shears consisting of a lower fixed blade firmly held by a bracket mounted on a bench; the upper blade is pivoted at the rear end, and the hand-operating lever is attached to the front end by a link system or by gearing.

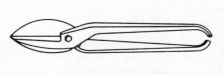

FIG.1 STRAIGHT SNIPS

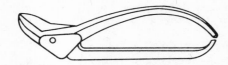

FIG.2 BENT SNIPS

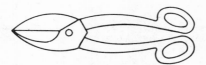

FIG.3 UNIVERSAL OR GILBOW SHEARS

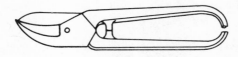

FIG.4 SCOTCH SHEARS

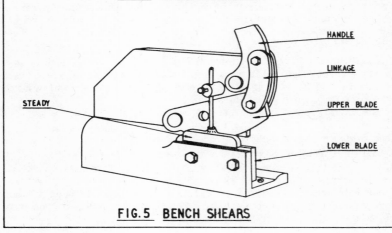

HANDLE

LINKAGE

STEADY

UPPER BLADE

LOWER BLADE

FIG.5 BENCH SHEARS

Bench Tools

Stakes

Stakes are made in a variety of shapes, sizes, and weights, consisting of steel forgings with each working face machined to the desired shape and highly polished. The stakes must be firmly supported by fitting them into a socket attached to the bench, or by holding them directly in the vice.

The choice of stake will depend upon the type of operation being carried out and the shape and size of the component being worked upon.

The following types of stakes will meet the needs of most general work.

Hatchet Stake

The hatchet stake shown in Fig. 6 is used for dressing edges, folding by hand, sharpening bends, and also for the tucking in of wired edges and joints.

Half-Moon Stake

The half-moon stake shown in Fig. 7 is used for the same types of operations as the hatchet stake but on cylindrical-shaped articles.

Combined Funnel and Side Stake

The combined funnel and side stake shown in Fig. 8 is used for shaping conical work, and for square to round transformers. The parallel section, i.e. the side stake, is used for making tube and also other work involving radii.

Bick Iron

The bick iron as shown in Fig. 9 is used for a wide variety of operations—shaping tapered work, knocking up, wiring and dressing edges.

Creasing Iron

The creasing iron as shown in Fig. 10 is used for swaging small work, hand wiring of flat sheets, forming clips and hinges. The flat surface can be used for dressing edges and squaring up worked joints.

Tinsmen's Mandrel

The tinsmen's mandrel as shown in Fig. 11 is made of cast iron or steel and can be firmly clamped to the bench. The rectangular section can be used for shaping and flanging square and rectangular work, while the radiused end is used for circular or elliptical work.

The square-tapered hole at one end locates stakes or heads.

Hand Hammers and Mallets

The sheet metal worker uses a wide variety of hammers and mallets of various shapes, sizes, and weights; several different types may be needed in order to make one relatively simple article.

The hammers are cast-steel forgings; the working faces are machined, and after hardening and tempering these faces are highly polished. The most commonly used types include:—

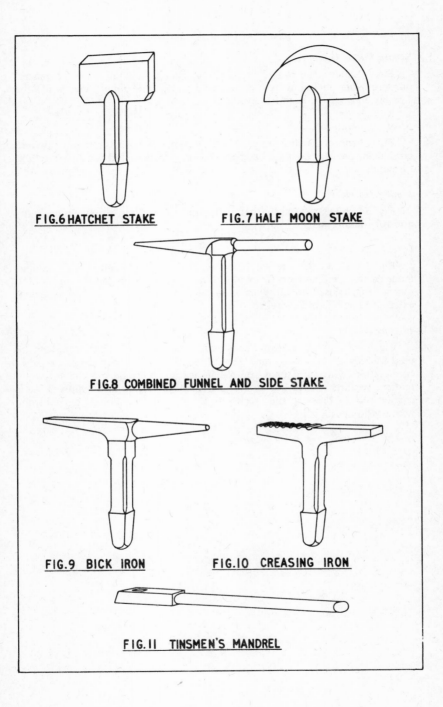

FIG.6 HATCHET STAKE

FIG.7 HALF MOON STAKE

FIG.8 COMBINED FUNNEL AND SIDE STAKE

FIG.9 BICK IRON

FIG.10 CREASING IRON

FIG.11 TINSMEN'S MANDREL

Square Faced Hammer

Fig. 12 shows the square faced or planishing hammer, used for general purpose work including wiring, dressing welds, and planishing, while the circular end may be used for riveting.

Stretching Hammer

Fig. 13 shows the stretching hammer, obtainable both as straight pein and cross pein, used for laying-off edges, for wiring flanges, and for the stretching of metal.

Paning Hammer

Fig. 14 shows the paning hammer, used for making paned down joints and for tucking wire.

Circular Mallet

Fig. 15 shows the circular boxwood mallet, fitted with a cane handle; made in various diameters from 40–110 mm in 6 mm steps, and from 100–150 mm in length; used for all types of flat work including setting and squaring, external flanging, and radiusing.

Bossing Mallet

Fig. 16 shows the boxwood bossing mallet; these pear-shaped mallets are used for raising, hollowing, and general internal work. They are also used in conjunction with sand bags for metal beating. Periodically the boxwood mallets require re-dressing to remove damage marks and chips. This is carried out by dressing the faces with a wood rasp, followed by polishing with sand-paper.

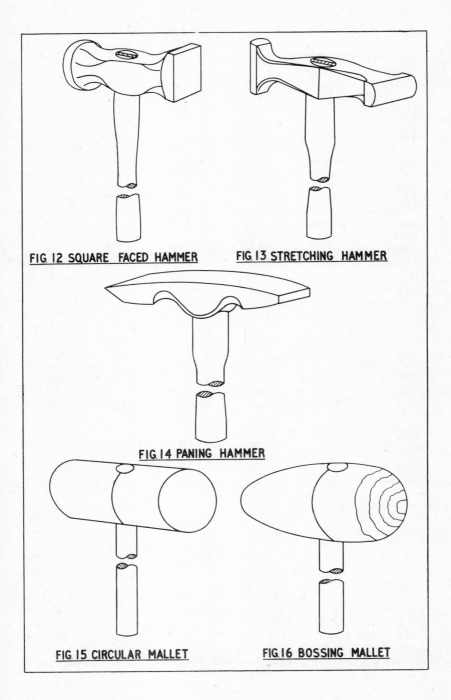

FIG. 12 SQUARE FACED HAMMER FIG. 13 STRETCHING HAMMER

FIG. 14 PANING HAMMER

FIG. 15 CIRCULAR MALLET FIG. 16 BOSSING MALLET

Machines for Sheet Metal Work

Guillotines

Guillotines used for the straight-line cutting of metal sheet vary in size from the small hand or foot-treadle types for cutting light-gauge materials to the heavy power-operated guillotines used for cutting the heavy-gauge materials.

Fig. 17 shows a typical treadle-type machine fitted with two hardened-steel blades 900 mm in length. The fixed lower blade is attached to the bed, and the moving blade (inclined to the fixed blade) is attached to a beam which has limited movement in the vertical plane. This movement is actuated by a foot-treadle; when the treadle is depressed the top blade descends and shears the metal at the point where it passes the lower blade. When the load is removed from the treadle strong springs return the beam to its initial position.

Adjustment is provided to give the desired amount of clearance between the faces of the two blades; the actual amount will be dependent on the thickness of the material to be cut. Correct setting is most important as this ensures a cleanly cut edge without burrs or radii.

When only a few pieces have to be cut, a scribed line on the material is set in alignment with the edge of the lower blade. When large numbers are required gauges can be set at front and rear, and on the bed, to ensure both squareness and correct size.

Safety precautions applicable to this type of machine must be rigidly observed. The blades must be adequately guarded at both front and rear, and guards should not be removed. Failure in this matter can cause most serious hand injuries. Great care is also required when using the foot-treadle to prevent the possibility of serious and painful foot accidents. Under no circumstances should more than one person be using a treadle guillotine at the same time. The material should be held firmly, and never attempt to cut material of a thicker gauge than the maximum thickness specified for a given machine.

Bending Rollers

Bending rollers, either hand-operated or power-driven, are used for bending flat metal sheet into cylindrical or part-cylindrical forms.

Fig. 18 shows the hand-operated machine consisting of a fabricated pressed-steel main frame supporting three rollers 50 mm in diameter and 950 mm long. The front two rollers known as 'pinch' or pressure rollers are set in vertical alignment, the upper one being adjustable in order to accommodate various thicknesses of material. The back roller is free to revolve in its own bearings, and can be adjusted to control the size of the radius of the bend.

The crank handle provides the initial turning motion to the bottom roller The function of these two front rollers is simply to apply sufficient pressure to the metal sheet to feed it on to the back roller which controls the radius of the cylindrical surface produced.

When rolling complete cylinders the finished cylinder is left around the bottom roller, therefore provision has to be made for its removal. The bottom roller is made to slip out of the main frame at one end, the movement being sufficient to enable the cylindrical component to be removed from the roller. This provision is called a slip roller.

The top and back rollers have several grooves of various radii at one end,

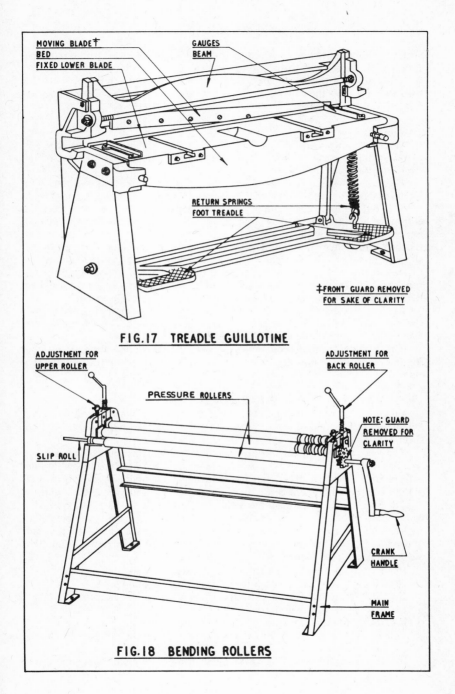

MOVING BLADE†
BED
FIXED LOWER BLADE

GAUGES
BEAM

RETURN SPRINGS
FOOT TREADLE

‡FRONT GUARD REMOVED
FOR SAKE OF CLARITY

FIG.17 TREADLE GUILLOTINE

ADJUSTMENT FOR
UPPER ROLLER

ADJUSTMENT FOR
BACK ROLLER

PRESSURE ROLLERS

NOTE: GUARD
REMOVED FOR
CLARITY

SLIP ROLL

CRANK
HANDLE

MAIN
FRAME

FIG.18 BENDING ROLLERS

and this allows a previously wired or folded sheet to be rolled to the required radius without damage to the work or machine.

The nature of the work carried out on this type of machine prevents the use of guards over the rollers, therefore extreme care must be taken otherwise fingers could be crushed.

Folding Machine

Hand- or power-operated folding machines are used extensively for carrying out operations which involve permanent deflection of sheet metal from one flat plane to another.

Fig. 20 shows the main details of a hand-operated folding machine with blades 900 mm in length and with a capacity of 25 mm maximum depth of fold.

The flat bed is rigidly supported in the main frame. A cam-operated clamping beam carrying a folding blade with an angular edge is located above and parallel with the bed. The piece of sheet to be folded is placed on the bed, and when the clamping beam is lowered and locked, it grips the sheet in position. The vertical folding beam which swivels on two trunnions located in the main frame, can be moved through an arc of sufficient magnitude to fold the sheet to the required form. This beam can be adjusted in the vertical plane to change the radius produced at the fold line.

Initially the sheet can be set between the bed and the clamping beam with the aid of a scribed line, or alternatively gauges can be set to ensure the accuracy of duplicate parts.

The folding beam handle must be firmly held when carrying out the folding operation. Care must also be taken when setting the fold line to the clamping beam.

Universal Swaging, Wiring, and Jennying Machine

Fig. 19 shows a hand-operated universal swaging, wiring, and jennying machine which is one of the most versatile and useful machines used by the sheet metal worker.

The main frame, which is firmly bolted to the bench, supports two driving spindles mounted one above the other, and geared together. The lower spindle is fixed in the vertical plane, but has sufficient adjustment in the horizontal plane to obtain alignment of the two wheels operating on the sheet metal.

The upper spindle is adjustable within small limits in the vertical plane. The rotary motion of the spindles is controlled by a hand-operated crank-handle.

Various pairs of wheels with differing profiles can be fitted to the end of the spindles; this enables many rotary operations to be carried out, and the most commonly used wheels would include:—

Fig. A   Wheels used for forming U-seatings for wire.

Fig. B   Closing wheels used for closing metal around wire.

Fig. C   Jennying wheels used for turning up small edges on circular blanks or cylinders.

Fig. D   Paning-down wheels used for paned down joints.

Fig. E   Swage wheels used to raise a bead or moulding on sheet metal to stiffen it.

Fig. F   Joggling wheels used for joggled joints on cylindrical work.

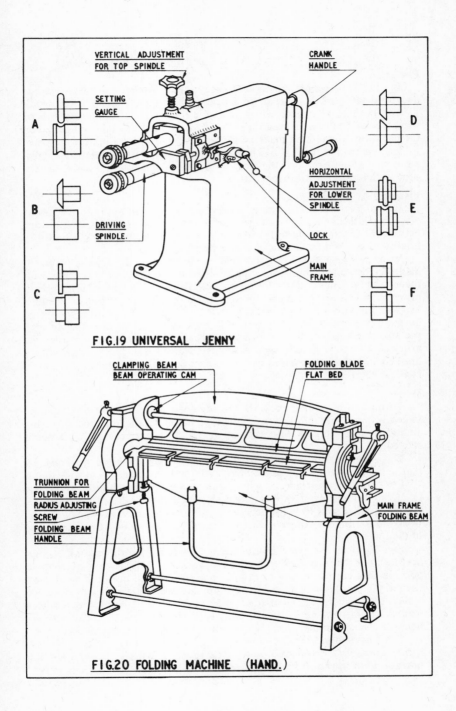

VERTICAL ADJUSTMENT
FOR TOP SPINDLE

CRANK
HANDLE

SETTING
GAUGE

A

B

DRIVING
SPINDLE.

C

HORIZONTAL
ADJUSTMENT
FOR LOWER
SPINDLE

LOCK

MAIN
FRAME

D

E

F

FIG.19 UNIVERSAL JENNY

CLAMPING BEAM
BEAM OPERATING CAM

FOLDING BLADE
FLAT BED

TRUNNION FOR
FOLDING BEAM
RADIUS ADJUSTING
SCREW
FOLDING BEAM
HANDLE

MAIN FRAME
FOLDING BEAM

FIG.20 FOLDING MACHINE (HAND.)

Sheet Metal Operations

Beading

Beading is the simplest method of increasing the strength, stiffness, appearance, and safety of the edge of an article made from thin gauge sheet metal.

The beading allowance which must be added to the developed size of sheet is equal to the actual bead size. Fig. 21(a) shows the bead line marked on the flat sheet; the folding machine is then set to give no radius and the sheet folded as shown in Fig. 21(b). The edge is then dressed with a boxwood mallet along the whole length of the bead as shown in Fig. 21(c). Finally the cut edge is closed as shown in Fig. 21(d).

Flanging

Flanging by hand is an operation carried out in order to produce edges of various widths and angles on flat or curved sheets. Flanges usually vary between 6–20 mm in width. If wider flanges are required the article is usually fabricated and not made from a single sheet.

When flanging flat sheet the folding machine is the most convenient method (Fig. 20). Flanging on cylindrical or shaped articles is more difficult than straight flanges, as the metal will need to be enlarged or stretched in order to gain sufficient metal for the larger radius. The depth of flange is marked out with a pair of dividers or odd-leg callipers; the sheet supported on the top of a suitable stake or metal block is rotated as it is dressed with the stretching hammer. This process is continued, gradually lowering the article until the required angle is almost reached, the flange being finally finished with the square-faced hammer; this sequence of operations is shown in Figs. 22(a), (b), (c).

Wiring

Wiring is a technique by which the edge of a piece of sheet metal can be folded around wire of a given diameter. This is another method of giving additional strength and stiffness to an article, and also provides a clean and safe edge.

The wiring operation may be carried out solely by hand methods, by machine, or sometimes by a combination of both methods.

For wiring straight sides which are bent in a folding machine an allowance of $2\frac{1}{2}$ times diameter of wire is added to the developed size of the sheet.

When the edge is to be stretched over by hand as in cylindrical or shaped work the normal allowance is 2 times diameter of wire plus 4 times thickness of the material.

Figs. 23(a)–(e) indicate the sequence of operations in wiring a straight edge. (a) Mark out the wire allowance on the flat sheet. (b) Set folding machine to give a radius corresponding to radius of wire, set bend line, and bend sheet beyond 90°. (c) Wire is placed in position and metal dressed with boxwood mallet. (d) Support the wired edge on a heavy metal plate and dress with a paning hammer (using end with radius). (e) Tuck the edge under with the opposite end of hammer. Finally straighten the edge with a boxwood mallet.

The universal machine as shown in Fig. 19 is frequently used to perform wiring operations on shaped work. The essential wheels required for this operation are shown in Figs. 19(a) and (b).

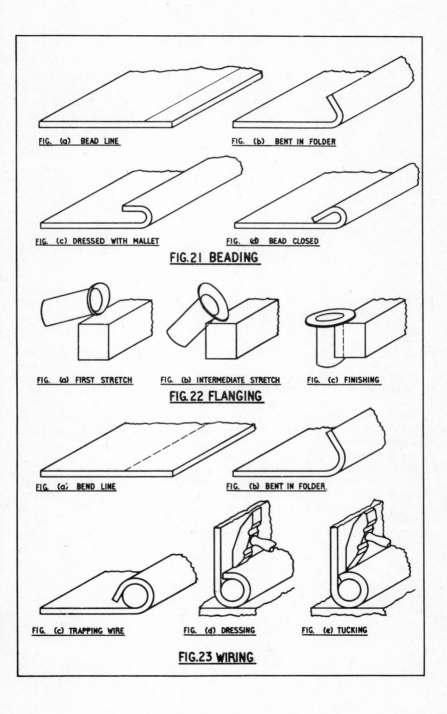

FIG. (a) BEAD LINE

FIG. (b) BENT IN FOLDER

FIG. (c) DRESSED WITH MALLET

FIG. (d) BEAD CLOSED

FIG.21 BEADING

FIG. (a) FIRST STRETCH

FIG. (b) INTERMEDIATE STRETCH

FIG. (c) FINISHING

FIG.22 FLANGING

FIG. (a) BEND LINE

FIG. (b) BENT IN FOLDER

FIG. (c) TRAPPING WIRE

FIG. (d) DRESSING

FIG. (e) TUCKING

FIG.23 WIRING

Sheet Metal Joints

Sheet metal can be joined together by several basic methods, and those most generally used include welding, brazing, riveting, soldering, and folded metal joints. The first three methods are more applicable to the heavier gauge materials and are therefore dealt with in the next chapter on metal joining.

Folded Metal Joints

Folded metal joints are made in a variety of different forms, each type having its own particular applications, although a completed workpiece might incorporate several types of joints. Those most commonly used include:—

Grooved Seam

A self-locking type of joint used to secure the edges of flat sheets or the edges of a shaped component without rivets or solder. In practice the grooved seam is soldered when the workpiece must be liquid proof.

When working with sheet metal of thickness 1 mm or above, the total seam allowance must be equal to 3 times width of seam, e.g. 5 mm width seam requires 15 mm allowance, i.e. 7 mm allowance on each edge. When working in heavier gauge materials the thickness of the material must also be taken into account.

Fig. 24(a) shows a developed sheet with the appropriate seam allowance added each side, and the width of seam marked from each edge. The two edges are then folded, one up and one down as in Fig. 24(b); these edges must be parallel to the sheet face. The folded edges are then hooked together as in Fig. 24(c) and interlocked by means of a grooving tool as shown in Fig. 24(d) The complete grooving tool is shown separately in Fig. 24(e). The recess in the end of the grooving tool is of the same shape as the finished joint. These tools are obtainable in sizes from 3·20 mm wide in steps of 1—5 mm. It is normal practice to select a tool 1·5 mm larger in size than the folding allowance. Finally the seam is closed with a boxwood mallet.

It can be seen from Fig. 24(d) that this joint is on the outside of the component; in some cases the joint is required inside the article as in Fig. 24(f). This operation is carried out by substituting a circular bar with a groove along its length in place of the grooving tool. This bar is used to support the inner face of the joint while the seam is closed with a suitable mallet.

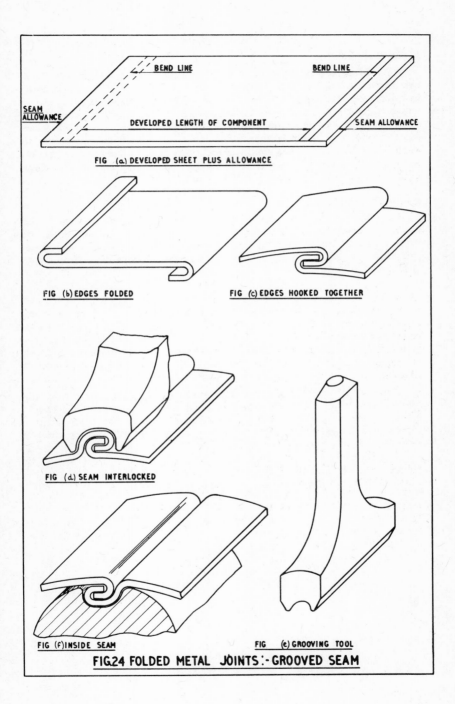

SEAM
ALLOWANCE

BEND LINE

BEND LINE

DEVELOPED LENGTH OF COMPONENT

SEAM ALLOWANCE

FIG (a) DEVELOPED SHEET PLUS ALLOWANCE

FIG (b) EDGES FOLDED

FIG (c) EDGES HOOKED TOGETHER

FIG (d) SEAM INTERLOCKED

FIG (f) INSIDE SEAM

FIG (e) GROOVING TOOL

FIG.24 FOLDED METAL JOINTS :- GROOVED SEAM

Paned Down Joint

A paned down joint is frequently used to secure two sections of sheet, e.g. two sections of pipe or ducting, or a conical section to a cylindrical section. Consider the latter example, and assume a 5 mm paned down joint is required. The cylindrical body is first flanged 5 mm wide and the conical section is flanged 10 mm wide, as shown in Fig. 25(a). Mark a bend line 5 mm from the cut edge of the 10 mm flange and turn another flange 5 mm wide at 90° as in Fig. 25(b). The cylindrical section is fitted into the conical section and the vertical flange is paned down to complete the joint as in Fig. 25(c). If the joint is to be liquid proof it will be also soldered.

Knock Up Bottom

The knock up bottom type of joint is a further development of the paned down joint, constructed in the same manner, but finally the metal edges are dressed over an additional 90° and will lie parallel to the sides of the body as shown in Fig. 25(d). This type of joint may be soldered depending on its application.

Slip on Joint

Frequently a circular base must be attached to a cylindrical body and the slip on joint is a convenient method of doing this. The base is cut to a diameter equal to the outside diameter of body plus 2 times depth of flange. The base is then flanged, fitted over the body, and is soldered to it as shown in Fig. 25(e).

Slip in Joint

The slip in joint is used for similar applications to the slip on, but the base is fitted inside the body instead of outside. The diameter of the base is equal to inside diameter of body plus 2 times depth of flange less 2 times thickness of material. Fig. 25(f) shows the slip in joint as constructed when soldered, also the arrangement of the joint when welded.

Fig. 25(f) shows the normal arrangement when the edges are to be soldered. For certain types of work a separate rim may be soldered on the outside of the bottom of the body to safeguard the base.

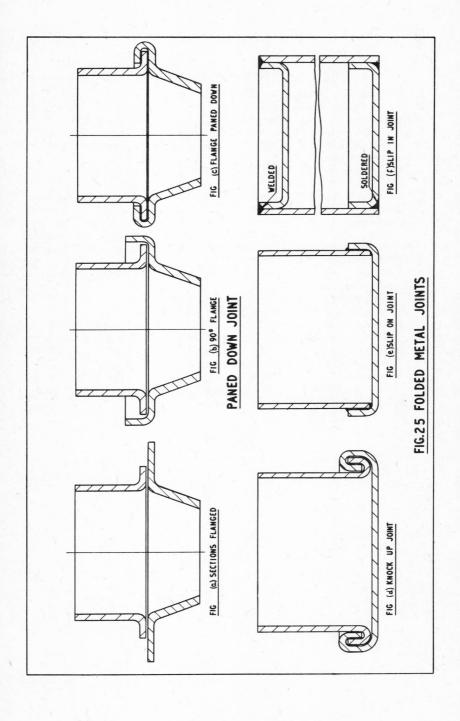

FIG (a) SECTIONS FLANGED

FIG (b) 90° FLANGE

FIG (c) FLANGE PANED DOWN

PANED DOWN JOINT

FIG (d) KNOCK UP JOINT

FIG (e) SLIP ON JOINT

WELDED

SOLDERED

FIG (f) SLIP IN JOINT

FIG. 25 FOLDED METAL JOINTS

Soft Soldering

Soldering is a traditional method of joining two metal surfaces, carried out by the fusing of an alloy of tin and lead known as solder. The melting temperature of the solder is lower than that of the metal being joined, therefore the molten solder flows between the mating surfaces filling the space between them, and as it solidifies forms an intermetallic compound with the surfaces of the joint.

This process may be subdivided into five basic operations:—

1. Fitting the parts. The mating parts should be carefully fitted: a clearance between $0·075$ and $0·125$ mm is sufficient to allow the solder to penetrate between the joint surfaces, and yet small enough to be completely filled by the molten solder; if the work is made from tinplate or if the metal is tinned prior to fitting, a clearance of $0·025$ mm is sufficient.
2. Cleaning the parts. The joint surfaces must be chemically clean if soldering is to be carried out in a satisfactory manner. All dirt, rust, paint, and grease must be removed, also any oxide film which forms on the surface of the metal when exposed to the air.
3. Applying a flux. Application of a suitable flux is necessary in order to attack and dissolve the oxide film on the surface of the metal and on the molten solder, and also to act as a screen to prevent any further oxidation during the actual soldering process. See Fig. 29.
4. Application of heat. Sufficient heat from a copper bit or from a blowpipe flame is essential to cause the solder to flow freely.
5. Removal of surplus solder.

Types of Fluxes

Zinc Chloride (Killed Spirits)

Made by dissolving granulated zinc in hydrochloric acid and may be used at full strength, or be diluted with about its own weight of water. As this type of flux leaves a crust near the joint which would cause rapid corrosion it is essential that the finished joint be throughly washed off in order to remove all traces of the flux.

Zinc chloride is a general-purpose flux and is suitable for soldering tinplate, copper, and brass, but not recommended for electrical joints and other work that cannot be efficiently washed to eliminate danger of corrosion.

Hydrochloric Acid

Hydrochloric acid used at half strength provides a useful flux for soldering zinc and galvanised articles. Equal proportions of this acid and zinc chloride make a suitable flux for soldering stainless steel. The completed joint must be thoroughly washed to remove all traces of the flux, and care must also be taken to avoid inhaling the dangerous vapour given off by this type of flux.

Paste Type (Acid)

As liquid fluxes tend to drain off the surface and possibly cause damage to other parts of the assembly it is sometimes more convenient to use flux in the form of paste.

The paste type fluxes consist of vaseline, tallow, or lanoline to which acids such as zinc chloride and ammonium chloride are added in various percentages.

Safe Type (Non-Corrosive)

A non-corrosive type of flux made from resin is widely used for soldering in order to avoid the possibility of the corrosive action associated with acid-type fluxes.

The resin may be used in several forms—crushed into a powder and sprinkled on the joint, or made into a liquid by dissolving the resin in methylated spirit and brushing the solution on the joint face; alternatively this type of flux may be prepared and applied in the form of paste.

The Soldering Bit

The traditional soldering bit most generally used for soldering the various types of sheet metal joints consists of a forged copper head of suitable section attached to an iron shank and held by means of a wooden handle. Fig. 26 shows the general-purpose type of copper bit, a square section reduced to a point at one end. Another very useful soldering bit, known as the hatchet head, is shown in Fig. 27.

Copper is used exclusively for the head because of its heat storage capacity and high thermal conductivity. The size of the head will govern the amount of heat which can be stored in it; the larger cross-section the greater the heat capacity. The weight of bit that can be conveniently handled is the limiting factor.

Preparation for use

Successful soft soldering depends largely on the condition of the copper soldering bit. The faces should be filed clean and square and the corners and the tip slightly radiused. The filed section must be then properly 'tinned' or wetted with solder. This can be carried out by heating the bit in a gas-heated soldering stove (Fig. 28) or coke fire. When the flame turns green remove the bit and dip in flux, or rub on a piece of sal ammoniac to remove oxide film, and then apply solder until faces are tinned. This operation must be repeated when the faces become tarnished or burnt. When the bit is prepared in this way the solder will run smoothly from the soldering bit to the workpiece.

Composition of Solder B.S. 219: 1959

The British Standard quoted above makes provision for a wide range of solders containing varying percentages of tin, lead, and antimony. Each grade is denoted by a letter of the alphabet, and of the fourteen different grades specified for general purposes, eight are classified as non-antimonial; the remaining six grades contain between $1 \cdot 0$ and $3 \cdot 0\%$ antimony.

The composition recommended for use on general sheet metal work when soldering by means of a copper bit is grade 'F' which contains equal proportions of tin and lead, liquid at 212°C and completely solid at 183°C.

Surface Development

The shape of most articles in sheet metal is based on a few geometrical forms either used singly or in combination. The forms most frequently used include the cube, prism, cylinder, cone, and pyramid. To make any of these forms the flat sheet must be rolled, folded, or worked into the desired shape, therefore the first requirement is the developed shape or pattern marked out on the flat sheet, and this development or pattern will include shape and size of notches, allowances for required joints, and allowances for wired edges and thickness of metal. The amount of time and care devoted to the marking-out and cutting-out of the pattern will be more than compensated by the production of a finished article which is accurate both in shape and dimensions.

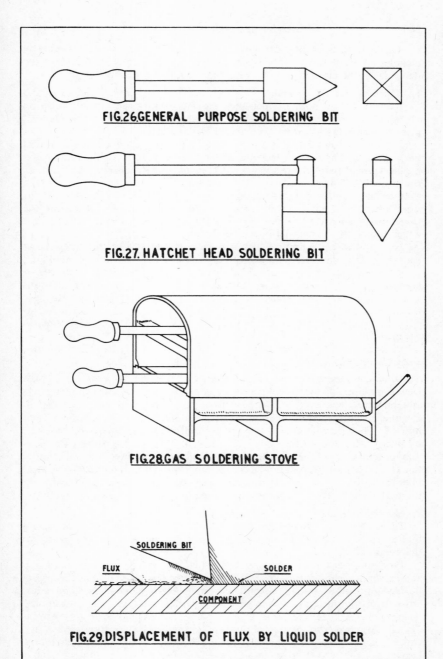

FIG.26.GENERAL PURPOSE SOLDERING BIT

FIG.27. HATCHET HEAD SOLDERING BIT

FIG.28.GAS SOLDERING STOVE

SOLDERING BIT

FLUX

SOLDER

COMPONENT

FIG.29.DISPLACEMENT OF FLUX BY LIQUID SOLDER

The pattern is usually developed from a working drawing or sketch by means of one of the three following methods; the actual method selected depends on the class of solid to which the required article belongs:—

1. *Parallel Line Development*

Patterns for all bodies which preserve a constant shape or cross-section throughout their length, and which belong geometrically to the class of prisms can be developed by the parallel line method.

Fig. 30(a) shows a square prism. When the four sides are opened out flat the resultant shape is a rectangle divided up into four smaller rectangles by the vertical parallel lines which correspond to the edges of the prism as shown in Fig. 30(b).

Consider the prism cut through obliquely as shown in Fig. 31(a). If the sides are opened out flat the cutting line can be traced by transferring the respective heights from Fig. 31(a) and then drawing the line a, b, c, d, e which intersects the parallel lines as shown in Fig. 31(b).

Next consider a cylinder which may be regarded as a prism with circular ends. Fig. 32(a) shows a cylinder with a series of equally spaced parallel lines drawn on its surface from end to end. If the circumference is then marked off along a horizontal base line by transferring the twelve numbered divisions 1–2, 2–3, 3–4, etc. the development of this curved surface is seen to be a rectangle in Fig. 32(b).

The length of the rectangle by calculation is equal to π times diameter of the cylinder.

If the cylinder is cut obliquely as at AB shown in Fig. 33(a) the developed shape can be obtained by the following method:—

Draw a circle representing circumference of the cylinder as shown in plan view Fig. 33(a); divide this circle into any convenient number of equal parts and number them accordingly. (Twelve equal parts used in this example). From each numbered point draw parallel vertical lines to intersect the joint line AB. The circumference is then marked off along the horizontal base line by transferring the twelve divisions 1–2, 2–3, 3–4, etc. from the plan view. From each point on the base line erect a perpendicular line. Draw horizontal lines from the intersection points on the joint line AB to intersect the vertical lines from the pattern. A curve drawn through these intersection points on the pattern will give the contour of the required oblique section. Fig. 33(b).

2. *Radial Line Development*

Patterns for all bodies converging to an apex, including frustums and bodies which form parts of cones or pyramids, can be developed by the radial line method.

First consider the right cone, one of the most common bodies in this group applicable to sheet metal work. Fig. 34 shows the elevation of a right cone ABH the development of which is a sector of a circle. Mark a semi-circle using radius OB and divide into any convenient number of parts (six in this example). Using radius AB describe arc B'A' any length, and draw line AB'. As the semi-circle BEH represents one-half of the base circumference, the six divisions BC, CD, etc. must be set off on arc B'A' twice, making a total of twelve divisions. Draw line from A to B^2 to complete the development of the right cone.

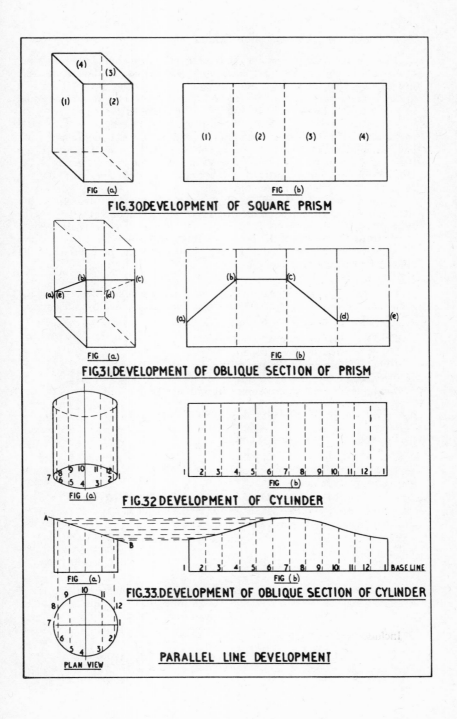

FIG (a)

FIG (b)

FIG.30.DEVELOPMENT OF SQUARE PRISM

FIG (a)

FIG (b)

FIG.31.DEVELOPMENT OF OBLIQUE SECTION OF PRISM

FIG (a)

FIG (b)

FIG.32 DEVELOPMENT OF CYLINDER

FIG (a)

FIG (b)

BASE LINE

FIG.33.DEVELOPMENT OF OBLIQUE SECTION OF CYLINDER

PLAN VIEW

PARALLEL LINE DEVELOPMENT

Next consider the pattern for the frustum of a right cone. Draw elevation as at ABH in Fig. 35. Mark off height of frustum as at JQ. Mark semi-circle using radius OB, and divide it into six equal parts. With radius AB describe arc B'A' and draw line AB'. Set off on arc B'A' twelve divisions each equal in length to BC. Draw line AB² and arc J¹J² to complete pattern.

Now consider the right cone cut obliquely. Set out elevation of cone ABH as shown in Fig. 36. On its base draw a semi-circle BEH representing half base circumference. Divide into six equal parts as BC, CD, DE, etc. From these points draw perpendiculars intersecting the base of the cone as at Cc, Dd, Ee, Ff, Gg; from points c, d, e, f, g, draw lines to the apex A. Draw line JQ at the appropriate position and angle.

From points Q, P, N, M, L, K, J, project horizontal lines out to the slant of the cone AB, and from these points on AB describe arcs on the pattern. With radius AB describe arc B¹A¹ and mark on it the twelve divisions equal in length to BC. Connect the points on B¹A¹ to the apex A. Draw a curve through the intersection points J¹, Q¹, J², to complete the contour of the pattern for this obliquely cut cone.

Calculations

Patterns are frequently required for right cones too large to be set out by the radial line method; in such cases dimensions can be obtained by calculations.

Consider the right cone shown in Fig. 34.

Let D = Base diameter of cone.
Let R = Slant height of cone.
If πD = Base circumference of cone.

Then length of pattern arc B¹B² $= \pi D$ . . . . . . (1)

Circumference of a circle radius R (enclosing 360°) $= 2\pi R$

Length of pattern arc (enclosing ϕ degrees) $= \dfrac{2\pi R\phi}{360}$ . . . . . (2)

Equating the values for (1) and (2) . . . . . . $\pi D = \dfrac{2\pi R\phi}{360}$

$$\therefore \quad \phi = \frac{\pi D 360}{2\pi R} = \frac{180D}{R}$$

Example   Let AO in Fig. 34   = 700 mm
Let BH in Fig. 34   = 500 mm
Find included angle of sector   = ϕ
Using Pythagoras Theorem:—

$$AB^2 = AO^2 + BO^2$$
$$= 700^2 + 250^2$$
$$= 490\ 000 + 62\ 500$$

$$\therefore \quad AB = \sqrt{552\ 500}$$
$$= 743 \text{ mm}$$

But AB = R = Radius of pattern

Included angle of sector $= \phi$

$$= \frac{180D}{R}$$
$$= \frac{180 \times 500}{743}$$
$$\phi \simeq 121°$$

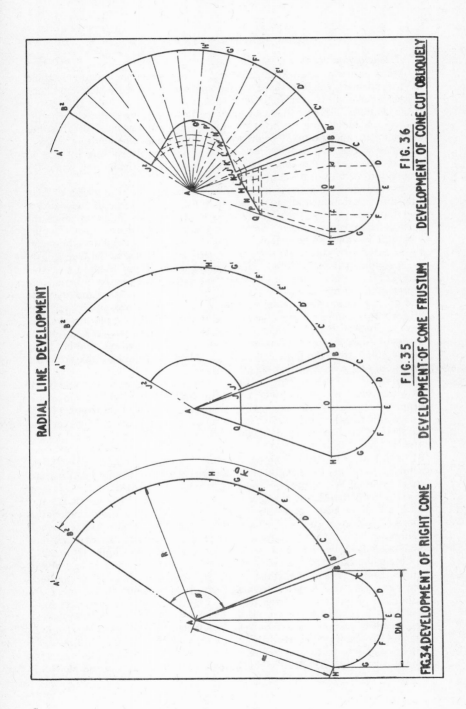

RADIAL LINE DEVELOPMENT

FIG.34, DEVELOPMENT OF RIGHT CONE

FIG.35 DEVELOPMENT OF CONE FRUSTUM

FIG.36 DEVELOPMENT OF CONE CUT OBLIQUELY

C

3. *Triangulation Method of Development*

Many bodies made in sheet metal are of complex design and are classified as 'transformers', i.e. the shape at one end transforms to a different shape at the other end, e.g. rectangle to a square, square to a circle, ellipse to a circle. Patterns for such bodies cannot be developed by either the parallel line or the radial line methods previously outlined. Surfaces of all solids belonging to the group of transformers can be divided up into a series of triangles whose size can be determined and then placed side by side in correct order until the complete pattern is produced, hence the name triangulation method of development.

In order to obtain the true size of each triangle, the true length of each side must be found and be placed in its correct position in the pattern, therefore two views of the object are essential, the elevation from which the vertical height of any line can be obtained, and the plan from which the plan length of any line can be obtained. If the plan length is placed at right angles to the vertical height of the same line the diagonal will give the true length.

A simple example of development by the triangulation method is shown in Fig. 37, a square body transformed to a circle. The plan shows that the centre of the circle coincides with the centre of the square, and that the diameter of the circle is smaller than the width of the square. If the circle was off-set (or of a different size) the method of development would be the same.

The circle in the plan view (Fig. 37) is divided into twelve equal parts; assuming the joint to be up the middle of the side marked A1, number these twelve points from the joint 1, 2, 3, 4, . . . 12. Extend the base line from the elevation, and erect a vertical-height line from point S to T.

To obtain the first triangle for the pattern take plan length A1 and mark off along the base line at right angles to the vertical height as shown (i). From this point draw a diagonal to point T, this gives true length of A1. Set off this length in the pattern and draw line A1 in a convenient place on the sheet. (Care needed to ensure the pattern will not run off the sheet.) Take true length AB from plan and from point A on pattern scribe arc. Next take B1 from plan and mark off along base line as shown (iii). Draw diagonal to point T. Take this true length of B1 and mark off from point 1 on pattern arc at point B. Where the two arcs intersect join B1 and AB.

To obtain the second triangle for the pattern take plan length B2 and mark off along base line as shown (ii). From this point draw diagonal to point T; this gives the true length of B2. Take this length and scribe arc from point B on pattern. From plan take length 1–2 and scribe arc on pattern from point 1. Draw line B2. Repeat the process with plan lengths B3 and 2–3 to obtain the third triangle. Repeat with plan lengths B4 and 3–4 to obtain fourth triangle. From plan take length BC and from point B on pattern strike arc; take true length C4 which is identical in length to B4, strike arc from point 4 on pattern; from point C where the two arcs intersect draw line from B to C and from C to 4. The remainder of the pattern can be developed by repeating the process previously outlined. When the final triangle EA1 is drawn, a free-hand curve through the points 1, 2, 3, 4, . . . 1 will complete the pattern. As explained earlier in the text any allowances for seams or laps must be added to this development. See Fig. 40, Example No. 3.

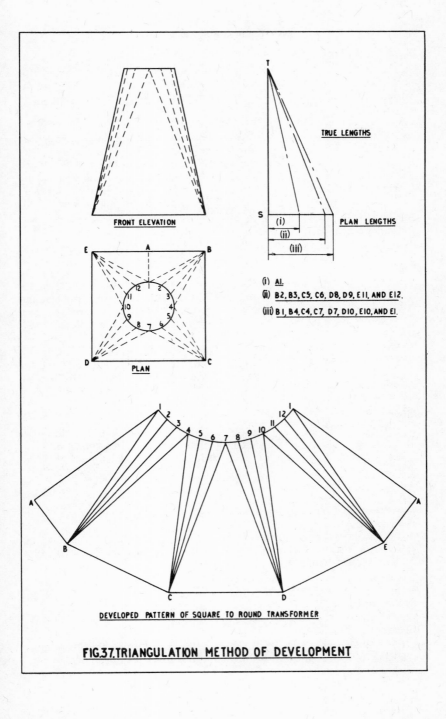

FRONT ELEVATION

TRUE LENGTHS

PLAN LENGTHS

S

(i)
(ii)
(iii)

E A B

12 2
11 3
10 4
9 5
8 7 6

PLAN

(i) A1.
(ii) B2, B3, C5, C6, D8, D9, E11, AND E12.
(iii) B1, B4, C4, C7, D7, D10, E10, AND E1.

DEVELOPED PATTERN OF SQUARE TO ROUND TRANSFORMER

FIG.37. TRIANGULATION METHOD OF DEVELOPMENT

Examples of Sheet Metal Work

The following examples of simple sheet metal work illustrate the development of several different geometrical forms with their appropriate allowances. A brief operation sequence is given for each example.

Example No. 1—Rectangular Tray   Fig. 38

1. Calculate developed sizes. (When calculating outside dimensions deduct $2 \times$ thickness of sheet from the length and width.) 2. Mark out on sheet and check dimensions. 3. Cut out developed shape and notch corners. 4. Bead edges. See Fig. 21(a)–(d). 5. Bend up sides (use folding machine Fig. 20 and hatchet stake Fig. 6). 6. Dress bends (use hatchet stake). 7. Square up sides (use boxwood mallet). 8. Solder laps (use soldering bit, Fig. 26). 9. Wash off flux. 10. Check all dimensions.

Example No. 2—Oil Bottle   Fig. 39

Body

1. Mark out developed shape, add seam allowance. See Fig. 24, p. 55. 2. Cut out developed shape and notch corners. 3. Break grain (use bending rollers, Fig. 18). 4. Prepare seam. 5. Form to shape. 6. Groove seam. 7. Solder seam on inside face. Wash off flux. 8. Check dimensions.

Bottom   Not shown separately on drawing, refer to Fig. 25(f).

1. Calculate blank size. 2. Mark out outside diameter and bend line for slip in joint. 3. Cut out. 4. Spin edge. 5. Flatten. 6. True depth of edge. 7. Check fit in body.

Rim

1 Calculate length, add lap. 2. Calculate width with bead allowance. 3. Mark out, cut out, and notch. 4. Break grain. 5. Bead edge. 6. Form to diameter. 7. Check fit on body. 8. Joggle lap. 9. Solder joint. 10. Wash off.

Top

1. Develop cone frustum (see Fig. 35), add laps, and grooved seam allowance.
2. Cut out and notch. 3. Break grain. 4. Prepare seam. 5. Form to shape. 6. Groove seam. 7. Solder seam on inside. 8. Wash off. 9. Lay off laps. 10. Check fit with body.

Neck

Operations as for rim.

Handle

1. Calculate length and width. 2. Mark out and cut out. 3. Bead edges. 4. Swage to fit over grooved seam. 5. Form to shape. 6. Check fit.

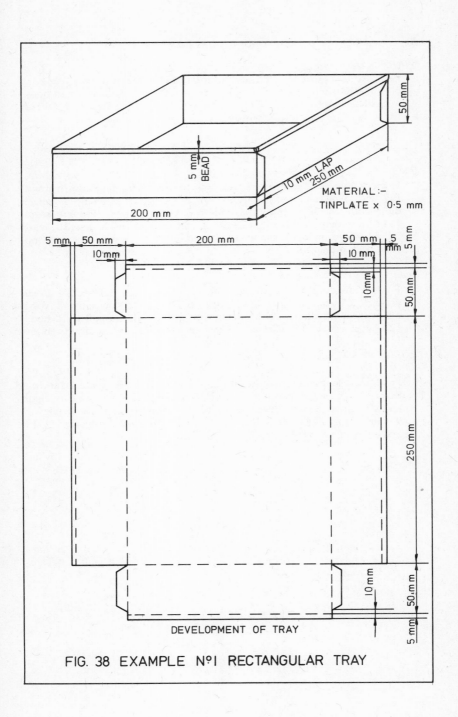

5 mm
BEAD

10 mm LAP
250 mm

50 mm

200 mm

MATERIAL :—
TINPLATE x 0·5 mm

5 mm | 50 mm | 200 mm | 50 mm | 5 mm
10 mm | | | 10 mm

5 mm

10 mm

50 mm

250 mm

10 mm

50 mm

5 mm

DEVELOPMENT OF TRAY

FIG. 38 EXAMPLE Nº1 RECTANGULAR TRAY

Assembly

Note all joints to be in line, and all joints to lap the same way.
1. Solder bottom to body. 2. Solder rim to body. 3. Solder top to body.
4. Solder neck to top. 5. Solder handle in position. 6. Wash off. 7. Test
for leaks. 8. Check all dimensions.

Example No. 3—Funnel   Fig. 40

Body

1. Mark out development of rectangle to circle (triangulation method,
Fig. 37). Add lap and seam allowances. 2. Mark notches. 3. Check
dimensions. 4. Break grain. 5. Cut out and notch. 6. Prepare seam.
7. Form to shape. 8. Groove seam. 9. Solder seam on inside face. 10. Wash
off. 11. True up body shape. 12. Lay off lap. 13. Level base and top.
14. Check dimensions.

Spout

1. Mark out developed shape, add laps. 2. Mark notch. 3. Check. 4. Break
grain. 5. Cut out and notch. 6. Form to shape. 7 Solder joint. 8. Wash
off. 9. True up shape. 10. Mark off lap (inside). 11. Lay off to fit body.
12. Level edges. 13. Check dimensions. 14. Fit and solder to body.
15. Wash off.

Rim

1. Calculate length and width; add lap and wire allowances. 2. Mark out
notches. 3. Check dimensions. 4. Cut out and notch. 5. Cut wire to length
and straighten. 6. Wire edge (off-set joint). 7. Bend to shape. 8. Joggle lap.
9. Check fit in body. 10. Solder joint. 11. Wash off. 12. Level rim. 13. Fit
and solder to body. 14. Wash off. 15. Check dimensions.

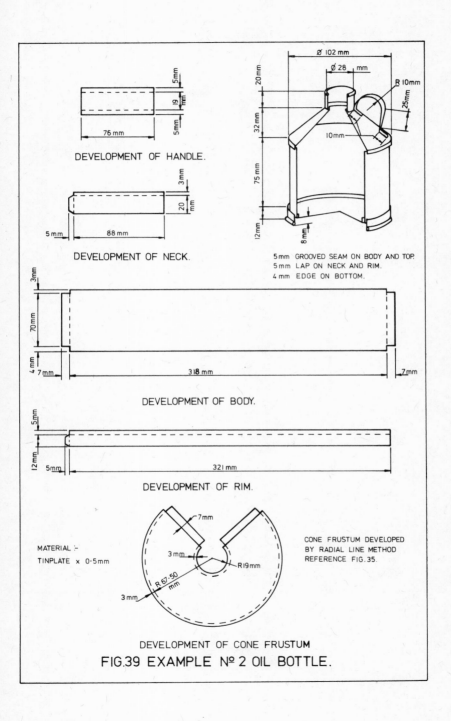

DEVELOPMENT OF HANDLE.

DEVELOPMENT OF NECK.

5mm GROOVED SEAM ON BODY AND TOP.
5mm LAP ON NECK AND RIM.
4mm EDGE ON BOTTOM.

DEVELOPMENT OF BODY.

DEVELOPMENT OF RIM.

MATERIAL :-
TINPLATE x 0·5mm

CONE FRUSTUM DEVELOPED
BY RADIAL LINE METHOD
REFERENCE FIG.35.

DEVELOPMENT OF CONE FRUSTUM

FIG.39 EXAMPLE № 2 OIL BOTTLE.

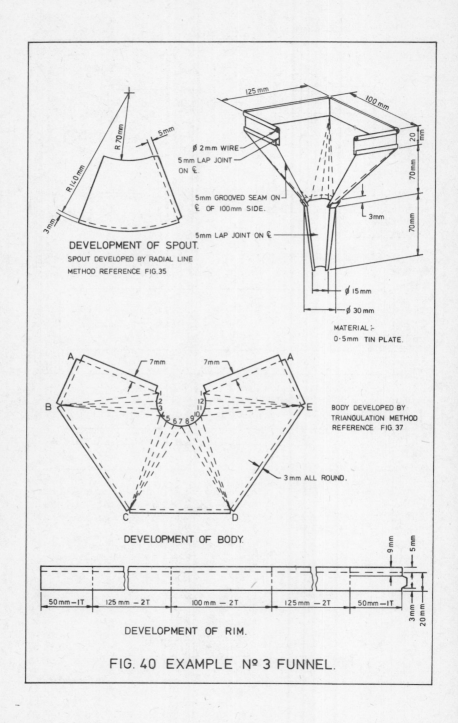

DEVELOPMENT OF SPOUT.

SPOUT DEVELOPED BY RADIAL LINE
METHOD REFERENCE FIG.35

R 70mm
R 140mm
5mm
3mm

125 mm
100 mm
20 mm
70mm
70mm

Ø 2mm WIRE
5 mm LAP JOINT
ON ₵.

5mm GROOVED SEAM ON
₵ OF 100mm SIDE.

5mm LAP JOINT ON ₵

3mm

Ø 15mm
Ø 30mm

MATERIAL :-
0·5mm TIN PLATE.

BODY DEVELOPED BY
TRIANGULATION METHOD
REFERENCE FIG. 37

7mm   7mm

A   A

B   E

1 2 3 4 5 6 7 8 9 10 11 12

3 mm ALL ROUND.

C   D

DEVELOPMENT OF BODY.

9 mm
5 mm

50mm —1T   125 mm — 2T   100 mm — 2T   125 mm — 2T   50mm —1T

3 mm
20 mm

DEVELOPMENT OF RIM.

FIG. 40 EXAMPLE Nº 3 FUNNEL.

CHAPTER THREE

METAL JOINING

Welding Processes

The general term 'fabricated product' is used to describe a wide range of engineering products made from metal sheet, plate, angle or channel sections, or other types of rolled sections which are joined together by means of a welding, brazing, or riveting process.

Welding is the most common method of fabricating and repairing metal products, therefore many different welding techniques have been developed to meet the requirements of modern industry. Two basic methods of fusion welding only are mentioned in this chapter.

Oxy-Acetylene Welding

The basic principle of the oxy-acetylene process is quite simple. When oxygen and acetylene gas are mixed in the correct proportions and ignited, a flame which reaches a temperature of over 3000°C is obtained, this being sufficient to melt all commercial metals. The edges of plates to be joined together are brought to the fusing temperature by heat generated with the aid of this oxygen/acetylene flame, while a filler metal in the form of a welding rod of suitable composition is fed into the joint. The molten edges of the plates and the filler metal flow together and upon cooling form one complete piece, the joint being as strong as the actual parent metal.

Two systems of oxy-acetylene welding are in general use: (i) Low Pressure; (ii) High Pressure.

Low-Pressure System

In this system acetylene is supplied at low pressure from a special generator by the action of water on calcium carbide. This low-pressure acetylene is purified, dried, and stored in a gas-storage holder, then as required is fed through the main supply line, into a hydraulic back-pressure valve, and then into the blow-pipe. The function of the back-pressure valve is to prevent oxygen from passing back into the acetylene-supply line and creating an explosive mixture.

The oxygen is supplied from a seamless, drawn-steel cylinder. It passes through a reducing valve and then on into a low-pressure blow-pipe. The latter is so designed that the high-pressure oxygen injects or draws the low pressure acetylene into the mixing chamber and then on to the tip of the nozzle where the mixture is burnt. The low-pressure blow-pipe is shown in Fig. 3(a). The low-pressure system has advantages when a large number of operators are continuously employed on repetition work and a large plant is therefore essential.

73

High-Pressure System

In the high-pressure system both the oxygen and the acetylene are supplied from seamless-steel cylinders, and the manufacturers claim the following advantages over the low-pressure system:—

(i)   Greater safety.
(ii)   Ease of adjustment.
(iii) Higher working efficiency, accounted for by the intimate mixture of gases in the blow-pipe, and the slightly higher flame temperature due to the high purity of the gas.
(iv)   Plant entirely portable, can be easily taken to any desired site.
(v)   Simplicity of operation.
(vi)   Accurate regulation of both oxygen and acetylene cylinders.

Standard Equipment

A high-pressure plant comprises the following items of equipment which are arranged as shown in Fig. 1.

(i)   Supply of oxygen in a steel cylinder *painted black*, into which is fitted an oxygen-pressure regulator.
(ii)   Supply of compressed acetylene in a steel cylinder *painted maroon*, into which is fitted an acetylene-pressure regulator.
       Note Acetylene gas is unstable when compressed to high pressures and is therefore contained in the cylinder dissolved in acetone. The cylinder is packed with a porous spongy material such as kapoc, asbestos, prepared charcoal, or other suitable material saturated with acetone, and the acetone absorbs large quantities of acetylene under pressure.
(iii) A high-pressure blow-pipe as shown in Fig. 3(b), equipped with a range of interchangeable nozzles suitable for welding the various types and thicknesses of metal.
(iv)   Two lengths of special non-porous rubber hose, one *blue* leading from the oxygen regulator to blow-pipe inlet marked 'O', the other *red* leading from the acetylene regulator to the blow-pipe inlet marked 'A'. Standard connections are fitted to the hose at both regulator and blow-pipe ends.
(v)   Keys to suit the cylinder-valve spindles.
(vi)   A supply of welding rods and fluxes; these are selected according to the type of metal being welded.
(vii) A pair of welding goggles fitted with lenses as recommended in B.S. 679; also protective clothing including a leather apron and a pair of gloves.
(viii) A welding table equipped with suitable firebricks, and a wire brush for cleaning the metal prior to welding.
(ix)   A spark lighter for igniting the blow-pipe.
(x)   A trolley for transporting cylinders and equipment.

Regulators

The reducing valve or pressure regulator used in both oxygen and acetylene cylinders perform two functions: (i) reduce the high cylinder pressure to the much lower working pressure used in the blow-pipe; (ii) maintain a steady working pressure in spite of variations in cylinder pressure.

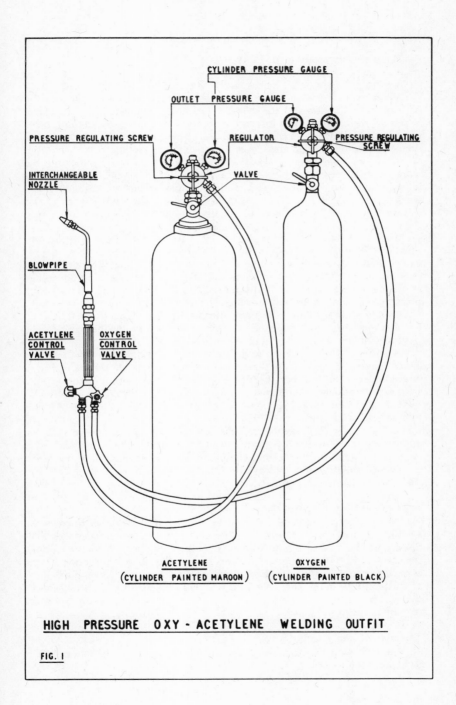

HIGH PRESSURE OXY-ACETYLENE WELDING OUTFIT

FIG. 1

These regulators are made in two types:—
(i) Single stage; and (ii) Double stage.

A sectional view of the single-stage oxygen regulator is shown in Fig. 2.

When the cylinder valve is opened gas flows from the cylinder into the base of the regulator and the cylinder pressure is indicated on the gauge. When the regulator screw is turned it compresses the spring S and the valve V is opened, and gas enters the body R; as the pressure rises it overcomes the spring-loaded diaphragm and closes the valve V, preventing further gas from entering. The outlet side is also fitted with a pressure gauge indicating the working pressure on the blow-pipe. As gas is drawn off on the outlet side, the springs lower the diaphragm and more gas enters the regulator. The working pressure is therefore controlled by the pressure on the springs and this can be varied by means of the adjusting screw, which is set initially to the pressure required for the work in hand.

With a two-stage regulator the gas from the cylinder flows into a high-pressure chamber and a spring-loaded diaphragm maintains it at a predetermined pressure. The gas passes into a second reducing chamber, the pressure being now controlled by the adjusting screw. The main advantage of the two-stage regulator is the more uniform flow of gas, the working pressure remaining constant until the cylinder is empty.

Both types of regulator are fitted with two pressure gauges, one indicating cylinder pressure, and the other working pressure on the blow-pipe. The oxygen cylinder gauge is graduated on one scale reading up to 280 bar, while a second scale reads up to 4000 lbf/in². The oxygen working pressure gauge may read up to 10·4 bar or 150 lbf/in². The gauge shown in Fig. 2 is graduated from 0–2 bar (0–30 lbf/in²) and is most suitable for normal welding operations. When flame cutting, a higher range gauge is used.

The acetylene working pressure gauge is graduated up to 41 bar (600 lbf/in²) inlet, and 2 bar (30 lbf/in²) outlet. A filter pad is fitted to the inlet of the acetylene regulator. It is most important to ensure that the adjusting screw is released (load removed from spring) before cylinder valve is opened. Failure in this respect can cause serious damage to the regulator.

These regulators must always be regarded as precision instruments and therefore be treated accordingly.

Selection of Blow-Pipe Nozzle

Blow-pipes are equipped with a series of different size nozzles to cover the welding requirements of different thicknesses of metal. These nozzles are classified according to the size of the outlet opening; as thickness increases so must the size of the nozzle opening be correspondingly larger. Selection of the correct nozzle, operating at the proper working pressure, is very important.

If the nozzle is too small the heat will be insufficient to fuse the metal to the required depth; if the nozzle is too large, the heat is too great and holes may be burnt in the metal.

Assembly of Equipment

The following sequence must be strictly adhered to if the equipment is to be assembled safely.

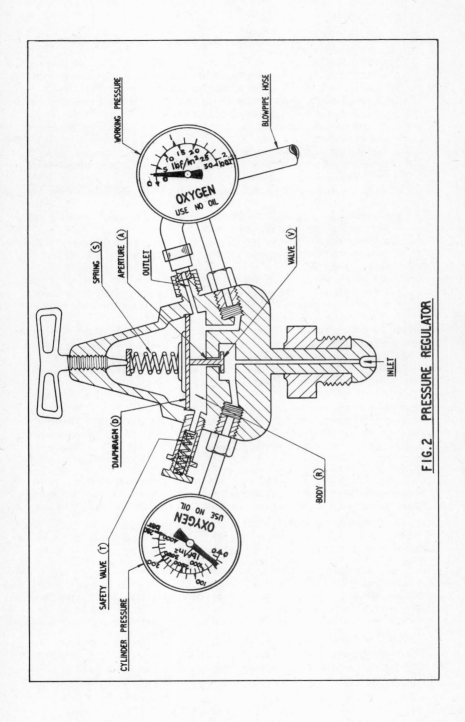

WORKING PRESSURE

BLOWPIPE HOSE

OXYGEN
USE NO OIL

SPRING (S)

APERTURE (A)

OUTLET

VALVE (V)

SAFETY VALVE (T)

DIAPHRAGM (D)

CYLINDER PRESSURE

OXYGEN
USE NO OIL

BODY (R)

INLET

FIG. 2 PRESSURE REGULATOR

1. Stand both the oxygen (*black*) and acetylene (*maroon*) cylinders in the upright position, and keep them in this position during use. Hold them firmly with the aid of a chain or strap.
2. Check to ensure that cylinder valves and regulator stems are free from oil and grease. Wipe with a clean cloth.
3. Blow out loose dirt from the cylinder valves by momentarily opening and closing them.
4. Screw regulators into their respective cylinders. The oxygen cylinder is threaded right-hand; the acetylene cylinder has left-hand threads. Use the proper wrench to tighten the nuts.
5. Blow the two rubber hoses through with compressed air to remove any dust or dirt.
6. Connect the *blue* hose to the oxygen-regulator outlet, and the *red* hose to the acetylene-regulator outlet.
7. Connect the opposite ends of the hoses to their respective inlets on the blow-pipe; the oxygen hose to inlet marked 'O' and acetylene hose to that marked 'A'.
8. Fit the appropriate size nozzle to the blow-pipe.
9. Open oxygen- and acetylene-cylinder valves slowly using the proper key. Test regulators for leaks using a soapy water solution; bubbles will reveal any leaks.
10. Set both regulators to the correct working pressures. Refer to chart supplied by the makers of the blow-pipe to ascertain these pressures.
11. Test hose connections for leaks at both regulator and blow-pipe.
12. Open oxygen and acetylene control valves on the blow-pipe and test nozzle connection for leaks.

Igniting Blow-pipe and Adjusting Flame

Successful gas welding will depend largely on the welder's ability to obtain the correct type of flame suitable for the job in hand. Three different types may be used in the oxy-acetylene process:—

1. *The Neutral Flame*   Fig. 3(c)

The neutral flame is obtained when just sufficient oxygen is passing through the blow-pipe in order to completely burn the acetylene and yet leave no excess oxygen. This flame is used for welding steel, cast iron, copper, and aluminium.

2. *The Oxidizing Flame*   Fig. 3(d)

The oxidizing flame is obtained when an excess of oxygen is forced into the mixture. This flame is used for welding brass and bronze.

3. *The Carburizing Flame*   Fig. 3(e)

The carburizing flame is obtained when an excess of acetylene is forced into the mixture. This type of flame can be readily identified by the three flame zones instead of the usual two seen in the other types mentioned. This flame is used for hard-facing, e.g. depositing stellite on valve seatings.

When igniting the flame, first open the blow-pipe acetylene control valve half to three parts of a turn. Hold the spark lighter about 25 mm away from the end of the nozzle and ignite the acetylene. Adjust the control valve

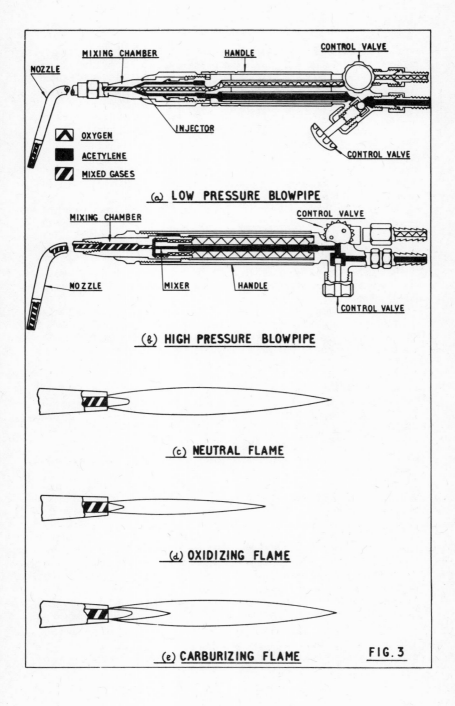

NOZZLE

MIXING CHAMBER   HANDLE   CONTROL VALVE

INJECTOR

OXYGEN

ACETYLENE

MIXED GASES

CONTROL VALVE

(a) LOW PRESSURE BLOWPIPE

MIXING CHAMBER   CONTROL VALVE

NOZZLE   MIXER   HANDLE

CONTROL VALVE

(b) HIGH PRESSURE BLOWPIPE

(c) NEUTRAL FLAME

(d) OXIDIZING FLAME

(e) CARBURIZING FLAME

FIG. 3

until a clean flame free from smoke is obtained. Gradually open the oxygen control valve until the desired type of flame is obtained, e.g. neutral, oxidizing, or carburizing. The flame may be harsh or quiet. The former is caused by forcing too much pressure of both gases into the blow-pipe nozzle and this is always undesirable.

The quiet flame is achieved by having the correct pressure of gases flowing into the nozzle. This is the ideal type of flame to ensure a continuous flow of molten metal without undue spatter.

Backfire and Flashback

A backfire will extinguish the flame with a loud 'pop' and can be due to several causes:—

1. Operating the blow-pipe with insufficient pressures for the size of the nozzle used.
2. The nozzle touching the surface of the work.
3. By overheating the nozzle.
4. Obstruction in the nozzle.

In the event of a backfire both control valves on the blow-pipe should be shut; after rectifying the fault relight the torch. (Remove torch from the heated metal.)

A flashback is a condition that results when the flame flashes back into the blow-pipe and burns with a hissing or squealing noise. This fault may be due to a clogged nozzle, or to the improper functioning of the control valves. In the event of a flashback shut off the acetylene-cylinder valve and then the oxygen before investigating the cause of the fault.

Welding Methods

The two methods employed in oxy-acetylene welding are: (i) leftward or forward; (ii) rightward or backward. The choice of method will depend upon the type of job, the nature and thickness of the material, type of joint, and accessibility.

(i)　Leftward welding is used for welding steel plates up to 5 mm thickness and for welding cast iron and some non-ferrous metals. The welding operation is commenced from the right-hand end of the plate, proceeding towards the left. The welding rod held at an angle of 30–40° precedes the blowpipe along the joint. The blow-pipe is held in the right hand making an angle of 60–70° with the work. A neutral flame is used, and the blow-pipe is given a side-to-side motion in addition to the forward movement; this ensures that both edges of plates being joined melt at the same rate. When a molten pool has been obtained the welding rod is periodically fed into the molten pool, not melted off directly from the flame. Fig. 4(a) shows the movement and relative position of the blow-pipe and welding rod in the leftward method.

(ii)　Rightward welding is used for welding plates exceeding 5 mm in thickness. In this method the welding operation is commenced from the left-hand end of the plate, proceeding towards the right. The welding rod held at an angle of 40–50° follows the blow-pipe along the joint. The blow-pipe is held at an angle of 40–50° with the work and is moved in a straight line, while

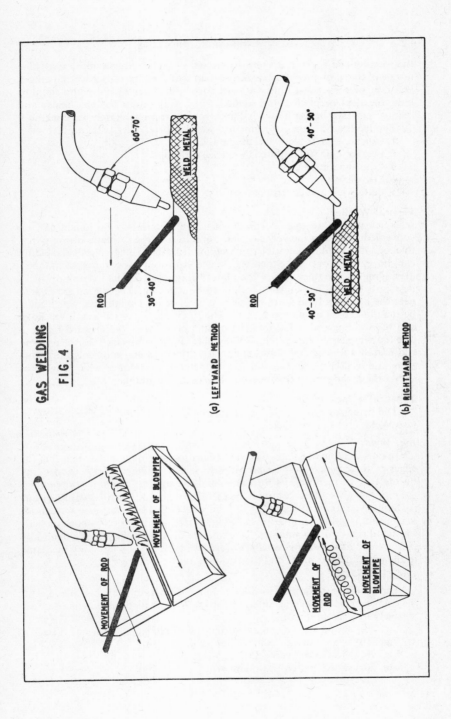

GAS WELDING

FIG. 4

ROD

60°–70°

30°–40°

WELD METAL

MOVEMENT OF ROD

MOVEMENT OF BLOWPIPE

(a) LEFTWARD METHOD

ROD

40°–50°

40°–50°

WELD METAL

MOVEMENT OF ROD

MOVEMENT OF BLOWPIPE

(b) RIGHTWARD METHOD

the welding rod is given a slight rotational or circular forward motion. The nozzle of the blow-pipe must be larger than that used for the leftward method, and the correct size welding rod is essential (diameter of rod being equal to half thickness of plate being welded). Fig. 4(b) shows the movement and relative position of the blow-pipe and welding rod in the rightward method.

The main advantages of rightward welding on thicker plate are:—
1. Quicker than the leftward method.
2. Less welding rod required (V-angle smaller).
3. Consumes less gas.
4. Less distortion.
5. Better view and control of the weld.

Vertical Welding

Vertical welding may be used when the material to be joined can be conveniently held in the vertical plane, and in the case of plates above 6 mm thickness the weld is accessible for welding from both sides. Vertical welding can be carried out by either the single- or double-operator techniques, depending on the thickness of the plates being welded. The maximum thickness possible by the single operator is about 8 mm. The plates are heated near the bottom of the joint, the blow-pipe piercing a small hole which must be maintained as welding proceeds. The fused metal runs beneath the hole, and the welding rod is fed into the molten pool as in the leftward method. The blow-pipe is given a small semi-circular upward movement as the welding rod precedes it. Fig. 5(a) shows the relative position and movement of blow-pipe and welding rod for the single-operator technique, while Fig. 5(b) shows the arrangement for the double-operator technique.

Types of Welded Joints

The principal types of welded joints include the Butt Weld, Fillet Weld, Lap Weld, and Corner Welds.

Butt Welds

In butt welding the plates to be joined are located in the same plane, but the edges of these plates may be prepared in several different ways, depending on the type of material, its thickness, and the welding method adopted.

Fig. 6 shows three common types of butt joints: (a) Plain Butt Joint; (b) Single Vee Joint; (c) Double Vee Joint. Fig. 6(d) shows the various methods of edge preparation suitable for mild-steel plates when welded by both the leftward and rightward techniques. To eliminate distortion the plates are initially tack welded at suitable intervals. A tack weld is made by applying the flame to the metal until it melts and then adding a little welding rod.

Fillet Welds

The plates to be joined in fillet welding are not in the same plane, and the joint can be of several different forms. A fillet type of joint is used extensively in structural work.

Fig. 7(a) shows the downhand or flat fillet weld.
Fig. 7(b) shows the horizontal fillet weld.
Fig. 7(c) shows the overhead fillet weld.
Fig. 7(d) shows the vertical fillet weld.

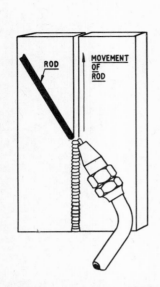

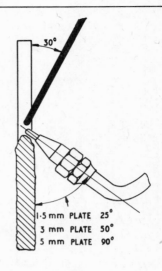

30°

1·5 mm PLATE 25°
3 mm PLATE 50°
5 mm PLATE 90°

FIG. 5 (a)   SINGLE OPERATOR VERTICAL WELDING.

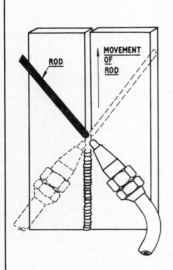

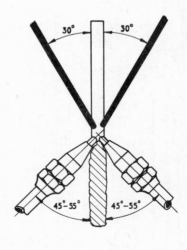

30°   30°

45°-55°   45°-55°

FIG. 5 (b)   DOUBLE OPERATOR VERTICAL WELDING

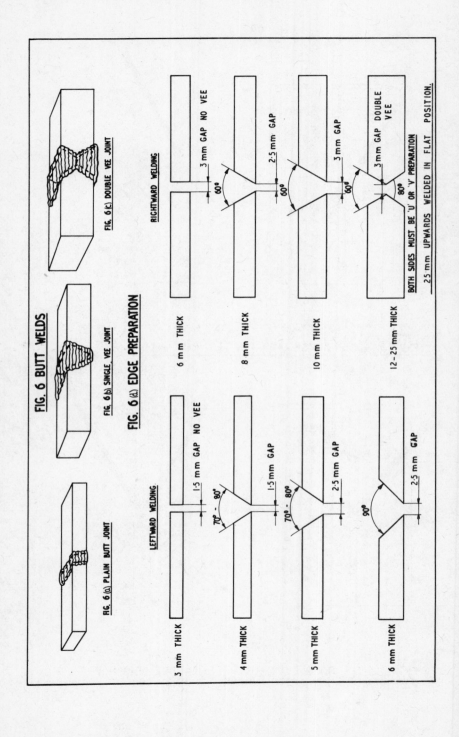

FIG. 6 BUTT WELDS

FIG. 6 (a) PLAIN BUTT JOINT

FIG. 6 (b) SINGLE VEE JOINT

FIG. 6 (c) DOUBLE VEE JOINT

FIG. 6 (d) EDGE PREPARATION

LEFTWARD WELDING

3 mm THICK — 1·5 mm GAP NO VEE

4 mm THICK — 70° - 80° — 1·5 mm GAP

5 mm THICK — 70° - 80° — 2·5 mm GAP

6 mm THICK — 90° — 2·5 mm GAP

RIGHTWARD WELDING

6 mm THICK — 3 mm GAP NO VEE

8 mm THICK — 60° — 2·5 mm GAP

10 mm THICK — 60° — 3 mm GAP

12 – 25 mm THICK — 80° — 3 mm GAP DOUBLE VEE

BOTH SIDES MUST BE 'U' OR 'V' PREPARATION

25 mm UPWARDS WELDED IN FLAT POSITION.

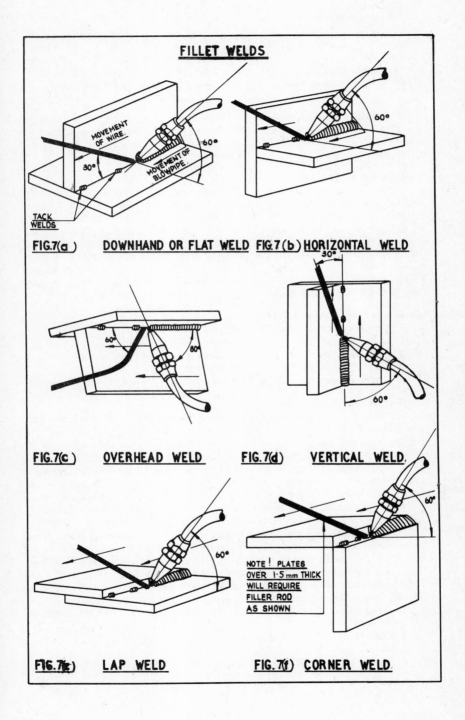

FILLET WELDS

FIG.7(a) DOWNHAND OR FLAT WELD FIG.7(b) HORIZONTAL WELD

FIG.7(c) OVERHEAD WELD FIG.7(d) VERTICAL WELD

FIG.7(e) LAP WELD FIG.7(f) CORNER WELD

NOTE! PLATES OVER 1·5 mm THICK WILL REQUIRE FILLER ROD AS SHOWN

Lap Welds

Overlapping plates can be conveniently welded by means of the lap joint as shown in Fig. 7(e). This type of joint is not as strong as the butt weld.

Corner Welds

The corner joint is used in the fabrication or repair of many types of product. The plates are set up as shown in Fig. 7(f) and are tack welded to keep them in position. The edges are then fused without a filler rod. If reinforcement is required then a filler rod will be used.

Welding Various Metals

In addition to the welding of mild steel, other metals can be satisfactorily welded by the oxy-acetylene process including cast iron, stainless steel, aluminium, copper, brass, and bronze. The basic technique will be the same as that already outlined for mild steel, but special provisions must be made, and precautions taken according to the requirements of the particular metal being welded: e.g. using the correct type of flux (flux not required on mild steel); correct type of welding rod; selection of the correct type of flame; size of nozzle in blow-pipe; holding the blow-pipe at the correct angle; pre- and post-heating of the workpiece; correct joint preparation.

Defects in Oxy-Acetylene Welds

The most common defects include:—

1. Lack of penetration.   5. Blowholes.
2. Lack of fusion.   6. Oxidation or carburization.
3. Lack of reinforcement.   7. Distortion.
4. Undercut sections.   8. Burnt metal due to use of oversize nozzle.

Oxy-Acetylene Flame Cutting

Iron and steel can be efficiently and cleanly cut by means of the oxy-acetylene flame-cutting process, a process which finds many industrial applications. The cutting is carried out with the aid of a special cutting blow-pipe which may be either hand operated or automatically controlled in a cutting machine. The blow-pipe is so designed that it will heat the metal to the ignition temperature and then direct a jet of high-pressure oxygen on to the metal. The metal is not melted but is cut by the chemical action of the oxygen on the heated metal.

The construction of a cutting blow-pipe is different to that used in the welding process. The fuel gases, oxygen and acetylene, are controlled by needle valves on the blow-pipe and the mixture of gases is injected into an outer orifice in the tip of the nozzle; this provides the heating flame. Another orifice in the centre of the nozzle permits the flow of high-pressure oxygen for the cutting. This cutting jet is controlled by a separate spring-loaded valve operated by a hand lever which when depressed releases the stream of high-pressure oxygen. The success of the cutting operation is dependent upon the following factors:—

1. Using the correct-size cutter nozzle according to the thickness of material to be cut.
2. Operating the blow-pipe at the correct oxygen pressure.
3. Using a clean nozzle.
4. Operating the blow-pipe at the correct cutting speed.

Brazing—Hard Soldering

Brazing is a joining process but it differs from welding due to the fact that the metal surfaces being joined are not fused together; the brazed joint is made by means of a thin film of suitable spelter which is caused to flow between the joint faces. The melting temperature of the spelter or silver solder is approximately 600°C, therefore the process can only be used to join articles whose melting temperature is well above this temperature. The types of brazed joints are somewhat limited, usually being confined to the lap- or fillet-type joints.

Prior to brazing, the parts to be joined must be fairly accurately fitted together, the joint faces thoroughly cleaned with a file and emery cloth, and be entirely free from all trace of oil or grease. The flux is mixed into a paste and is applied to the joint faces, sufficient heat is obtained from a coal gas and compressed-air torch to cause the flux to run with a watery appearance. The filler metal in the form of small particles or as a rod is applied to the hot metal and by capillary action follows the flux through the joint, sealing it completely. Upon the completion of the brazing operation the flux must be removed, usually with boiling water.

Bronze Welding

Bronze welding is the name given to a metal-joining process which is intermediate between brazing and fusion welding. The parts are not fused during the process, and the faces to be joined are not closely fitted, much more filler metal being used than in the brazing process. The advantages of bronze welding include, the speed with which very strong joints can be made, less distortion than in fusion welding, and the ability to join dissimilar metals. For light-gauge materials, fillet and lap joints are favoured, but for thicker materials the joint preparation is the same as that needed for fusion welding.

Prior to bronze welding the joint faces or edges are cleaned by shot blasting, grinding, or by a file to at least 12 mm back from the joint edge. The welding torch is held at the same angle as in fusion welding, the root of the joint being brought to a dull-red heat, approximately 900°C. The bronze filler rod is heated in the flame of the torch and dipped in flux; the molten filler rod is tinned to the parent metal; and the joint is completed by a succession of runs until sufficient reinforcement is achieved.

Electric-Arc Welding (Metallic-Arc)

Another important method of fusion welding used extensively in modern practice is based on the electric-arc principle, whereby intense heat is obtained from an electric current which creates an arc of flame between a metal electrode and the plates which are to be welded. The heat so produced is sufficient to fuse the edges of the plates at the joint forming a small pool of molten metal; additional molten metal from the tip of the electrode is deposited into the molten pool. When the molten pool solidifies it forms a strong welded joint.

The electric supply needed for this type of welding may be either direct current (d.c.) or alternating current (a.c.); both systems possess certain advantages depending on the purpose for which they are employed. Many different types and sizes of electric welding machines are now available, and two of the most generally used are the d.c. Generator and the a.c. Transformer.

D.C. Generators   Figs. 8(a) and 8(b)

With a d.c. welding machine the electric current is produced by means of a generator which is driven by a petrol or diesel engine, or alternatively is driven by an a.c. or d.c. electric motor.

The engine-driven generator-set can operate quite independently of any electrical supply, and for this reason is used on site work where no mains supply of electricity is available.

The motor-driven type of generator-set is chiefly used for the type of welding work performed inside a workshop, and is therefore often permanently mounted on the floor, but the portable type of set is also available. The electric motor provides a good, constant speed-drive for the generator, and is not affected by the load imposed upon it.

A.C. Transformers

The a.c. welding machine employs a transformer instead of a generator to provide the required welding current. See Fig. 8(c).

The a.c. Transformer as its name implies is an instrument which transforms or steps down the voltage of the normal mains electrical supply to a voltage suitable for welding, i.e. between 80 and 100 volts.

Unlike the d.c. Generator the a.c. Transformer has no moving parts and for this reason is usually referred to as a static plant.

The advantages claimed for the a.c. welding plant are:—

1. Low initial cost.
2. No moving parts, therefore negligible maintenance.
3. Higher electrical efficiency.
4. Easy to transport.

The disadvantages are few but important:—

1. Coated electrodes must always be used.
2. Voltage higher than in d.c. system, therefore risk of shock greater.
3. Welding of non-ferrous materials more difficult than with d.c. system.

Electric Welding Equipment

1. A d.c. Generator or an a.c. Transformer.
2. A properly designed electrode-holder (Fig. 9) possessing the following features:—

(a) Light in weight to reduce fatigue.
(b) Well insulated.
(c) Well balanced.
(d) Must not overheat.
(e) Locate and eject the electrode easily.

3. Two lengths of flexible cable to carry the current to and from the work. One cable runs from the welding plant to the electrode holder; the other from the plant to the work bench known as the ground cable. The diameter of these cables will be governed by the voltage and the distance it has to be carried from the machine.
4. A wide selection of different-gauge electrodes of various materials.

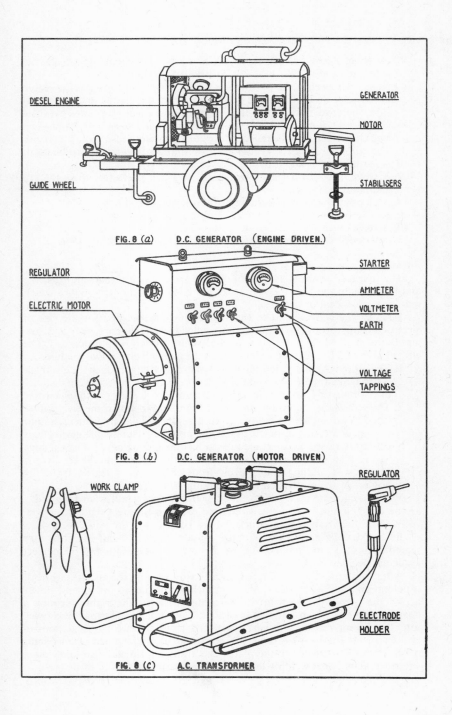

DIESEL ENGINE

GENERATOR

MOTOR

GUIDE WHEEL

STABILISERS

FIG. 8 (a)   D.C. GENERATOR (ENGINE DRIVEN.)

REGULATOR

STARTER

AMMETER

ELECTRIC MOTOR

VOLTMETER

EARTH

VOLTAGE
TAPPINGS

FIG. 8 (b)   D.C. GENERATOR (MOTOR DRIVEN)

WORK CLAMP

REGULATOR

ELECTRODE
HOLDER

FIG. 8 (c)   A.C. TRANSFORMER

5. A head shield or face screen fitted with special coloured lenses as recommended in B.S. No. 679. See Figs. 11(a) and 11(b).

Note An electric arc produces a brilliant light and gives off invisible ultra-violet and infra-red rays which are very dangerous to the eyes and skin, therefore never attempt to look at the arc with the naked eye. The helmet type of head shield fits over the head, and leaves both hands free. The face screen provides adequate protection, but needs holding by hand. The coloured lenses are classified according to the amperes to be used.

6. A leather apron and a pair of gloves.
7. A welding booth designed to protect all other personnel from the arc glare and radiation.
8. A chipping hammer for the removal of slag from the weld.
9. A wire brush to clean the weld, and to remove spatter.
10. A steel bench insulated from the booth.
11. A wooden duckboard to safeguard the welder from damp floors.

Striking the Arc

The first step towards successful electric-arc welding is learning to strike and to maintain the arc, and run a straight bead of metal, techniques which require a good deal of practice.

First set the control unit to the correct current specified for the size of electrode being used. (The value recommended by the makers is only approximate; the final setting is made as the welding operation proceeds.) The electrode is then brought into contact with the plate by one of two methods:—

1. The tapping-motion method as shown in Fig. 10(a) in which the electrode is brought straight down on the plate and instantly withdrawn a distance of 3–5 mm, this distance being equal to the core diameter of the electrode.
2. The scratching method as shown in Fig. 10(b) in which the electrode is tilted at an angle and is then given a slight circular movement similar to that of striking a match. As in the previous method the electrode is promptly raised a distance equal to its diameter, otherwise it will stick to the plate. If the electrode does stick the holder should be given a sharp twist; failing this the electrode should be released from the holder, or the electric current should be switched off.

Welding currents may vary from 20–600 amperes; and for striking a d.c. arc on open circuit 55–60 volts is required, whilst an a.c. set requires 80–100 volts. Once the arc has been struck the arc voltage will drop to 20–25 volts.

Before striking an arc the operator should have his head shield or face screen in position and observe the arc through the glass filters of the correct grade as specified in B.S. 679.

After mastering the art of quickly and easily striking the arc the electrode is held at an angle of 60–70° to the plate, while it is moved evenly and slowly across the plate starting from the left edge towards the right, forming a continuous bead which must be even, free from holes, and penetrating well into the parent metal. The heat generated from the arc forms a pool of molten metal in the plate and the electrode begins to melt, transferring metal from the electrode to the plate. This transfer of metal also takes place against gravity when welding in the overhead position.

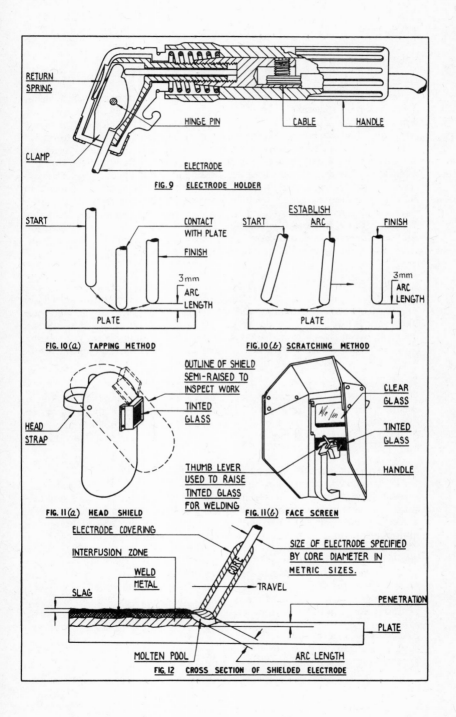

RETURN SPRING

HINGE PIN

CABLE

HANDLE

CLAMP

ELECTRODE

FIG. 9   ELECTRODE HOLDER

START

CONTACT WITH PLATE

FINISH

3 mm ARC LENGTH

PLATE

FIG. 10 (a)   TAPPING METHOD

ESTABLISH

START   ARC   FINISH

3mm ARC LENGTH

PLATE

FIG. 10 (b)   SCRATCHING METHOD

OUTLINE OF SHIELD SEMI-RAISED TO INSPECT WORK

TINTED GLASS

HEAD STRAP

FIG. 11 (a)   HEAD SHIELD

CLEAR GLASS

TINTED GLASS

HANDLE

THUMB LEVER USED TO RAISE TINTED GLASS FOR WELDING

FIG. 11 (b)   FACE SCREEN

ELECTRODE COVERING

INTERFUSION ZONE

WELD METAL

SLAG

CORE

TRAVEL

SIZE OF ELECTRODE SPECIFIED BY CORE DIAMETER IN METRIC SIZES.

PENETRATION

PLATE

MOLTEN POOL

ARC LENGTH

FIG. 12   CROSS SECTION OF SHIELDED ELECTRODE

Essential Factors

The following factors govern successful arc welding:—

1. *The correct choice of electrode*

In selecting the most suitable electrode, consideration must be given to the position of the weld, type of metal being welded, size of the electrode, type of joint, and current settings. The main groups of electrodes include mild steel, high-carbon steel, special alloy steel, cast iron, and non-ferrous, classified as bare, and flux-covered electrodes. The bare electrodes have a very light coating which affords some protection against oxidation of the surface.

The flux-covered or shielded electrode has a heavy coating of several chemical substances which protect the molten metal from oxidation and helps to keep the arc steady. When this type of electrode melts, the coating produces a shield of gas around the molten metal, safeguarding it against the atmosphere. Some of the coating also forms a slag over the molten pool which also serves as a protection against oxidation. Fig. 12 shows a cross-section of a flux-covered electrode in the process of welding.

2. *The correct length of arc*

The correct length of arc will depend on the type of electrode used, and also upon the nature of the welding operation. As previously stated the length of arc is approximately equal to the core diameter of the electrode. If the arc is too long a wide irregular bead is produced with insufficient fusion between the plate and the electrode metal. When the arc is too short insufficient heat is generated to melt the plate properly, and the electrode will also stick frequently, resulting in a very uneven bead.

3. *The correct speed of travel*

The speed of travel of the electrode across the work must be slow to ensure sufficient penetration without excessive build-up of the bead. When the speed is too fast the molten pool solidifies rapidly and impurities are retained in the weld. If the speed is too slow excessive metal produces a high and wide bead.

4. *The correct current*

The correct amperage in accordance with the size of the electrode used is most important. When the amperage is too great the electrode melts fast, causing a large pool of molten metal and excessive spatter. If the amperage is too low the heat generated will be insufficient to melt the plate and the molten pool will be small, resulting in lack of fusion.

Arc-Welding Positions

Arc-welding operations can be carried out with the work in almost any position, but the degree of skill required of the welding operator will vary considerably depending on the position of the joint, e.g. flat or downhand position, horizontal, vertical, or overhead position.

Flat or Downhand Position

The welding operation is simplified when the joint is in the flat position: gravity assists the transfer of metal from the electrode to the work, better penetration is obtained, and the operation can be performed more quickly with less fatigue.

Typical examples of downhand or flat position welding include the following standard joints:—

Lap Joints

The lap joint is a relatively simple joint. Two flat plates requiring no special edge preparation are placed one on top of the other, the actual amount of overlap depending on the plate thickness. The minimum overlap is equal to four times plate thickness. Single-weld lap joints as shown in Fig. 13(a) are suitable for lightly loaded structures. Double-weld lap joints as shown in Fig. 13(b) are necessary when greater strength is required. The joint may be single pass, i.e. one layer of beads, or it may be multiple pass. i.e. two or more layers of beads along the joint seam, each bead overlapping the other. The latter is usually used on plates over 10 mm thick, and in cases where strength is a major consideration.

Fillet Joints

The down-hand fillet or tee joint is shown in Fig. 14(a). The vertical plate is tack-welded in position on the horizontal plate, and then finally welded by either the single-pass or the multiple-pass techniques, depending on the strength of joint required. Fig. 14(b) shows the double-fillet joint, i.e. both sides of the vertical plate being welded.

Corner Joints

Both outside and inside corner joints as shown in Fig. 15(a) and (b) may be welded in the downhand position. After tack welding the plates in position a single bead may be run along the joint; heavy stock will require a series of beads to fill the corner.

Butt Joints

Fig. 16(a) shows the 'closed' square butt joint suitable for plates up to a maximum thickness of 3 mm, the edges of the two plates being in direct contact.

Fig. 16(b) shows the 'open' square butt joint suitable for plates up to 6 mm in thickness, the gap between the two edges being equal to half plate thickness.

In other types of butt joint the edges of the two plates need some preparation prior to welding, and this would be carried out by machining, or with the aid of a flame-cutting torch.

Fig. 17(a) shows the single vee-joint suitable for plates up to 15 mm in thickness. The included angle of the vee should not exceed 60°.

Fig. 17(b) shows the double vee-joint recommended for plates over 15 mm thick. This type of edge preparation is more expensive than that of the single vee, but the additional cost may be off-set by considerable saving in the amount of deposit metal needed to fill the joint.

Fig. 18(a) shows the single U-joint used for thicker-size plates. U-joint edge-preparation involves expensive machining costs, but these are largely off-set when welding thick plates by a corresponding reduction in welding costs.

Fig. 18(b) shows the double U-joint used on plates of 25 mm thickness and above.

DOWNHAND POSITION

LAP JOINTS

FIG. 13 (a) SINGLE WELD

FIG. 13 (b) DOUBLE WELD

FILLET JOINTS

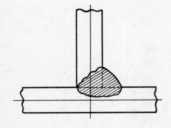

FIG. 14 (a) SINGLE JOINT

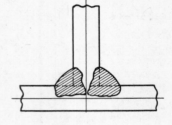

FIG. 14 (b) DOUBLE JOINT

CORNER JOINTS

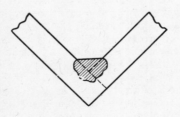

FIG. 15 (a) INSIDE JOINT

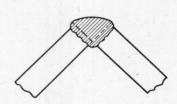

FIG. 15 (b) OUTSIDE JOINT

BUTT JOINTS.

THICKNESS 3mm MAXIMUM

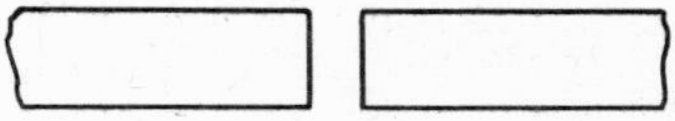

THICKNESS 6mm MAXIMUM

FIG.16.(a) CLOSED SQUARE BUTT

FIG.16.(b) OPEN SQUARE BUTT

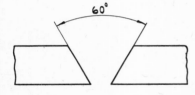

THICKNESS UP TO 15mm MAXIMUM

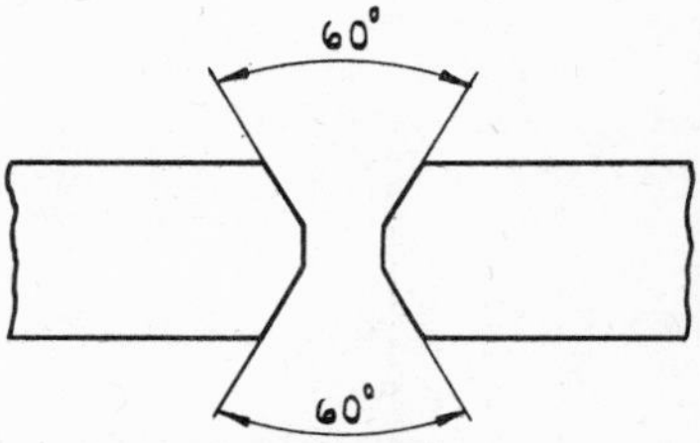

THICKNESS OVER 15mm

FIG.17.(a) SINGLE VEE

FIG.17.(b) DOUBLE VEE

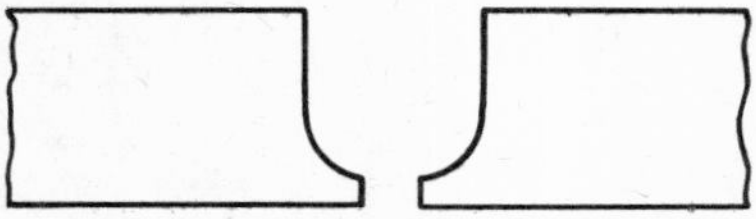

THICKNESS 15-25mm

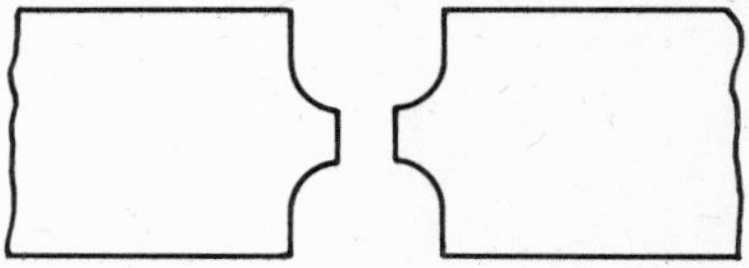

THICKNESS 25mm AND ABOVE.

FIG.18.(a) SINGLE "U" JOINT

FIG.18.(b) DOUBLE "U" JOINT

The Horizontal Position

There are many welding applications where the plates cannot be arranged in the flat or downhand position, therefore some work is performed in the horizontal position, i.e. the joint is on a vertical plate with bead line in the horizontal plane.

All the types of joint outlined in the section on flat or downhand welding can be welded in the horizontal position. Examples of these joints are shown in Figs. 19(a), (b), (c).

The Vertical Position

Frequently when fabricating or repairing work the weld must be carried out in the vertical position, i.e. the plates and the bead line are in the vertical plane. A vertical weld may be carried out either by depositing beads in the upward or downward direction. Downward welding is suitable for thin-gauge materials, but on plates above 6 mm, upward welding is more practical.

Figs. 20(a), (b), (c) show examples of the various joints in the vertical position.

The Overhead Position

Welding in the overhead position is a most difficult operation; often the welder must work in a cramped position, and he is also working against the downward pull of gravity tending to cause the weld metal to drop. Despite this, many excellent welds are made in the overhead position.

Gas Welding—Nozzle Sizes
(B.O.C. Lightweight Welding Blowpipe)

Mild Steel Thickness	Nozzle Size	Operating Pressure Acetylene	Oxygen
mm		bar	bar
1·00	1	0·14	0·14
1·25	2	0·14	0·14
2·00	3	0·14	0·14
2·50	5	0·14	0·14
3·15	7	0·30	0·30
4·00	10	0·30	0·30
5·00	13	0·30	0·30
6·30	18	0·50	0·50
8·00	25	0·50	0·50

Metallic-Arc Welding
Current Guide

Electrode Size	Current (amperes)
mm	
1·6	40/60
2·0	60/80
2·5	80/100
3·15	100/125
4·0	140/160
5·0	180/200
6·3	210/240

Note

The size of nozzle given for a particular thickness of mild steel is for general guidance only, and will vary according to the skill of the welder, the mass of metal, and the technique employed. Pressures may also be varied slightly.

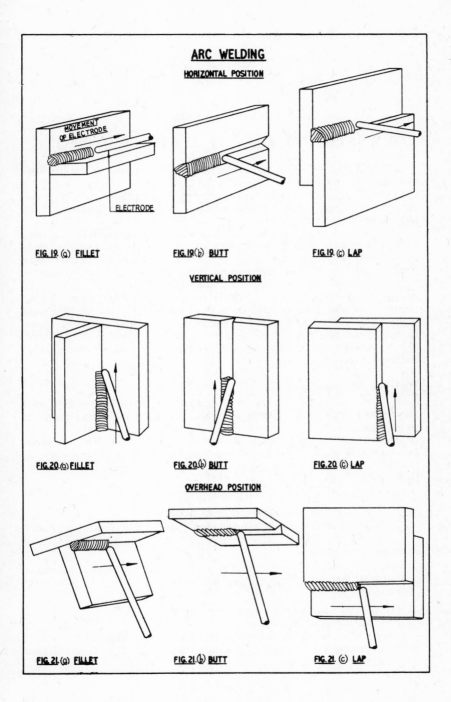

ARC WELDING

HORIZONTAL POSITION

MOVEMENT OF ELECTRODE

ELECTRODE

FIG. 19. (a) FILLET

FIG. 19 (b) BUTT

FIG. 19. (c) LAP

VERTICAL POSITION

FIG. 20. (a) FILLET

FIG. 20 (b) BUTT

FIG. 20. (c) LAP

OVERHEAD POSITION

FIG. 21. (a) FILLET

FIG. 21. (b) BUTT

FIG. 21. (c) LAP

D

CHAPTER FOUR

CLASSIFICATION OF MACHINE TOOLS

The basic types of tools mentioned in Chapter One such as the file, saw, hammer, and chisel have been used by the hand of the craftsman over many centuries. The quality of articles produced with the aid of such tools depended entirely on the manual skill of the individual craftsman manipulating them, and the quantity produced was always very limited.

A revolutionary change came towards the end of the eighteenth century with the advent of machine tools. The development of these machines prior to 1850 may be attributed to a few men of exceptional vision and technical ability, including Wilkinson, Bentham, Brunel, Maudsley, and Whitworth.

During the last hundred years the machine tool has radically transformed production methods, largely replacing the work of the human hand with far greater speed and precision. The constant development of the machine tools made modern mass production possible, and in turn this capacity to manufacture abundantly and cheaply determines modern living standards, therefore the machine-tool industry is often referred to as 'the driving force of technical advance'.

What is a Machine Tool?

A machine tool may be briefly defined as a power-driven machine used for producing a variety of shapes and sizes in metal by cutting away the excess metal.

This simple definition eliminates all forms of hand-operated tools, wood-working machinery, and power presses as used in forming operations.

Its Function

The basic function of any machine tool is of a two-fold nature:—

1. To hold and control the metal being machined.
2. To support and control the cutting tools which remove the excess metal.

Its Primary Requirements

Machine tools are manufactured in a large variety of types and designs, and all fulfil the above function, yet initially a machine may be selected to meet some primary requirement.

1. Precision, to give very accurate production.
2. Speed, giving rapid production.
3. Versatility, adaptable to wide range of machining operations.
4. Simplicity, operation, and control easier, and less skilled labour required.

Methods of Classification

The range and variety of modern machine tools are so great that some form of classification is essential. Three simple methods are briefly mentioned.

1. According to purpose for which used

(a) *Single purpose:* Machines of simple design, possessing the minimum of fitments and attachments, simple in operation, and the initial cost is comparatively low. Such machines are capable of performing one type of operation on numerous types of different components. Built as a standard product by many machine-tool manufacturers. Typical examples under this heading would include: Drilling, Surface Grinding, and Slotting machines.

(b) *Multi-purpose:* Machines designed to perform a wide range of operations, and made as a standard product by many machine-tool builders. The initial cost is more than that of a single-purpose machine but the extra capital expenditure is usually justified by the additional range of operations that can be performed, and the greater utilisation in a general engineering machine shop. Such machines are often described as Universal Machines and include: Universal Milling and Universal Grinding Machines and standard Centre Lathes.

(c) *Special purpose:* Machines designed and manufactured to perform one specific operation on one type of component which is required in large numbers. Such operations have usually proved very difficult, time consuming, or impossible on the standard machines referred to previously. The initial cost of a special-purpose machine is always high, but if the number of components can be guaranteed and there is no possibility of changes in their design, then the extra cost may be more than off-set by savings which accrue from reduction in machining times and scrap percentages. The useful life of a special-purpose machine is governed by the demand for the component it produces.

Examples of such machines used in aero-engine manufacture would include: Turning machines for cutting the cooling fins on a cylinder barrel; Profile machines for cutting the port forms in a cylinder sleeve; Grinding machines designed to perform various operations on turbine blades.

2. According to the type of cutting agent used

(a) Machines using single-point tools, e.g. Turning machines, Shaping and Planing machines, Boring and Slotting machines.

(b) Machines employing multi-tooth cutters, e.g. all types of Milling machines, Gear Cutting machines, and Broaching machines.

(c) Machines employing abrasive grinding wheels, e.g. all types of Grinding machines, including Cylindrical, Surface, Thread, Gear, and Cutter Grinding machines.

3. **According to the type of surface produced**

(a) Plane or flat surfaces, e.g. Shaping, Planing, Slotting, Face Milling, and Surface Grinding.

(b) Surfaces of revolution, e.g. cylindrical forms produced on Turning machines, Boring machines, Cylindrical Grinding machines, and Drilling machines.

(c) Combination of surfaces, e.g. surfaces produced on Profiling and Die-sinking machines, Gear Cutting and Gear Grinding machines.

Formation of machined surfaces

In the second method of classification, reference was made to the three main cutting agents; any one of these might be used to produce the surfaces mentioned in the third method by varying the combinations of cutting tool and workpiece movements. The most common applications would include the following:—

1. Single-point tool with reciprocating movement.
   Workpiece held stationary—transverse feed.
   Principle of Shaping. Fig. 1.
2. Single-point tool held stationary—transverse feed.
   Workpiece reciprocates.
   Principle of Planing. Fig. 2.
3. Single-point tool held stationary—longitudinal or transverse feed.
   Workpiece revolving.
   Principle of Turning. Figs. 3(a) and 3(b).
4. Single-point tool revolving.
   Workpiece stationary—longitudinal or transverse feed.
   Principle of Horizontal Boring. Figs. 4(a) and 4(b).
5. Multi-tooth cutter revolving.
   Workpiece travelling—longitudinal, transverse, or vertical feed.
   Principle of the various forms of Milling. Figs. 5(a) and 5(b).
6. Multi-tooth cutter revolving—axial feed.
   Workpiece stationary.
   Principle of Drilling. Fig. 6.
7. Non-revolving multi-tooth cutter—axial feed.
   Workpiece stationary.
   Principle of Broaching. Fig. 7.
8. Abrasive Grinding Wheel.
   Workpiece reciprocating—transverse feed.
   Principle of Horizontal Surface Grinding. Fig. 8.
9. Abrasive Grinding Wheel—transverse feed.
   Workpiece revolving.
   Principle of Ring Grinding machine. Fig. 9.
10. Abrasive Grinding Wheel.
    Workpiece revolving—longitudinal traverse—transverse feed.
    Principle of Cylindrical Grinding. Figs. 10 and 11.

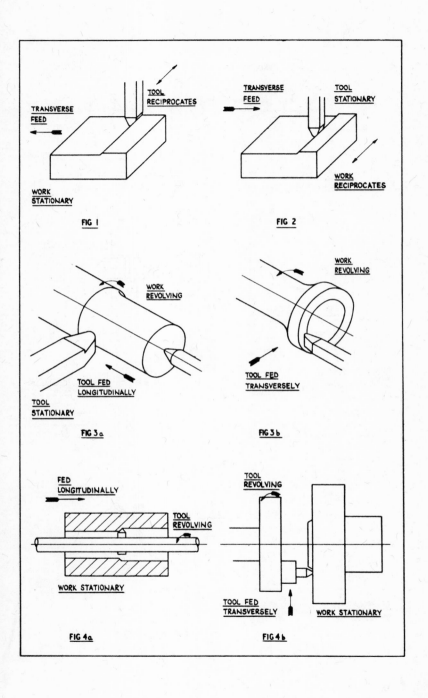

TOOL
RECIPROCATES

TRANSVERSE
FEED

WORK
STATIONARY

FIG 1

TRANSVERSE
FEED

TOOL
STATIONARY

WORK
RECIPROCATES

FIG 2

WORK
REVOLVING

TOOL FED
LONGITUDINALLY

TOOL
STATIONARY

FIG 3a

WORK
REVOLVING

TOOL FED
TRANSVERSELY

FIG 3b

FED
LONGITUDINALLY

TOOL
REVOLVING

WORK STATIONARY

FIG 4a

TOOL
REVOLVING

TOOL FED
TRANSVERSELY

WORK STATIONARY

FIG 4b

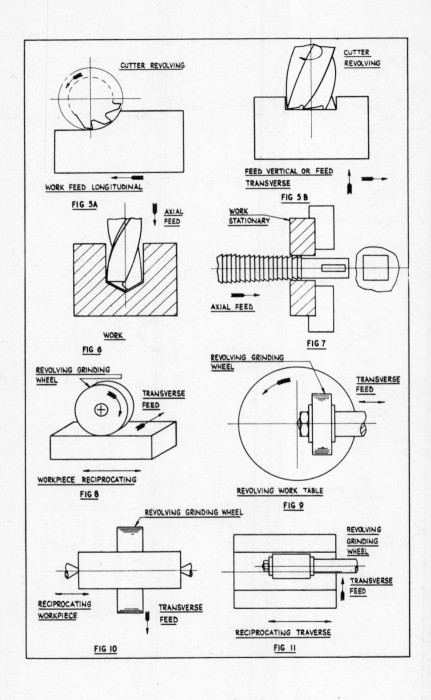

CUTTER REVOLVING.

WORK FEED LONGITUDINAL

FIG 5A

CUTTER REVOLVING

FEED VERTICAL OR FEED TRANSVERSE

FIG 5 B

AXIAL FEED

WORK

FIG 6

WORK STATIONARY

AXIAL FEED

FIG 7

REVOLVING GRINDING WHEEL

TRANSVERSE FEED

WORKPIECE RECIPROCATING

FIG 8

REVOLVING GRINDING WHEEL

TRANSVERSE FEED

REVOLVING WORK TABLE

FIG 9

REVOLVING GRINDING WHEEL

RECIPROCATING WORKPIECE

TRANSVERSE FEED

FIG 10

REVOLVING GRINDING WHEEL

TRANSVERSE FEED

RECIPROCATING TRAVERSE

FIG 11

Forming and Generating

The foregoing examples of surface formation may be classified as generated surfaces or formed surfaces, and in certain cases a combination of both.

A surface which is produced by a combination of machine movements, and whose truth and accuracy is entirely dependent on these movements is said to be generated. Such surfaces are in no way related to the tool or cutter shape.

Examples of generated surfaces include Fig. 1, Fig. 2, Figs. 3(a) and 3(b). Figs. 4(a) and 4(b).

Surfaces which are obtained directly from the shape of the tool, cutter or grinding wheel are said to be formed surfaces. A typical example is shown in Fig. 7.

Some surfaces are produced by a combination of both generating and forming principles.

In Fig. 5(a) the flatness of the surface in the transverse direction is dependent on the accuracy of the cutter form, and any inaccuracies of the cutter will produce corresponding inaccuracies in the flatness of the work.

In Fig. 3(a) if a form tool replaced the standard turning tool, and was fed into the revolving workpiece, the diameter produced would be generated, but the shape of the groove is a copy of the tool shape, and may be regarded as a forming process.

When cutting a screw thread in the lathe with a single-point tool, the thread form is a replica of the tool shape, and is therefore a formed surface. The helix angle of the thread is obtained by rotation of the workpiece and travel of the carriage (the relationship controlled by gearing driving the leadscrew), and must be considered as a generating process.

Copying

Many modern machine tools employ the copying principle where the movement of tool or cutter is synchronised with a tracing pin or stylus which is in contact with a master form or template. The tool reproduces a shape which is an exact replica of the master. The latter can be quickly changed when setting the machine for a different type of component. See p. 155.

Tool Life

Any tool or cutter operating under set conditions of cutting speed, feed rate, and depth of cut, will cut efficiently for a period of time, but at some stage it will cease to cut satisfactorily and will need re-grinding. The length of time required to bring about this failure in cutting action is known as tool life, and is dependent on a number of variable factors:—

1. Type of cutting-tool material and its heat treatment.
2. The composition and properties of material being cut.
3. The cutting speed selected.
4. Amount of metal to be removed.
5. Shape of the tool or cutter and its angles.
6. The rigidity of workpiece, tool, and machine.
7. The condition of machine.
8. Quality of the surface finish required.

Metal-Cutting Materials

The materials used for the manufacture of cutting tools and cutters must of necessity be stronger and harder than the material to be cut, and tough enough to withstand the shock loads imposed during the cutting operation. In addition they must resist abrasion, retain a keen cutting edge, and retain their hardness at the high temperatures developed during cutting.

No one cutting-tool material possesses all these desirable qualities, therefore a number of cutting materials have been developed to suit different applications, and are briefly classified below:—

1. *Tool Steels*
    (a) High-carbon steel (0·9–1·3%).
Fully hardened and suitably tempered.

Retains cutting edge up to approximately 225°C, therefore only very limited cutting speed permissible, hence its limited application in modern machine-shops.

(b) High-speed steel, fully heat treated.

An alloy steel containing tungsten between 14–22% as the main alloying element, with small percentages of chromium, vanadium, and cobalt.

Retains cutting edge up to approximately 660°C, therefore much higher cutting speeds are permissible. Used for all standard tools.

Molybdenum is also used as the main alloying element in certain types of high-speed steel, and is used in combination with tungsten in others.

2. *Cast Non-Ferrous Tool Materials*
Cast alloys consisting of about 50% cobalt, plus varying percentages of chromium, molybdenum, vanadium, and carbon. Such alloys are cast into final form, and cannot be forged or heat treated.

Owing to the cast structure they are extremely brittle and are never used as solid tools or cutters, but are used in the form of tool tips or inserted cutter teeth. They possess excellent wearing, heat-resisting, and corrosion-resisting properties. Stellite is a well-known material in this group.

3. *Sintered- or Cemented-Carbide Tool Materials*
Produced by powder metallurgy, pulverised carbides of tungsten, tantalum and titanium are mixed with cobalt or nickel, and placed in dies; compressed by hydraulic pressure, and then sintered in a hydrogen atmosphere in carefully controlled electric furnaces. They are ground to shape, followed by the final sintering operation. Sintered carbide is fully hard when cooled to room temperature. Despite its hardness and high resistance to heat this material possesses a tensile strength only equivalent to about 50% that of high-speed steel and is used in the form of tool tips or inserted cutter teeth. The cutting speeds with these materials are from 3–6 times those used with high-speed steel. Increased tool life between re-grinding is also obtained.

4. *Diamond Cutting Tools*
Commercial diamonds mounted in special tool holders are frequently used for the final machining operations on non-ferrous materials such as aluminium and copper alloys, and whitemetals. High cutting speeds and very fine cuts and feeds are employed, which give extremely good surface finish and dimensional accuracy.

5. *Abrasive Grinding Wheels* (Dealt with in Chapter on Grinding Machines).

Machinability of Work Material

The composition, structure, and properties of the different work materials all influence their machinability. The term machinability is used to describe the various aspects of metal cutting and includes the ease or difficulty encountered in obtaining specific results such as a given tool life, desired quality of surface finish, rate of stock removal, chip formation, and power consumed.

The main properties which influence machinability include tensile strength, hardness and ductility, in some cases these may be modified by suitable heat treatment, or by cold working to improve machinability. A wide range of speed and feed rates is provided on modern machine tools to meet the varying requirements of differing materials.

Some of the new materials are virtually unmachinable apart from grinding, hence the need for new techniques in forming these materials, e.g. high-nickel-content alloys.

Cutting Speed

The rate at which the cutting edge passes over the work, expressed in metres per minute. The strict SI unit would be the metre per second, but the minute is always adopted as the unit time in cutting speed calculations for reasons of practical convenience.

Cutting Speed for Turning Operations

The surface speed of the work in respect of the tool. Obtained by multiplying the circumference of the work (in metres) by the speed in rev/min.

Expressed $C.S. = \dfrac{\pi.D.N}{1000}$ metres per minute.

$$\text{when } D = \text{Diameter in millimetres.}$$
$$N = \text{Revolutions per minute.}$$
$$C.S. = \text{Cutting Speed (metres per minute).}$$

Example: Find cutting speed of 50 mm diameter bar at 140 rev/min.

$$C.S. = \frac{22 \times 50 \times 140}{7 \times 1000} = 22 \text{ m/min.}$$

Generally in practice we need the rev/min in order to set the machine to cut a given material at the permissible cutting speed. This is obtained from the above formula.

$$\text{If } C.S. = \frac{\pi.D.N}{1000} \text{ then } N = \frac{C.S. \times 1000}{\pi \times D}$$

Example: Find rev/min suitable for turning 50 mm diameter bar at 30 m/min.

$$N = \frac{C.S. \times 1000}{\pi \times D} = \frac{30 \times 1000 \times 7}{22 \times 50} = 191 \text{ rev/min.}$$

Cutting Speed for Drilling

The formula given above for turning will apply to drilling, but D will be diameter of drill instead of diameter of work.

Example: Find rev/min. suitable for 12 mm diameter drill to cut at 15 m/min.

$$N = \frac{C.S. \times 1000}{\pi \times D} = \frac{15 \times 1000 \times 7}{22 \times 12} = 398 \text{ rev/min.}$$

Cutting Speed for Milling

The speed of periphery of cutter expressed in metres per minute.

$$C.S. = \frac{\pi.D.N}{1000} \text{ when } D = \text{Diameter of Cutter (mm)}$$

$$N = \text{Revolutions per minute.}$$
$$C.S. = \text{Cutting speed (m/min).}$$

Example: Find the approximate rev/min suitable for milling a mild-steel component when using a 100 mm diameter plain milling cutter. Assume cutting speed of 25 m/min.

$$C.S. = \frac{\pi.D.N}{1000} \qquad \therefore N = \frac{C.S. \times 1000}{\pi \times D}$$

$$N = \frac{25 \times 1000 \times 7}{22 \times 100} = \underline{80 \text{ rev/min.}}$$

Cutting Speed for Shaping and Planing

The reciprocating action on these machines involves a cutting stroke and a return stroke. Starting from rest, the cutting stroke reaches a maximum cutting speed and slows down to rest. On the return stroke the same thing happens but in a shorter total time.

This double stroke is called one cycle, and the rate of cutting is expressed as cycles per minute.

Accurate estimation of cutting speed is difficult, but the following method will give an approximate guide:

$$\frac{\text{Permissible cutting speed for material being cut (m/min)}}{2 \times \text{Length of Stroke required (in metres)}}$$

= Number of cycles per minute.

Example: Find the number of cycles per minute suitable for shaping a cast-iron plate, length of stroke 250 mm. Assume permissible cutting speed for cast iron = 18 m/min.

$$\text{Then cycles/min} = \frac{C.S. \text{ (m/min)}}{2 \times \text{Length of Stroke (m)}}$$

$$= \frac{18 \times 1000}{2 \times 250} = \underline{36 \text{ cycles/min.}}$$

Approximate guide to cutting speeds when using high-speed-steel tools and cutters.

Materials to be cut	Cast Iron	Mild Steel	Cast Steel	High-Speed Steel	Alloy Steels	Brass	Aluminium
Cutting speed (m/min)	18–24	24–30	15–18	12–15	9–18	30–60	150–300

Cutting Feed

In most machining operations the width of the tool or cutter is considerably less than the width of surface to be machined, therefore a feed motion is required. The magnitude of movement given per revolution or per reversal of the work is known as Feed Rate.

Feed Rate for Turning

The distance the tool moves along the bar, or across the face per revolution of the work, expressed in millimetres per revolution of work, or expressed as number of cuts per 25 mm travel. As a general rule fairly coarse feeds are used for roughing operations, and fine feeds when finishing. (0·4 mm/rev = 62·5 cuts per 25 mm of travel.)

Feed Rate for Drilling

The rate at which the drill travels through the workpiece, expressed in millimetres per revolution of the drill, e.g. 0·12 mm per revolution of drill or as 208 revolutions per 25 mm of travel. The amount of feed per revolution will depend largely on the size of drill and would be increased when using larger drills.

Feed Rate for Shaping and Planing

The rate at which the tool advances per cycle, expressed in millimetres per cycle.

Feed Rate for Milling

The rate at which the work advances past the cutter, expressed in millimetres per minute. As milling cutters vary so much in size and strength no general rules can be laid down, and estimates of feed rate are based on a permissible load per tooth of cutter.

Therefore Feed Rate = Feed per tooth × Number of teeth × rev/min (mm/min).

The following table shows approximate feed per tooth when using high-speed-steel cutters:—

Material to be cut	Face Mills	Helical Mills	Slotting and Side Mills	End Mills	Form-Relieved Cutters	Circular Saws
Cast Iron	0·28– 0·41	0·20– 0·33	0·15– 0·23	0·15– 0·20	0·08– 0·13	0·08 0·10
Mild Steel	0·25– 0·30	0·20– 0·25	0·15– 0·18	0·13– 0·15	0·08– 0·10	0·08
Cast Steel	0·30	0·25	0·18	0·15	0·10	0·08
H.S. Steel	0·20	0·18	0·13	0·10	0·08	0·08
Alloy Steel	0·15	0·13	0·10	0·08	0·05	0·05
Brass	0·23– 0·56	0·18– 0·46	0·15– 0·33	0·13– 0·28	0·08– 0·18	0·05– 0·13
Aluminium	0·51	0·46	0·33	0·28	0·18	0·13

Economical Tool Life

The most economical tool life for any machining operation is largely a compromise between maximum rates of production and maximum length of time between re-grinding. The latter will vary considerably from one machine to another. It generally depends on time required to remove a tool from the machine, the cost of re-grinding, and the cost of re-setting, therefore it follows that simple tools and machines require a shorter tool life than more complicated set-ups.

For example, 30 minutes might be economically sound for a facing operation on a centre lathe or a shaping machine—90 minutes necessary for a turret lathe or milling machine, and 300 minutes for a full automatic machine.

Bearing these facts in mind, it is often more economic to reduce cutting speed rather than increase it, the loss in production rate being more than compensated by savings on re-grinding and re-setting.

CHAPTER FIVE

TURNING MACHINES

The Centre Lathe

Originally designed about 1797 by Henry Maudsley who developed the principle of both the sliding carriage and the leadscrew. During the intervening years many improvements and refinements have been introduced, yet a modern centre lathe still retains the basic principles of Maudsley's machine.

The centre lathe is one of the most versatile machine tools, but it is not suitable for rapid mass production and is therefore used most extensively in toolrooms and experimental departments for prototype work. Many other types of turning machines have been developed from the centre lathe to suit mass-production needs, and will be briefly mentioned later in this chapter.

Basic Cutting Operations

The basic cutting operations performed on a centre lathe are fourfold:—

1. Turning to circular form. Fig. 3(a), p. 101.
2. Facing. Fig. 3(b), p. 101.
3. Screw-cutting.
4. Drilling and boring.

Size of Lathes

Lathe sizes are designated by:—

1. Height of centres above bed.
2. Maximum length of work that can be held between centres.
3. Swing-over bed (twice height of centres).
4. Swing-over saddle; this is considerably less than swing-over bed.

Thus a 200 × 900 mm lathe would swing a job 400 mm in diameter over bed, and accommodate a job up to 900 mm in length between centres.

The American manufacturers usually state the maximum swing, e.g. 400 × 900 mm.

Main Details of Centre Lathe

Fig. 1 indicates the main details common to all centre lathes and includes:—

The Lathe Bed

The bed is the foundation member of the machine, most generally made in cast iron, although some modern manufacturers use alloy irons, steel inserts, or flame-hardened beds.

The most common bed design is an open box section suitably braced by cross ribs to give the rigidity and strength which is so essential to resist the bending and twisting stresses imposed during cutting. The bed may be considered as a girder supported at both ends and loaded at the section where cutting is taking place.

The upper faces of the bed are accurately machined and ground to form guide surfaces or 'ways' for both the carriage and the tailstock. These surfaces are subjected to severe conditions of wear due to the abrasion and scoring which takes place during the normal operation of the machine.

Several different forms of bed guide-ways are available; three common types are:—

1. Flat guides. Fig. 2.
2. Inverted Vee guides. Fig. 3.
3. Inverted Vee and Flat guides. Fig. 4.

The advantages claimed for vee guides are automatic-adjustment, gravity keeping the mating surfaces in contract, less tendency for the saddle to wedge when cross winding, side strips not required, and metal particles do not adhere to slide surfaces. The main disadvantages are the lack of bearing area, which results in rapid wear; in addition the inverted vees cause weakness in the saddle.

In practice it would appear that flat beds are most suitable when conditions demand heavy cutting and coarse feeds, and vee-shaped beds when precision work is being performed.

The Headstock

The headstock is the medium through which rotary motion is transmitted to the workpiece. It is securely located on the left-hand end of the lathe bed. Most modern headstocks are of the 'all-geared' type incorporating the main driving spindle, its bearings, and the special change mechanisms to give a range of cutting speeds.

A simple type of all-geared headstock is shown in Fig. 5(a). The drive is obtained from a constant-speed electric motor coupled by vee belts and pulley to a driving shaft carrying the sliding cluster of gears A.B.C. A centre shaft carries three fixed gears D.E.F., while a second cluster of sliding gears G.H.K. is located on the main machine spindle. Two fork-ended selectors actuated by hand levers conveniently placed on the headstock enable the operator to quickly select the required speed. A metal plate attached to the headstock will indicate the appropriate lever positions for the full range of speeds.

The gears and the splined shafts carrying them are made from heat-treated alloy steel, both accurately ground. Adequate lubrication is provided by means of a fully automatic force-feed system. A multi-plate clutch controls the main spindle operated by the stop-and-start lever.

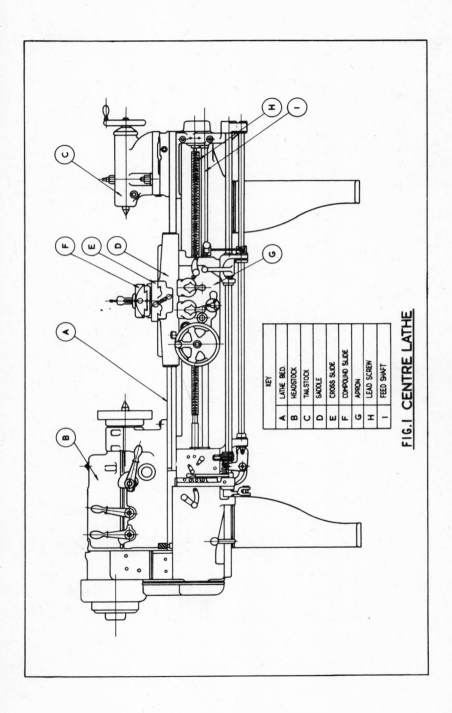

KEY	
A	LATHE BED.
B	HEADSTOCK
C	TAILSTOCK
D	SADDLE
E	CROSS SLIDE
F	COMPOUND SLIDE
G	APRON
H	LEAD SCREW
I	FEED SHAFT

FIG.I CENTRE LATHE

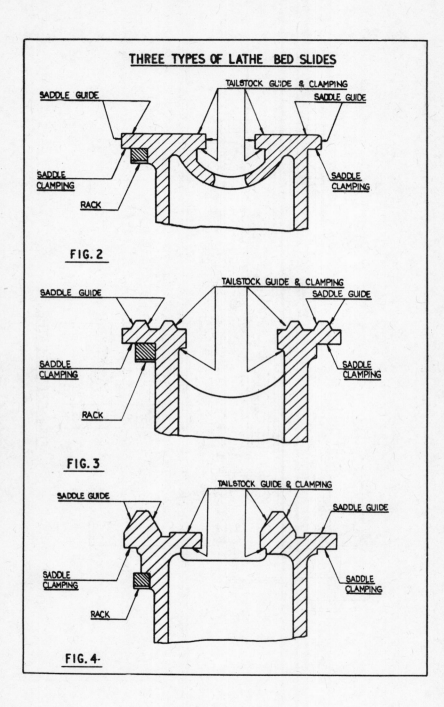

THREE TYPES OF LATHE BED SLIDES

FIG. 2

SADDLE GUIDE
TAILSTOCK GUIDE & CLAMPING
SADDLE GUIDE
SADDLE CLAMPING
RACK
SADDLE CLAMPING

FIG. 3

SADDLE GUIDE
TAILSTOCK GUIDE & CLAMPING
SADDLE GUIDE
SADDLE CLAMPING
RACK
SADDLE CLAMPING

FIG. 4

SADDLE GUIDE
TAILSTOCK GUIDE & CLAMPING
SADDLE GUIDE
SADDLE CLAMPING
RACK
SADDLE CLAMPING

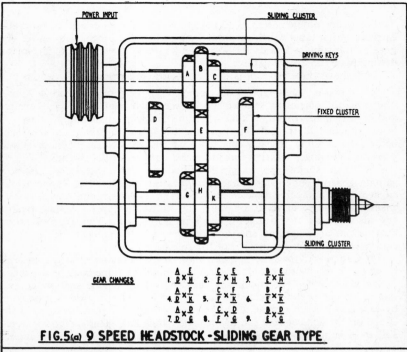

POWER INPUT

SLIDING CLUSTER

DRIVING KEYS

A B C

FIXED CLUSTER

D E F

G H K

SLIDING CLUSTER

GEAR CHANGES

1. $\frac{A}{D} \times \frac{E}{H}$ 2. $\frac{C}{F} \times \frac{E}{H}$ 3. $\frac{B}{E} \times \frac{E}{H}$

4. $\frac{A}{D} \times \frac{F}{K}$ 5. $\frac{C}{F} \times \frac{F}{K}$ 6. $\frac{B}{E} \times \frac{F}{K}$

7. $\frac{A}{D} \times \frac{D}{G}$ 8. $\frac{C}{F} \times \frac{D}{G}$ 9. $\frac{B}{E} \times \frac{D}{G}$

FIG.5(a) 9 SPEED HEADSTOCK - SLIDING GEAR TYPE

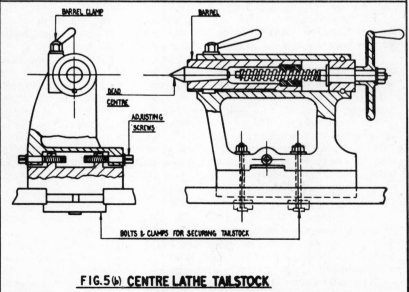

BARREL CLAMP

BARREL

DEAD CENTRE

ADJUSTING SCREWS

BOLTS & CLAMPS FOR SECURING TAILSTOCK

FIG.5(b) CENTRE LATHE TAILSTOCK

The main spindle is hollow to accommodate bar material; the front end carries a Morse taper which provides accurate location for the live centre. The nose of the spindle locates the work-holding device, e.g. chuck, face-plate, driving plate, or special fixture.

Fig. 6 shows three types of lathe-spindle nose in current use:—

(a) Improved screw-type; a development from the original screwed nose. The threaded portion is sandwiched between two plain locating diameters and its length controlled, so that when the chuck or other holding device is being attached to the spindle nose, the two plain locations must register before the matting threads engage. This ensures correct alignment, and prevents the danger of cross-threading and damage to the threads.

(b) Taper spigot-type, originally fitted on American lathes, is now gaining general popularity. The spigot has an International Taper, which engages with a tapered hole in the chuck or other holding device; a key ensures a positive drive. A retaining nut holds the taper together axially, and also acts as an extractor when separating them. This type of fitting provides an accurate and speedy location, and also reduces the length of chuck overhang beyond the end of the spindle.

(c) Cam lock-type; the spindle nose has six equally spaced clearance holes which receive the cam lock studs projecting from the back of the chuck or faceplate. When the chuck has been centralised by the shallow conical spigot, and three studs located in the spindle flange, it is locked in position by cam locks which engage in the recess in the studs; these firmly hold the chuck on the conical seat and against the flange face. This method is quick and most suitable where frequent changes of holding device are required.

The Tailstock

The tailstock shown in Fig. 5(b) is located on the right-hand end of the lathe bed, and is movable along the bed guide-ways; bolts and clamps securely hold the tailstock in any desired position.

The barrel is hollow, at one end a morse-taper bore locates the dead centre, and also provides the location for drill and reamer shanks. The opposite end of the barrel carries a feed screw actuated by the handwheel; this gives the longitudinal movements. By means of the locking device, the barrel may be securely held in any desired position.

The main body is made in two separate parts, the upper portion can be adjusted transversely relative to the base by means of two adjusting screws. This adjustment is necessary to align the dead centre held in the tailstock with the live centre in the headstock. It also provides one method of taper turning shallow tapers on components held between centres. See methods of taper turning, p. 124.

The Carriage

The carriage is a complete assembly which includes saddle, apron, cross-slide, compound-slide rest, and the tool box or tool post.

The complete unit may be traversed along the bed guide-ways, either by manual control or under power feed. When traversed manually, movement is controlled by a handwheel operating a pinion which engages with the rack attached to the front of the bed. When traversed under power feed, the pinion

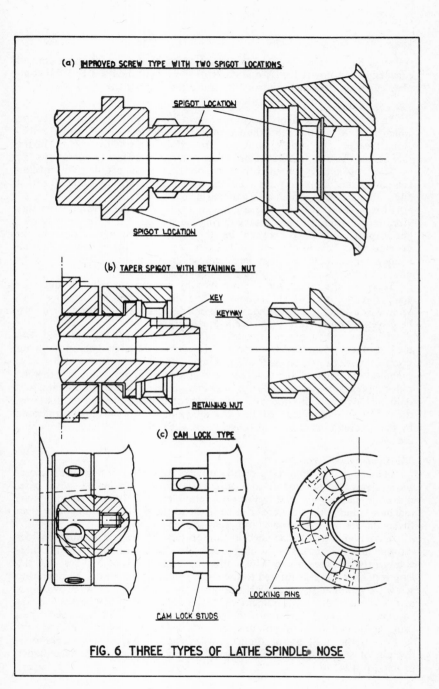

(a) IMPROVED SCREW TYPE WITH TWO SPIGOT LOCATIONS.

SPIGOT LOCATION

SPIGOT LOCATION

(b) TAPER SPIGOT WITH RETAINING NUT

KEY

KEYWAY

RETAINING NUT

(c) CAM LOCK TYPE

CAM LOCK STUDS

LOCKING PINS

FIG. 6 THREE TYPES OF LATHE SPINDLE NOSE

is driven by the feed-shaft and the apron gears. Two separate levers control engagement of power feeds; one controls the longitudinal feed of the complete carriage, the other controls the transverse feed of the cross-slide.

The Cross-Slide

The cross-slide controls the movement of the cutting tool in a direction which is at 90° to the bed. The carriage governs the movement of the tool along the bed, i.e. 'sliding' while the cross-slide controls the motion of the tool across the bed, i.e. 'surfacing' often referred to as facing operations.

The cross-slide is attached to the upper face of the saddle by a dovetail vee slide; the desired fit between the two is obtained by some form of adjustable gib-strip, which also compensates for wear.

Free travel is required, but any slackness in the saddle dovetail will cause vibration, chatter, and inaccuracy during machining. The gib-strip may be a flat strip of metal fitted between the stationary and moving portions of the dovetail slide, held in position and adjusted by grub-screw pressure; alternatively a tapered gib-strip may be fitted, which is adjusted longitudinally by one screw located in the front face of the cross-slide.

Travel of the cross-slide is controlled by a screw, usually of square or acme thread form, which engages with a nut attached to the slide; this screw has a hand lever attached at one end for manual operation, or it may be driven by power feed through the apron gears.

Accurate measurement of slide movement can be readily obtained with the aid of a graduated sleeve fitted to the cross-slide screw behind the hand lever. Full use should be made of this fitment, and a wise operator will always calculate the value of the divisions in relation to slide movements, thereby reducing measurement checks and obtaining more accurate production, and reduction of scrap. It should be also noted that when reading graduations, the reduction in diameter will be twice the value of tool movement indicated by the graduations. Care is also necessary when initially setting and locking the sleeve.

The Compound-Slide

The compound-slide rest which is attached to the upper face of the cross-slide carries the tool box or tool post. Located on a graduated swivel base, this slide may be set to travel at an angle relative to the centre-line of the machine spindle, thus the tool can be made to move in directions other than those allowed by the carriage and cross-slide movements.

A circular tee-slot machined in the top face of the centre-slide provides movement for the heads of the clamping bolts when swivelling the compound-slide to the required angle. Most lathes have hand-operated slides, and the length of tool travel is limited to the short length of thread on the operating screw. A graduated sleeve is also fitted to the operating screw, providing a means of accurate measurement of tool movement when the slide is set parallel or at right angles to machine spindle. Special care is needed when using graduated sleeve in conjunction with angular setting of the slide.

One of the most useful applications of the compound-slide is the production of short tapers, either external or internal. See methods of taper turning, p. 124.

The Feed Shaft

The feed shaft referred to in a previous section provides the feed motion which is transmitted to the carriage and cross-slide. It is driven directly by gearing from the main machine spindle, or more frequently through a separate feed gear-box which provides a wide range of different feed rates to suit the requirements of various machining operations.

The Leadscrew

In order to cut a screw thread, the longitudinal carriage movement must be accurately related to the revolutions of the workpiece. This is achieved by means of the leadscrew, which passes through the apron, and is driven by gearing from the main spindle or through the feed gear-box. A movable half-nut in the apron enables the carriage to be directly connected to the leadscrew when cutting a thread.

Tool Posts

One feature of centre-lathe work is the wide range of different cutting operations that can be carried out on a single component, e.g. turning diameters, facing flanges, forming recesses, chamfering, drilling, boring, screw-cutting (external and internal), knurling, etc., involving a very large number of different shaped tools. It is essential therefore that the tool post should be of simple design yet quick in operation to facilitate speedy tool changing and setting.

Fig. 7 shows three types of tool post in current use:—

(a) The clamp-type tool post, commonly fitted on small British lathes and on many Continental machines. A single clamp plate swivels on a central bolt, and is supported by a compression spring. The rear end of the clamp is supported by an adjustable jacking screw, which eliminates the need for clamp packing. The tool is set for height with packing strips of various thickness, and secured by means of the part spherical washer and clamping nut. This arrangement ensures firm clamping despite slight variations in height of tool and jacking screw.

(b) The pillar-type tool post is used by many manufacturers both in this country and abroad. A vertical pillar swivels in a rectangular plate which slides into the tee-slot machined in the upper face of the compound-slide rest. A vertical slot in the pillar admits the tool shank, and the required height of the cutting edge is obtained by sliding the boat-shaped piece on the part spherical ring located on top of the compound-slide. A square-headed clamping-bolt in the pillar secures the tool in the desired position. The chief advantage of this type of tool post is the speedy adjustment for position and height of the cutting tool.

(c) Four-station tool post (four-way tool box), consisting of a square block of steel with a spigot base locating in the upper face of the compound-slide. Four milled slots in the vertical faces of the block provide the location for four separate tools, rigidly held by set screws. A spring-loaded indexing-pin in the face of the compound-slide accurately locates the post in any one of the four positions. A central clamping bolt operated by a ball handle locks or unlocks the post. In order to index the post, the clamping screw

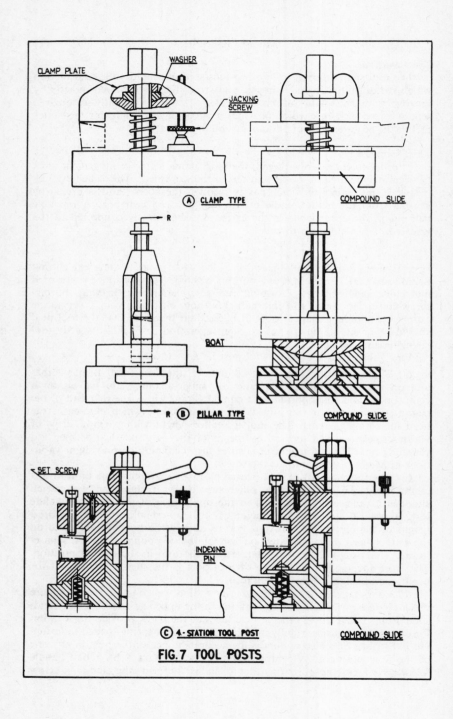

(A) CLAMP TYPE

CLAMP PLATE

WASHER

JACKING SCREW

COMPOUND SLIDE

R

(B) PILLAR TYPE

BOAT

COMPOUND SLIDE

SET SCREW

INDEXING PIN

(C) 4-STATION TOOL POST

COMPOUND SLIDE

FIG. 7 TOOL POSTS

is released, lifting the post clear of the locating pin; the box is then turned to the appropriate position and re-locked. This type of post is very useful for repetitive work; the tools are quickly brought into operation for consecutive operations, and if used in conjunction with the graduated index on the cross-slide, a great deal of measurement can be eliminated.

Turning Tools and Tool Angles

The cutting tools used on all types of turning machines, boring machines, shapers, and planers are known as 'single-point' tools, i.e. the tool has a single cutting edge at one end only. Such tools may be broadly divided into groups:—

1. *Solid Tools:* the cutting edge being integral with the shank. The cutting end is forged to the approximate shape, and finally ground to its final form. Such tools are generally made from high-speed steel.

Fig. 8 shows in plan view a selection of tools made by this method.

2. *Tool Tips:* made from either high-speed steel, stellite, or cemented carbides, are brazed or welded to a low-carbon steel shank. The cutting edges of these tools consist mainly of straight lines, eliminating most of the curves and radii associated with the more traditional turning tools.

Typical tipped tool shapes are shown in Fig. 9.

3. *Tool Bits or Inserts:* located in a tool holder or a boring bar and held by adjusting screws or clamps. Only a small amount of the expensive cutting-tool material is required, and this can be quickly removed from the tool holder when re-grinding is necessary.

Tool Angles

Although the shape and contour of lathe tools vary considerably, all tools must be ground in such a way that the main cutting angles are maintained. These angles are referred to as rake and clearance angles.

Rake Angles

Front (or Top) Rake Fig. 10(a)

Defined as the slope of the cutting face backwards from the front cutting edge. Its actual value varies according to the material being cut: generally a larger front rake for the free-cutting materials, e.g. soft steel and aluminium; small front rake for the crystalline materials, e.g. cast iron and cast brass.

Side Rake Fig. 10(b)

Defined as the slope of the cutting face relative to the end face of workpiece, measured from the horizontal plane.

True Rake

Actual slope of the cutting face as presented to the work; generally a combination of the front and side rake angles.

Negative Rake

The rake angle is defined as positive if the front cutting angle (front clearance plus wedge angle) is less than 90°, and defined as negative if the front cutting angle is greater than 90°.

Rake angles influence chip formation, tool wear, cutting force, surface finish, and permissible cutting speed.

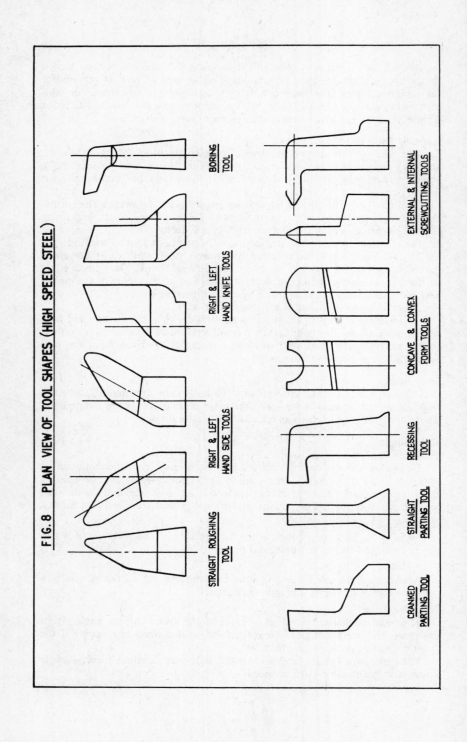

FIG. 8   PLAN VIEW OF TOOL SHAPES (HIGH SPEED STEEL)

STRAIGHT ROUGHING TOOL

RIGHT & LEFT HAND SIDE TOOLS

RIGHT & LEFT HAND KNIFE TOOLS

BORING TOOL

CRANKED PARTING TOOL

STRAIGHT PARTING TOOL

RECESSING TOOL

CONCAVE & CONVEX FORM TOOLS

EXTERNAL & INTERNAL SCREWCUTTING TOOLS

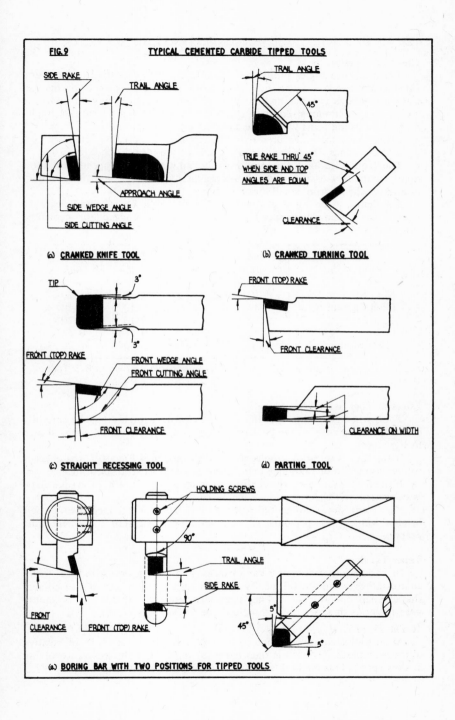

FIG. 9   TYPICAL CEMENTED CARBIDE TIPPED TOOLS

SIDE RAKE
TRAIL ANGLE
APPROACH ANGLE
SIDE WEDGE ANGLE
SIDE CUTTING ANGLE

(a) **CRANKED KNIFE TOOL**

TRAIL ANGLE
45°
TRUE RAKE THRU' 45°
WHEN SIDE AND TOP
ANGLES ARE EQUAL
CLEARANCE

(b) **CRANKED TURNING TOOL**

TIP
3°
3°
FRONT (TOP) RAKE
FRONT WEDGE ANGLE
FRONT CUTTING ANGLE
FRONT CLEARANCE

(c) **STRAIGHT RECESSING TOOL**

FRONT (TOP) RAKE
FRONT CLEARANCE
CLEARANCE ON WIDTH

(d) **PARTING TOOL**

HOLDING SCREWS
90°
TRAIL ANGLE
SIDE RAKE
FRONT CLEARANCE
FRONT (TOP) RAKE
5°
45°
5°

(e) **BORING BAR WITH TWO POSITIONS FOR TIPPED TOOLS**

Clearance Angles

The clearance angles should be just sufficient to ensure that the front and side faces of the tool do not rub on the work. Excessive clearance means that the cutting edge is weak and insufficiently supported. Minimum clearance will ensure maximum strength at the cutting edge (compare clearance angles on woodworking tools with those suitable for metal cutting).

Front clearance—measured from the front of the tool. Fig. 10(a).

Side clearance—measured from the side of the tool. Fig. 10(b).

The front clearance for cylindrical turning with high-speed-steel tools is approximately 6–10°; boring tools might require 15°, with a secondary clearance when boring small diameter holes.

The figures given below give an approximate guide for rake and clearance values when using high-speed-steel tools, angles reduced for cemented carbide tools.

Material to be cut	Front Clearance	Side Clearance	Front Rake	Side Rake
Mild Steel	8–10°	6–10°	18–20°	18–20°
High Carbon Steel	6–8°	6–8°	6–10°	6–10°
Cast Iron	8–10°	6–10°	5–10°	7–10°
Brass	6–8°	6–8°	0–5°	0–5°
Aluminium	8–10°	8–10°	25–40°	15–20°

Note: The B.S. specification for single point tools is given in B.S. 1886: 1952.

Effect of Tool Setting

Tools when ground to specific rake and clearance angles must be carefully set with cutting edge on the horizontal centre-line of the workpiece as shown in Fig. 10(e).

If the tool is set above the centre-line as shown in Fig. 10(f) the effect is to increase value of rake angle and decrease value of front clearance.

If the tool is set below the centre-line as shown in Fig. 10(g) the rake angle is decreased and clearance angle increased.

Fig. 10(h) shows tangential setting, the angles being operative at their original values; this principle is more common in capstan and turret-lathe practice.

Taper Turning

In addition to machining flat surfaces, and surfaces of cylindrical form, centre lathes are quite frequently used to turn or bore surfaces of conical shape. Such operations are known as taper turning. The most commonly used methods of taper turning include the following:—

1. *The Form Tool*

A flat tool accurately ground to the required angle is carefully set relative to the workpiece. The tool is then fed in by hand while the work is revolving at slow speed. This method is confined to tapers of short length.

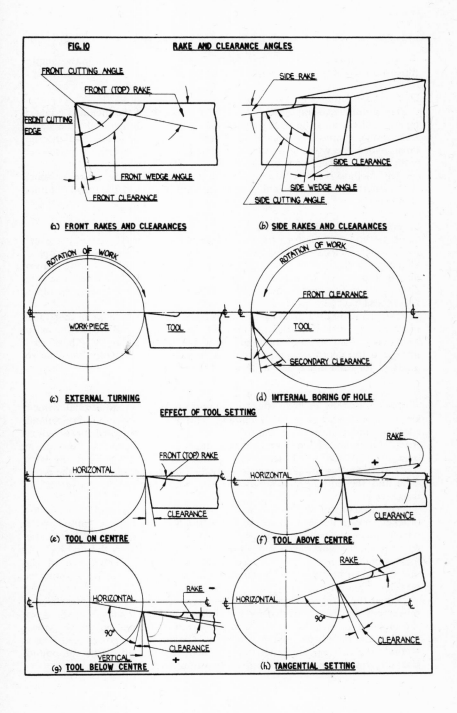

FIG. 10   **RAKE AND CLEARANCE ANGLES**

FRONT CUTTING ANGLE

FRONT (TOP) RAKE

FRONT CUTTING EDGE

FRONT WEDGE ANGLE

FRONT CLEARANCE

SIDE RAKE

SIDE CLEARANCE

SIDE WEDGE ANGLE

SIDE CUTTING ANGLE

(a) **FRONT RAKES AND CLEARANCES**

(b) **SIDE RAKES AND CLEARANCES**

ROTATION OF WORK

WORK-PIECE

TOOL

(c) **EXTERNAL TURNING**

ROTATION OF WORK

FRONT CLEARANCE

TOOL

SECONDARY CLEARANCE

(d) **INTERNAL BORING OF HOLE**

EFFECT OF TOOL SETTING

HORIZONTAL

FRONT (TOP) RAKE

CLEARANCE

(e) **TOOL ON CENTRE**

HORIZONTAL

RAKE

+

CLEARANCE

−

(f) **TOOL ABOVE CENTRE**

HORIZONTAL

RAKE −

90°

CLEARANCE

VERTICAL +

(g) **TOOL BELOW CENTRE**

HORIZONTAL

RAKE

90°

CLEARANCE

(h) **TANGENTIAL SETTING**

The machining of the 45° chamfers on examples shown later in the chapter illustrate this method. See Figs. 16 and 17.

2. *Compound Slide* Fig. 11

The graduated compound slide is set to one-half of the included angle of taper required, and the tool is traversed by the hand-operated slide screw. This simple method is equally applicable for both external and internal tapers when the work is located in a chuck, and for external tapers when work is held between centres.

This method is limited because of the short length of tool travel, confined to the length of slide screw, and due to the hand operation, the finish obtained is inferior.

3. *Off-setting Tailstock* Fig. 12

A method suitable for producing long shallow external tapers on a workpiece which is located between centres. The tailstock centre is set out of alignment with the headstock centre, and the amount of taper for a given length between centres will depend on the magnitude of the off-set. The total amount of tailstock movement is somewhat limited, therefore steep tapers are impossible.

The main disadvantage of this method is the excessive wear that takes place in the work centres, especially at the tailstock end, resulting in inaccuracies. Also when turning duplicate parts, unless the length of each piece and the depth of centre holes are identical, the tailstock must be readjusted for each individual workpiece.

4. *Taper-Turning Attachment* Fig. 13

Many modern centre lathes are equipped with an additional fitment known as the taper-turning attachment. This fitment provides a convenient, speedy, and accurate method of producing conical-shaped parts whose machining might include taper turning, taper boring, or taper screw-cutting operations. These attachments vary considerably in design, but the basic function is always the same, i.e. to provide a lateral movement to the cross-slide and the cutting tool simultaneously with longitudinal movement of the carriage.

The attachment shown in Fig. 13 is of simple design and consists of a bracket (A) firmly secured to the lathe bed, which carries a guide-bar (B) which can be swivelled to the required angle (half included angle of taper required on the workpiece) and is locked in this position. A sliding block (C) locates on the guide-bar and is also attached to the cross-slide by a link (D) and locked in position at (E). The cross-slide operating nut is disconnected by releasing a set-screw (F).

When the lathe carriage is now traversed along the bed the cross-slide movement will be controlled by the sliding-block as it moves up or down the inclined guide-bar, and the tool will produce a taper on the workpiece equal to the inclination of the guide-bar. The automatic power feed is used to drive the carriage, and the cut is applied with the aid of the compound-slide which is set at 90° to its normal position.

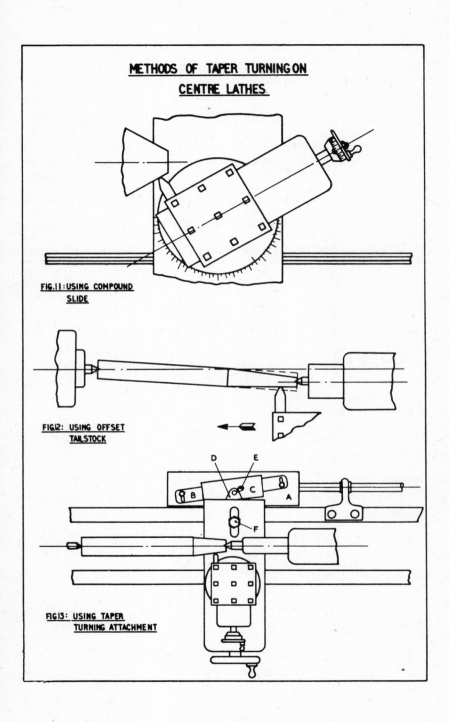

METHODS OF TAPER TURNING ON CENTRE LATHES.

FIG.11: USING COMPOUND SLIDE

FIG.12: USING OFFSET TAILSTOCK

FIG.13: USING TAPER TURNING ATTACHMENT

Screw Cutting

A centre lathe equipped with single-point tools is frequently used for cutting external and internal screw threads on components that have been turned and bored on the machine. This ensures accuracy and eliminates the need for a second operation on another type of machine. The principle of screw-cutting on the lathe is the ratio between the thread on the leadscrew and the thread to be cut. In other words the traverse of the screwing-tool controlled by the rotation of the leadscrew must be accurately related to the rotation of the work controlled by the main spindle. To obtain such a relationship the lead-screw must be geared to the main spindle.

Fig. 14 shows this gearing in the form of a simple train, i.e. 1 Driving Gear revolving at the same speed as the main spindle, 1 Driven Gear attached to the leadscrew, and 1 Idler Gear between the other two which has no effect on gear ratio. When the driving and driven gears have an equal number of teeth, i.e. 1:1 gear ratio, the thread cut on the work should be of identical pitch to that of the leadscrew.

Pitch = Distance from a point on one thread to the corresponding point on the next.
e.g., 1·25 mm, 1·50 mm, 2·00 mm, 2·50 mm, 3·00 mm pitch.

Lead = Distance nut travels in one revolution.
With a single-start thread Lead = Pitch.
With a multi-start thread Lead = Pitch × Number of starts.
e.g. 2 mm pitch × 4 starts = 8 mm Lead.

To cut a thread of a different Lead to that of the leadscrew the ratio of gearing

$$= \frac{\text{Lead of screw to be cut}}{\text{Lead of leadscrew}}$$

$$= \frac{\text{Driving gear}}{\text{Driven gear}}$$

A standard range of gears could be 20 teeth to 100 teeth in steps of ten.

Example 1.

Find a suitable gear ratio to cut 3 mm pitch on a lathe with a 6 mm pitch leadscrew.

$$\text{Ratio} = \frac{\text{Lead of screw to be cut}}{\text{Lead of leadscrew}}$$

$$\frac{3}{6} = \frac{30}{60} = \frac{\text{Driving gear}}{\text{Driven gear}}$$

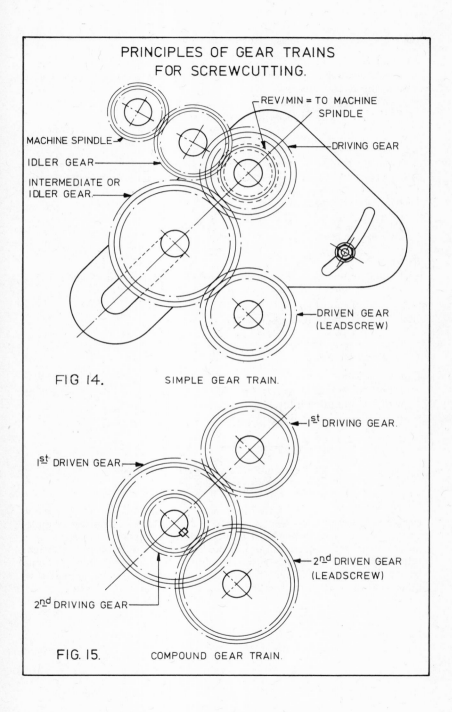

PRINCIPLES OF GEAR TRAINS
FOR SCREWCUTTING.

REV/MIN = TO MACHINE
SPINDLE

MACHINE SPINDLE

IDLER GEAR

INTERMEDIATE OR
IDLER GEAR.

DRIVING GEAR

DRIVEN GEAR
(LEADSCREW)

FIG 14.   SIMPLE GEAR TRAIN.

1st DRIVING GEAR.

1st DRIVEN GEAR

2nd DRIVEN GEAR
(LEADSCREW)

2nd DRIVING GEAR

FIG. 15.   COMPOUND GEAR TRAIN.

Example 2.

Find a suitable gear ratio to cut a $1 \cdot 50$ mm pitch screw on a lathe with a $6 \cdot 0$ mm pitch leadscrew.

$$\text{Ratio} = \frac{\text{Lead of screw to be cut}}{\text{Lead of leadscrew}} = \frac{1 \cdot 5}{6 \cdot 0} = \frac{30}{120}$$

$$= \frac{30 \times 40}{60 \times 80}$$

This is a compound train of gears, as shown in Fig. 15, i.e. four gears instead of three—two driving and two driven gears; all four govern the ratio.

$$\text{Ratio in (2)} = \frac{30 \times 40}{60 \times 80}$$

1st driving gear = 30   1st driven gear = 60
2nd driving gear = 40   2nd driven gear = 80

Example 3.

Find a suitable gear ratio to cut a $3 \cdot 0$ mm pitch screw on a lathe with a $12 \cdot 5$ mm pitch leadscrew.

$$\text{Ratio} = \frac{\text{Lead of screw to be cut}}{\text{Lead of leadscrew}} = \frac{3}{12 \cdot 5} = \frac{30}{125}$$

$$\text{Ratio} = \frac{10 \times 3}{25 \times 5} = \frac{20 \times 60}{50 \times 100} = \frac{\text{Driving gears}}{\text{Driven gears}}$$

Example 4.

Find a suitable gear ratio to cut a 10 mm pitch $\times$ 3-start thread on a lathe with a 6 mm pitch leadscrew.

$$\text{Lead} = \text{Pitch} \times \text{Number of starts} = 10 \times 3 = 30 \text{ mm}$$

$$\therefore \text{Ratio} = \frac{\text{Lead of screw to be cut}}{\text{Lead of leadscrew}} = \frac{30}{6}$$

$$= \frac{5 \times 6}{2 \times 3} = \frac{50 \times 60}{20 \times 30} = \frac{\text{Driving gears}}{\text{Driven gears}}$$

The examples are sufficient to illustrate the method of calculating the gear ratio required to cut a screw thread of a given lead when using a simple-change gear type of lathe. Most modern centre lathes are equipped with a quick-change gear mechanism or gearbox providing a wide range of different ratios, and thus the frequent setting up of gear trains is eliminated. It should be appreciated, however, that in both the simple-change gear method and the quick-change gearbox method the fundamental principle is the same.

Cutting Metric Threads on a Lathe with an English Leadscrew

Screw threads based on the metric system of measurement may be produced on a lathe with a standard leadscrew according to the British system of measurement. An additional gear with 127 teeth is essential, and the formula for calculating the gear ratios is derived as follows:—

If 1 inch is $= 25 \cdot 4$ mm

Then a thread of 1 mm lead $= 25 \cdot 4$ threads per inch (T.P.I.)

If leadscrew had 1 T.P.I.

Then gear ratio required to cut 1 mm lead

$$= \frac{\text{Lead of screw to be cut}}{\text{Lead of leadscrew}} = \frac{\frac{1}{25 \cdot 4}}{1} = \frac{1}{25 \cdot 4} \times \frac{5}{5} = \frac{5}{127}$$

If instead of 1 mm lead we wish to cut thread of x mm lead, the above ratio is multiplied by x.

$$\therefore \text{Ratio} = \frac{5x}{127}$$

If instead of 1-thread-per-inch leadscrew we have an n-thread-per-inch leadscrew.

$$\text{Then Ratio} = \frac{5x.n}{127} = \text{General Formula for any metric thread.}$$

Example:

Find suitable gear ratio for cutting the following threads on a British lathe with a 4-thread-per-inch leadscrew.

(a) $1 \cdot 5$ mm lead; (b) $2 \cdot 5$ mm lead; (c) $4 \cdot 2$ mm lead.

(a) $x = \frac{3}{2}$, n $= 4$. $\text{Ratio} = \frac{5x.n}{127} = \frac{5 \times 1 \cdot 5 \times 4}{127} = \frac{30}{127} = \frac{\text{Driving gear}}{\text{Driven gear}}$

(b) $x = \frac{5}{2}$, n $= 4$. $\text{Ratio} = \frac{5x.n}{127} = \frac{5 \times 2 \cdot 5 \times 4}{127} = \frac{50}{127} = \frac{\text{Driving gear}}{\text{Driven gear}}$

(c) $x = 4 \cdot 2$, n $= 4$. $\text{Ratio} = \frac{5x.n}{127} = \frac{5 \times 4 \cdot 2 \times 4}{127} = \frac{84}{127}$

As no 84 wheel is available, use compound train:—

$$\text{Ratio} = \frac{84}{127} = \frac{7 \times 12}{127} \quad \text{Multiply by 10} = \frac{70 \times 12}{10 \times 127}$$

$$\text{Multiply by 5} \quad = \frac{70 \times 60}{50 \times 127} = \frac{\text{Driving gears}}{\text{Driven gears}}$$

E

Basic Turning Operations and Methods of Location

On the following pages three examples of simple turning work are given, and these show method of holding the material, the tools used, and sequence of operations.

Example 1. Location Pin, Fig. 16

Made from standard rolled bar, located in four-jaw independent chuck— re-set in chuck for the 2nd operation.

Example 2. End-Mill Blank, Fig. 17

Material located in chuck for facing and centre-drilling, located between centres and driven by carrier and driving plate for the 3rd and 4th operation.

Example 3. Arbor Collar, Fig. 18

This example includes drilling, boring, and reaming; also illustrates the use of a location stump turned in position, ensuring true location of the component in the final turning operation.

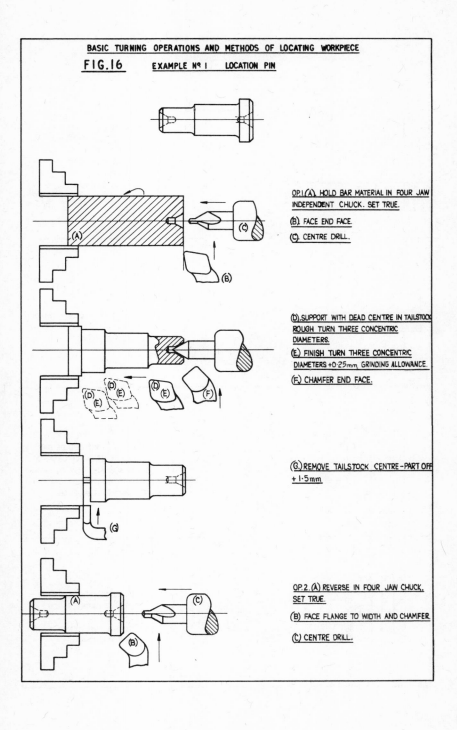

BASIC TURNING OPERATIONS AND METHODS OF LOCATING WORKPIECE

FIG.16   EXAMPLE Nº 1   LOCATION PIN

OP.1.(A). HOLD BAR MATERIAL IN FOUR JAW INDEPENDENT CHUCK. SET TRUE.

(B). FACE END FACE.

(C). CENTRE DRILL.

(D). SUPPORT WITH DEAD CENTRE IN TAILSTOCK ROUGH TURN THREE CONCENTRIC DIAMETERS.

(E). FINISH TURN THREE CONCENTRIC DIAMETERS +0.25mm GRINDING ALLOWANCE.

(F). CHAMFER END FACE.

(G). REMOVE TAILSTOCK CENTRE – PART OFF + 1.5mm

OP.2.(A) REVERSE IN FOUR JAW CHUCK, SET TRUE.

(B) FACE FLANGE TO WIDTH AND CHAMFER.

(C) CENTRE DRILL.

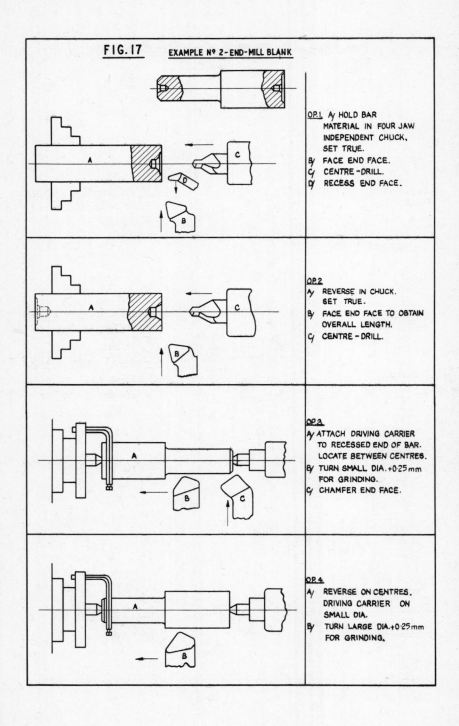

FIG. 17

EXAMPLE Nº 2 - END-MILL BLANK

OP.1. A/ HOLD BAR
MATERIAL IN FOUR JAW
INDEPENDENT CHUCK,
SET TRUE.
B/ FACE END FACE.
C/ CENTRE - DRILL.
D/ RECESS END FACE.

OP.2
A/ REVERSE IN CHUCK.
SET TRUE.
B/ FACE END FACE TO OBTAIN
OVERALL LENGTH.
C/ CENTRE - DRILL.

OP.3
A/ ATTACH DRIVING CARRIER
TO RECESSED END OF BAR.
LOCATE BETWEEN CENTRES.
B/ TURN SMALL DIA. +0·25 mm
FOR GRINDING.
C/ CHAMFER END FACE.

OP.4
A/ REVERSE ON CENTRES.
DRIVING CARRIER ON
SMALL DIA.
B/ TURN LARGE DIA. +0·25 mm
FOR GRINDING.

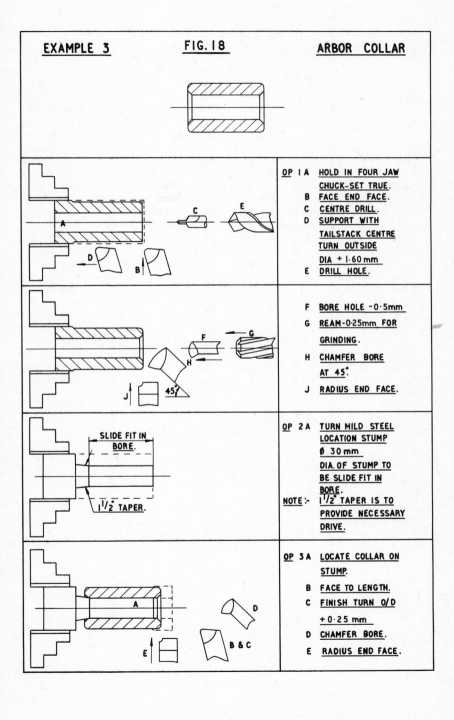

EXAMPLE 3   FIG. 18   ARBOR COLLAR

OP 1 A HOLD IN FOUR JAW CHUCK–SET TRUE.
B FACE END FACE.
C CENTRE DRILL.
D SUPPORT WITH TAILSTACK CENTRE TURN OUTSIDE DIA + 1.60 mm
E DRILL HOLE.

F BORE HOLE –0.5mm
G REAM–0.25mm FOR GRINDING.
H CHAMFER BORE AT 45°.
J RADIUS END FACE.

OP 2 A TURN MILD STEEL LOCATION STUMP Ø 30 mm DIA. OF STUMP TO BE SLIDE FIT IN BORE.
NOTE :- 1½° TAPER IS TO PROVIDE NECESSARY DRIVE.

SLIDE FIT IN BORE.

1½° TAPER.

OP 3 A LOCATE COLLAR ON STUMP.
B FACE TO LENGTH.
C FINISH TURN O/D + 0.25 mm
D CHAMFER BORE.
E RADIUS END FACE.

Toolmaker's Buttons and Button Boring

When a jig-boring machine is not available, holes can be bored to close limits of accuracy both for size and position by means of toolmaker's buttons and a standard centre lathe.

Fig. 19(a) shows a sectional view of a jig-button, a small cylindrical steel bush accurately ground on the circumference and end faces, the hole being about 3 mm larger in diameter than the retaining screw. These buttons can be set by end measurement (gauge blocks, micrometer, or vernier height gauge), with far greater precision than that possible by marking-out methods.

A simple button-boring example is shown in Fig. 19(b), representing a jig-plate requiring two 16 mm diameter holes in the positions shown. The sides of the plate marked A and B and the two faces are accurately machined flat and at right angles to each other. The centres of the two 16 mm diameter holes are then established by marking-out, and two holes are drilled and tapped on these centres to suit the retaining screws. The two jig-buttons are set in their approximate positions and lightly clamped by the screws.

The jig-plate is located on a surface plate and the first button is set concentric with the desired hole position by first taking measurements from the datum face B with a set of gauge blocks as shown in Fig. 19(c). This is repeated in respect of the dimension from datum face A, allowance being made in each case for half button diameter. When the correct setting is obtained the first button is securely clamped, and the second button is set in a similar manner, measurements being taken from datum face B and from the first button. After setting, the second button is securely clamped. The jig-plate with the two jig-buttons in position is then lightly clamped to the face-plate of a centre lathe and the first button is set true by means of a dial indicator as shown in Fig. 19(d). When this button is running true the jig-plate is firmly clamped on the face-plate and the jig-button is removed.

The small tapped hole is opened out with a standard 12 mm diameter drill, followed by a single-point boring tool to enlarge the hole to its final size.

The jig-plate is then re-set on the face-plate to bring the second button on the centre of rotation; when set true with the dial indicator the plate is securely clamped, this button is removed, and the second hole is drilled and bored to the required size.

It should be noted that after boring the first hole it is always wise to insert a plug gauge and check the setting of the remaining button to ensure no movement has taken place during the machining operation.

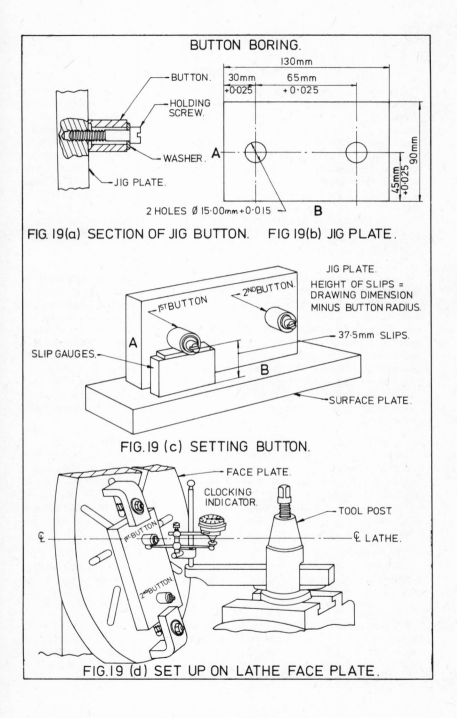

BUTTON BORING.

BUTTON.

HOLDING SCREW.

WASHER. A

JIG PLATE.

130mm

30mm +0·025   65mm +0·025

90mm

45mm +0·025

2 HOLES Ø 15·00mm +0·015   B

FIG. 19(a) SECTION OF JIG BUTTON.   FIG 19(b) JIG PLATE.

JIG PLATE.

HEIGHT OF SLIPS = DRAWING DIMENSION MINUS BUTTON RADIUS.

2ND BUTTON.

1ST BUTTON

A

37·5mm SLIPS.

SLIP GAUGES.

B

SURFACE PLATE.

FIG. 19 (c) SETTING BUTTON.

FACE PLATE.

CLOCKING INDICATOR.

TOOL POST.

1ST BUTTON

⊄ LATHE.

2ND BUTTON

FIG. 19 (d) SET UP ON LATHE FACE PLATE.

Turret and Capstan Lathes

The productive capacity of a standard centre lathe is limited by the necessity for frequent tool changes, and the corresponding measurement of individual dimensions. Therefore to meet the needs of batch or quantity production, turning machines of modified design, incorporating a revolving multi-tool holder locating a range of cutting tools, have been introduced. These tools can be initially set for the production of a particular component by skilled craftsmen, and the large numbers of duplicate parts are machined at high-production rates by semi-skilled operators. Turret and capstan lathes may be classified as semi-automatic machines, other types have been developed to work on a fully automatic cycle.

A typical capstan lathe is shown in Fig. 20. It follows centre lathe design in respect of bed, headstock, saddle, and cross-slide, but its special features include:—

1. *The Turret*

This fits on the right-hand end of the bed in the position occupied by the tailstock on the centre lathe. It is mounted on an auxiliary slide which moves longitudinally in a sub-bed which can be moved along the main bed and locked in desired position. The turret movement is confined to the relatively short length of the auxiliary slide. The turret is of hexagonal shape, providing six locating faces for tool attachments. An automatic indexing device is provided so that each turret face can be aligned with the machine spindle as it is required. Stops which can be set to limit the movement of each tool are coupled to the turret indexing mechanism so that they remain in correct relationship to the tools they control. The star-handle provides a manual control of the turret which can be also traversed under power feed.

2. *The Cross-Slide*

Similar in design to the centre-lathe cross-slide but the compound-slide is omitted. A four-way tool box is located directly on the cross-slide, and is manually indexed to bring each of the four tools into the correct position. In addition a rear tool post is provided which is generally used for parting-off or for forming operations. Such tools are held in the inverted position. Stops are fitted to limit cross-slide tool movements, but these are manually selected for each tool.

3. *The Saddle*

Similar to the centre-lathe saddle but incorporating stops which control longitudinal movement of tools held in the cross-slide tool boxes. These stops are selected manually.

4. *Headstock*

An all-geared headstock which usually incorporates a device whereby certain speeds may be changed without disengaging the clutch. A reversing mechanism is also fitted; this is essential for producing left-hand threads and for tapping.

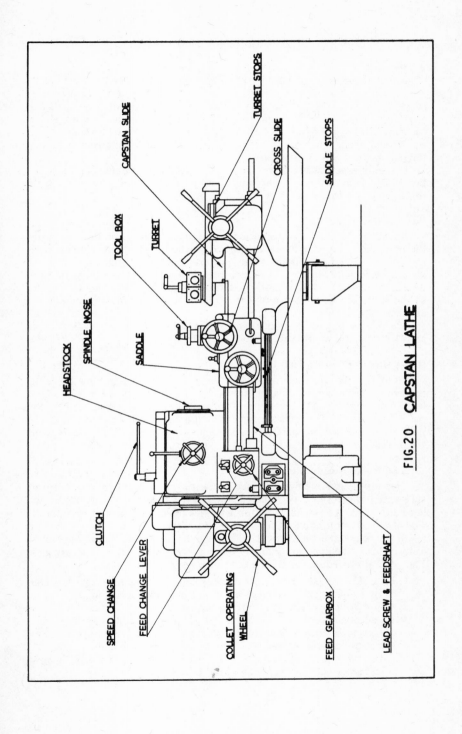

HEADSTOCK

SPINDLE NOSE

CLUTCH

SPEED CHANGE

FEED CHANGE LEVER

COLLET OPERATING
WHEEL

FEED GEARBOX

LEAD SCREW & FEEDSHAFT

SADDLE

TOOL BOX

TURRET

CAPSTAN SLIDE

TURRET STOPS

CROSS SLIDE

SADDLE STOPS

FIG.20 CAPSTAN LATHE

5. Bar Feed Mechanism

Much of the work produced on the capstan lathe is made from bar stock. An attachment extends away from the spindle at the rear of the headstock to support and feed this material forward at the appropriate intervals. This bar feed mechanism consists of a metal tube with a wood lining through which the standard bar passes. A plunger actuated by wire ropes and weights bears on the end of the bar, and when the work-holding device is released, pushes the bar forward to a pre-set bar-stop.

Expanding collets are most frequently used for gripping bar material, but chucks can be fitted for holding castings and forgings and other items too large to pass through the hollow spindle. See p. 143.

Box Turning Tools

As far as possible all turning on the capstan lathe is carried out from the hexagon turret, especially when large batches are being machined. With the aid of special tool holders the various types of cutting tools may be set with adequate support to ensure repetitive accuracy in the parts produced. This is not always possible if turning is done from the cross-slide, as the stops are less positive and the 'feel' can vary from one operator to another.

Several special tool holders are available; these are known as Box Tools and the most commonly used include the following:—

Roller Steady Centring Tool Fig. 21

Used for the accurate centre-drilling of components which are subsequently finished by external grinding. The two top rollers are set to bear lightly on the bar and the bottom roller is quickly adjusted to give the required pressure. The rollers ensure that the bar is running true, and that the centre-hole will be concentric, and this avoids the likelihood of drill breakages.

Inverted Roller Steady Box Tool Fig. 22

This tool is mounted on the face of the turret and consists of an arm of substantial dimensions to which is attached a bracket. This holds two hardened-steel rollers and a platform to which the cutting tool is clamped. The rollers are adjustable to suit various diameters.

In operation the tool produces the diameter required, whilst the rollers follow closely behind and run on the turned portion thus supporting it. The general procedure for setting the roller box is as follows:—

1. Turn short length of bar to diameter required, using tool on cross-slide, or by using stepped parting tool as shown in example. Fig. 32.
2. Adjust rollers to just run on this pilot diameter.
3. Set cutting edge of tool on horizontal centre-line of bar with front face of tool in advance of the rollers by approximately $1 \cdot 5$ mm.
4. Press tool against diameter of pilot, and clamp in position.
5. Take trial cut and check diameter. If adjustment is necessary it must be made on the cutting tool and not on the rollers.

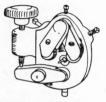

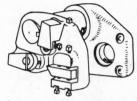

FIG.21 ROLLER STEADY
CENTRING TOOL

FIG.22 INVERTED ROLLER
STEADY BOX TOOL

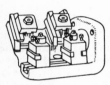

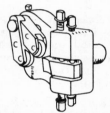

FIG.23 FLAT STEADY BOX
TOOL
FLANGE TYPE

FIG.24 ROLLER STEADY
ENDING TOOL

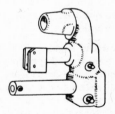

FIG.25 FLOATING REAMER
HOLDER

FIG.26 SOLID KNEE TURNING
TOOL

Flat Steady Box Tool Fig. 23

Similar in some ways to the roller steady box, but the rollers are replaced by vee-steadies. These are particularly useful when turning such materials as brass where the chips produced are small and would be rolled into the surface by the rollers on a roller steady box. The size of cut is more restricted but it is possible to turn more than one diameter by using two tools and the appropriate steadies. The setting procedure is similar to that outlined for the roller steady box.

Roller Steady Ending Tool Fig. 24

Many jobs require a special form on their end face, i.e. the radius on the end of a bolt. This can be readily produced with a roller steady ending tool which consists of two hardened-steel rollers which contact the finished diameter of the work and are closely followed by a form tool which produces the desired shape on the end of the component. The setting is similar to that of the roller box except the cutting tool is set behind the rollers instead of in front.

Solid Knee Turning Tool Fig. 26

When machining components which are located in a chuck, the knee turning tool allows turning and boring to be performed simultaneously. A boring bar locates in the central hole, while a turning tool is held in the overhead bracket. The support bush locates on the overhead support-bar projecting from the headstock, and this ensures rigidity of the set-up.

Floating Reamer Holder Fig. 25

The flange type of floating reamer holder shown in Fig. 25 is an essential item of equipment used on the capstan lathe for holding machine reamers of various diameters. When a hole has been drilled, or drilled and bored, the reamer is finally used to ensure accurate size and good surface finish.

The shank of the reamer is located in the floating holder by means of standard split-adaptor bushes or by morse-taper sockets.

The floating holder makes the reamer self-centring in relation to the hole already drilled or bored, thereby ensuring an accurate hole both dimensionally and in surface finish.

Coventry Die-Head Fig. 27

Most external threads produced on the capstan lathe are cut with the aid of a self-opening die-head. The 'Coventry' die-head is a typical example, and will produce threads accurate in size and form with a good surface finish. In addition they retain their setting over a long period, and being self-opening do not require reversing off the finished thread.

The cutting dies or chasers are made in sets of four, each die being numbered, and they are located in a clockwise order in the accurately ground slots in the die-body (Fig. 27 shows only two of the four dies in position) and are retained by the cover plate.

The die-head is gripped by its shank in the machine turret, and is closed by operating the locking arm which allows the detent pin to engage in a slot at the back of the scroll. The detent-pin lever has two positions, one for the roughing cut and the other for the finishing cut.

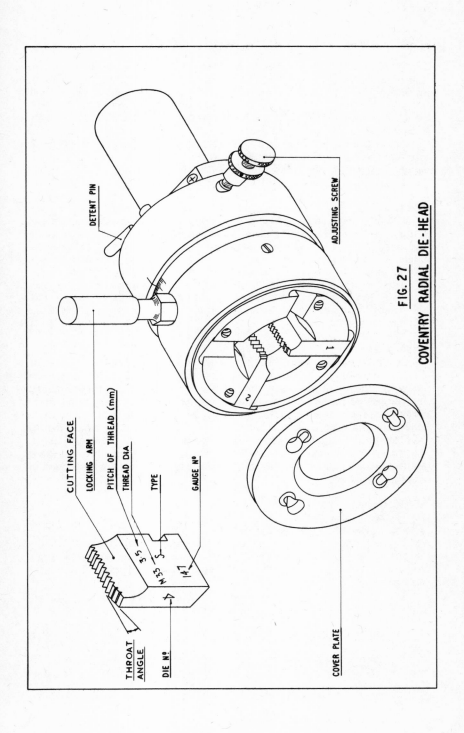

DETENT PIN

ADJUSTING SCREW

CUTTING FACE

LOCKING ARM

PITCH OF THREAD (mm)

THREAD DIA

TYPE

GAUGE Nº

M 33

3·5

S

147

THROAT ANGLE

DIE Nº

COVER PLATE

FIG. 27

COVENTRY RADIAL DIE-HEAD

When initially setting the die-head the detent pin lever is put in the finishing (or minus) position, and the adjusting screw is turned until the indicator line is one divison on the plus side of the zero-marking; this will allow final sizing to a screw gauge. The dies are then eased on to the work which has been turned to a few hundredths of a millimetre oversize, light pressure being maintained to overcome resistance of the capstan-slide. The forward travel of the head is usually arrested by a capstan-slide stop; the dies continue to screw forward for a short distance on the bar until the scroll is pulled off the detent pin, when the opening springs 'snap' the die-head open.

Die Grinding

The dies are ground on the throat or lead angle while held in a special fixture, all four dies being ground in one setting to ensure uniformity. A choice of four throat angles is available—15°, 20°, 33°, and 45°; the 20° angle is considered standard, and the others are used in special cases, e.g. 15° for tough materials, 33° and 45° for threading close to a shoulder.

After several grindings the height of the die is affected and it becomes necessary to regrind the top cutting face. Again a special fixture is required, the height being established by a gauge used in conjunction with the gauge number marked on the die.

Types of Die

Coventry dies are supplied in a range of sizes and types. They are made to suit die-heads from 6 mm to 114 mm, these sizes being the maximum diameter which will pass right through the head. Die thread forms may be milled, ground, or lapped, depending upon the degree of precision required. They are produced with various rake angles to suit different materials; a letter stamped on the die face indicates the sort of work for which the die is most suitable, e.g. S—mild steel and wrought iron; B—brass or plastics, etc. In addition to normal vee-threads, acme, and buttress threads, single and multi-start can be cut. Tapered threads can also be cut with the aid of a special die-head.

Work Holding

The work produced on capstan lathes can be broadly divided into two groups: 1. Bar Work; 2. Chuck Work.

1. Bar work, i.e. work produced from standard rolled bar is usually held in some form of collet chuck, which incorporates a one-piece spring collet to give accurate, positive, and rapid location. These collet chucks may be manually or air operated.

Three different types of chucks are in use. Fig. 28(a) shows the draw-in type. The external taper on the spring collet fits into a mating taper in the chuck, and as the collet is drawn back it exerts a powerful grip on the bar. The action of this type of collet tends to draw the bar back from the setting stop.

Fig. 28(b) shows the push-forward-type collet chuck. A forward movement of the spring collet into the taper bore of the chuck closes the collet

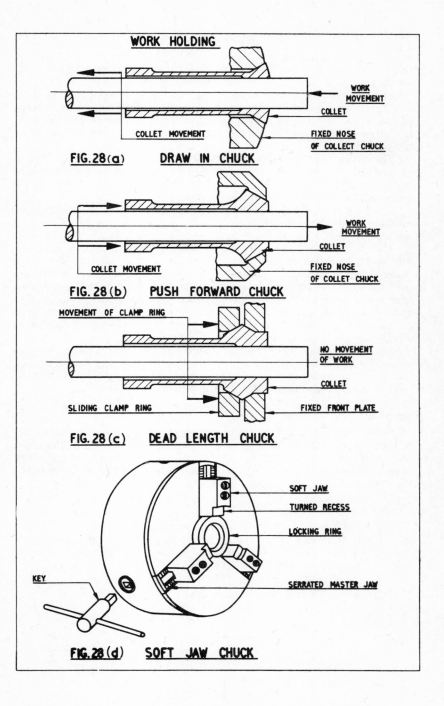

WORK HOLDING

FIG. 28 (a)   DRAW IN CHUCK

WORK MOVEMENT

COLLET

COLLET MOVEMENT

FIXED NOSE OF COLLECT CHUCK

FIG. 28 (b)   PUSH FORWARD CHUCK

WORK MOVEMENT

COLLET

COLLET MOVEMENT

FIXED NOSE OF COLLET CHUCK

FIG. 28 (c)   DEAD LENGTH CHUCK

MOVEMENT OF CLAMP RING

NO MOVEMENT OF WORK

COLLET

SLIDING CLAMP RING

FIXED FRONT PLATE

FIG. 28 (d)   SOFT JAW CHUCK

SOFT JAW

TURNED RECESS

LOCKING RING

KEY

SERRATED MASTER JAW

on to the bar, providing the necessary grip. This action has the opposite effect to that of the draw-in type and tends to press the bar firmly into the setting stop.

Fig. 28(c) shows the dead-length-type chuck. Linear movement of collet and bar is prevented by the fixed front plate, the sliding clamp ring working against the external taper of the spring collet. This type of chuck is particularly suitable for air operation, and gives the most accurate control of bar position.

The spring collet will only efficiently hold bar which is within $+0·125$ mm of nominal size. When holding hot-rolled bar the draw-in-type chuck can be fitted with separate pads in place of the split collet, and these pads will accommodate bar with $+0·75$ mm of nominal size.

2. Chuck work, i.e. work whose maximum diameter is greater than the machine-spindle bore, therefore held in either a self-centring or independent jaw chuck.

The three-jaw self-centring type is used most frequently, and can be fitted with hardened or soft jaws. The hardened jaws are used for rough material, e.g. hot-rolled bar, castings, forgings, etc.; the soft jaws are normally used for second operations, the diameter to be located in the jaws having been machined in the first operation. The soft jaws are bored out in position and will accurately locate work on diameter and length with minimum risk of damage. When boring the jaws the chuck must be firmly locked to prevent vibration.

Fig. 28(d) shows a three-jaw chuck fitted with soft jaws. A ring is clamped in position at the back of the jaws, and the location diameter for the work is then bored to the appropriate size. After boring the ring is removed and the work located on diameter and back face in the turned recess.

Turret Lathes

Similar to the capstan in general design and principles of operation, but of much larger capacity. The main difference is in the design of the turret tool holder; this is mounted on a saddle which slides along the full length of machine bed as shown in Fig. 29. Compare this with Fig. 30 which shows the limited travel of the capstan tool holder.

Capstan Lathe Tool Layout

Fig. 31 shows a plan view of a tool layout suitable for the manufacture of a batch of special bolts. The corresponding sequence of operations is shown in Fig. 32 utilising six turret tool stations, two tools located in the four-way tool box, and one tool in the rear tool post.

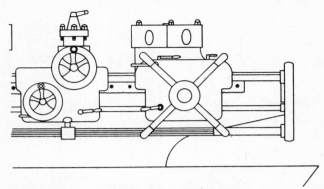

FIG. 29   COMBINATION TURRET LATHE

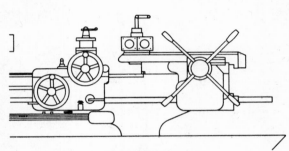

FIG. 30   CAPSTAN LATHE

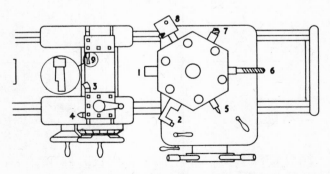

FIG. 31   CAPSTAN LATHE TOOL LAYOUT

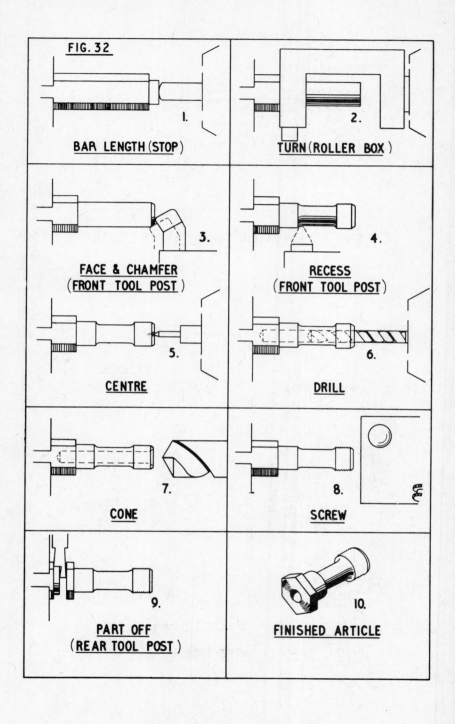

FIG. 32

1. BAR LENGTH (STOP)

2. TURN (ROLLER BOX)

3. FACE & CHAMFER (FRONT TOOL POST)

4. RECESS (FRONT TOOL POST)

5. CENTRE

6. DRILL

7. CONE

8. SCREW

9. PART OFF (REAR TOOL POST)

10. FINISHED ARTICLE

CHAPTER SIX

MILLING MACHINES

In less than fifty years after the introduction of Maudsley's centre lathe the early types of milling machine were being developed, and the first decade of the twentieth century saw the introduction of a horizontal milling machine similar in basic design to the modern column-and-knee machine. In more recent years many other types of milling machine have been developed to meet the needs of modern industry.

Definition

Milling may be defined as a machining process for the removal of excess metal by means of revolving multi-tooth cutters (or mills), each tooth taking its share of the cut as the workpiece is fed in a suitable direction while in contact with the cutter.

Basic Milling Operations

1. Machining flat or plane surfaces, parallel or at right angles to base face.
2. Machining plane surfaces at an angle relative to base face.
3. Machining keyways or slots.
4. Machining circular forms.
5. Machining irregular-shaped forms or profiles.
6. Machining gear teeth, and thread forms.
7. Machining helical flutes and grooves.
8. Machining holes (drilling and boring).

The above list of basic operations indicates the versatile nature of the milling process; in addition intricate forms can be produced automatically and independently of the skill of the operator after the machine and cutters have been initially set for quantity production.

Classification of Milling Machines

Milling machines may be broadly classified into three main groups:—

1. Column-and-Knee-type machines.
2. Manufacturing or Bed-type machines.
3. Special-type machines.

Column-and-Knee Milling Machine

The most commonly used type of milling machine, whose name is derived from two of its main elements, i.e. the main frame or column and the projecting knee which carries the saddle and work-table. These machines are very versatile, providing three independent movements to the workpiece, longitudinal, transverse, and vertical, and are therefore used extensively in tool-rooms, experimental departments, and in many production shops for milling a wide range of small and medium-size components. Owing to a lack of rigidity they are not the most suitable type of machine for milling heavy production work.

Column-and-knee machines are made in three styles:—
1. Plain Horizontal Machine.
2. Universal Machine.
3. Vertical Machine.

Plain Horizontal Machine

The main elements of the plain horizontal machine are shown in Fig. 1.

Column

A vertical hollow casting which houses the driving mechanism, usually a constant-speed motor with vee-belt drive to a main shaft, controlled by a friction clutch and through sliding gears to the main spindle. The sliding gears can be selected by moving a dial or lever on the outside of the column. The front face of the column is accurately machined and this locates and guides the knee in its vertical travel. Integral with the column is a projecting foot which forms the machine base, supporting the knee elevating screw and also providing a reservoir for the coolant.

Spindle

A hollow variable-speed spindle is located in the column in a horizontal position. The spindle nose is bored to a standard taper (small or large international taper), providing accurate location for the milling cutter arbors. The spindle flange carries driving keys which locate in slots in the arbor flange, providing a positive drive.

Overarm

The overarm is accurately located on the top face of the column, providing support and correct alignment for the cutter arbor, and is adjustable in the horizontal plane to accommodate arbors of various lengths.

One arbor steadily attached to the outer end of the overarm provides a bearing for the cutter arbor; additional steadies may be utilised to give added support and rigidity.

Knee

The knee is the second largest unit of the machine, located and guided on the column face. It is supported by the elevating screw which provides the vertical movement. In turn the knee supports the saddle and the work-table. A cross-shaft driven from the column provides power feed to both saddle, work-table, and elevating screw. These feeds may be varied to suit a wide range of milling operations.

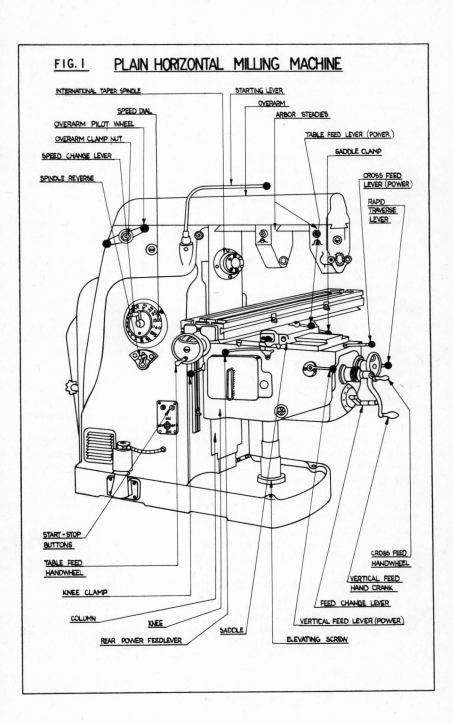

FIG. 1   PLAIN HORIZONTAL MILLING MACHINE

INTERNATIONAL TAPER SPINDLE

SPEED DIAL

OVERARM PILOT WHEEL

OVERARM CLAMP NUT

SPEED CHANGE LEVER

SPINDLE REVERSE

STARTING LEVER

OVERARM

ARBOR STEADIES

TABLE FEED LEVER (POWER.)

SADDLE CLAMP

CROSS FEED LEVER (POWER)

RAPID TRAVERSE LEVER

START - STOP BUTTONS

TABLE FEED HANDWHEEL

KNEE CLAMP

COLUMN

KNEE

REAR POWER FEEDLEVER

SADDLE

ELEVATING SCREW

CROSS FEED HANDWHEEL

VERTICAL FEED HAND CRANK

FEED CHANGE LEVER

VERTICAL FEED LEVER (POWER)

Saddle

A one-piece casting located and guided by the horizontal guiding surfaces on the knee. The saddle supports the work-table and provides transverse movement to the workpiece; it may be manually operated or traversed by automatic feed.

Table

The work-table operating in the saddle guide-ways provides the longitudinal movement to the work. The work may be clamped directly on the table, or be held in one of a number of attachments or fixtures. The working surface of the table is accurately machined, and is provided with a series of tee-slots which carry the tee-bolts for clamping, and also locate the tenons on the base of fixtures and attachments, ensuring speedy alignment.

Universal Milling Machines

The general construction of the universal machine is very similar to that of the plain machine; the chief difference lies in the design of the saddle. The universal saddle is made in two parts: the upper portion which supports the table can be swivelled in a horizontal plane relative to the lower portion attached to the knee. This additional feature increases the usefulness of the machine, especially for helices, e.g. milling the flutes in twist-drills and milling cutters, and teeth in helical gears. Such work is performed with the aid of a universal dividing head which ensures accurate circular division (see later section on Dividing Head).

Vertical Milling Machine Fig. 2

Many features of the vertical machine are identical to the plain horizontal, the obvious difference being the position of the spindle which is in the vertical plane instead of the horizontal; from this the machine derives its name.

The vertical spindle is mounted in a sliding head which can be moved up or down the upper column face by hand or power feed. Some machines are fitted with a swivel head, and this enables the spindle axis to be set at an angle relative to the table.

The vertical machine is chiefly used for milling operations that cannot be conveniently performed on the other types of machines, e.g. profiling internal and external surfaces, milling die-plates and moulds; and drilling and boring holes in jigs and fixtures.

Various attachments are used on the vertical machine for holding the work, including the dividing head and rotary table.

Manufacturing or Bed-Type Milling Machines

These machines are designed to meet the needs of quantity production of duplicate parts. Their chief characteristic is the fixed table support or bed which is carried directly on the foundations, an arrangement which provides for greater rigidity than the column-and-knee design.

The standard machines are made in two basic types:—

1. Single-spindle machines.

FIG. 2

PLAIN VERTICAL MILLER

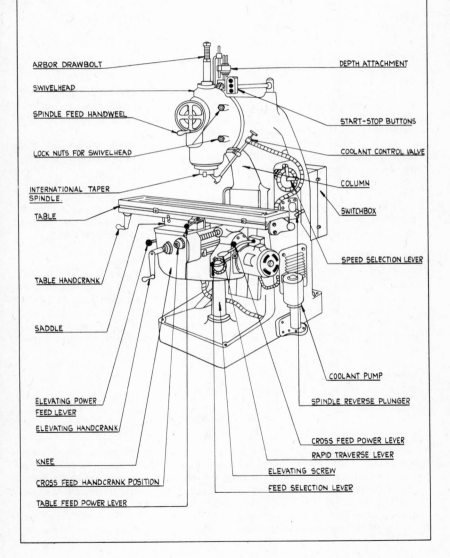

ARBOR DRAWBOLT

SWIVELHEAD

SPINDLE FEED HANDWEEL

LOCK NUTS FOR SWIVELHEAD

INTERNATIONAL TAPER SPINDLE.

TABLE

TABLE HANDCRANK

SADDLE

ELEVATING POWER FEED LEVER

ELEVATING HANDCRANK

KNEE

CROSS FEED HANDCRANK POSITION

TABLE FEED POWER LEVER

DEPTH ATTACHMENT

START-STOP BUTTONS

COOLANT CONTROL VALVE

COLUMN

SWITCHBOX

SPEED SELECTION LEVER

COOLANT PUMP

SPINDLE REVERSE PLUNGER

CROSS FEED POWER LEVER

RAPID TRAVERSE LEVER

ELEVATING SCREW

FEED SELECTION LEVER

2. Duplex milling machines—two horizontal spindles located on opposite sides of the table.

The main elements of these machines are shown in Fig. 3.

Column

The main vertical member which is attached to the side of the bed forming the main frame of the machine. Guide-ways on the vertical face of the column locate and guide the spindle-carrier unit, and also provide vertical adjustment of the cutter spindle.

The base of the column houses the electric motor and gearing which drives the spindle.

Spindle Carrier

The spindle carrier, as its name implies, carries the cutter spindle and slides on the vertical face of the column, providing the necessary vertical adjustment for cutter setting. The spindle which fits in a quill can be also adjusted to set the cutter relative to the work.

Both vertical and crosswise adjustments are manually controlled, and after the cutters are initially set the spindle carrier and spindle are securely locked in position to maintain accuracy during cutting.

Bed

The table support or bed of box construction which stands directly on the floor ensures that the work-table is solidly supported. It also houses the feed-drive mechanism, and forms a reservoir for the coolant fluid.

Work-Table

The work-table is located in guide-ways on the upper face of the bed, providing the longitudinal movement for the workpiece. The top face of the table is provided with tee-slots for alignment and clamping purposes.

Generally these machines operate on a fully automatic cycle the table movement being hydraulically operated and governed by pre-set trip stops mounted on the front face of the table. The system allows for rapid movement of the table during the non-cutting part of the cycle.

On the Duplex machine with two spindle carriers that can be adjusted independently it is possible to carry out two identical milling operations on either face of the workpiece in one traverse of the table.

Special-Type Machines

1. **Plano Milling Machine** Fig. 4

A machine designed to carry out milling operations on large heavy components. It has a box-type bed, reciprocating table, elevating cross-slide, and side pillars very similar in appearance to the planing machine, from which it derives its name. Two cutter heads are located on the cross-slide, and one on each side pillar. A separate drive is required for each cutter spindle, arranged by means of an electric motor and gearbox which provides a range of cutting speeds to suit various types of material and cutter diameters.

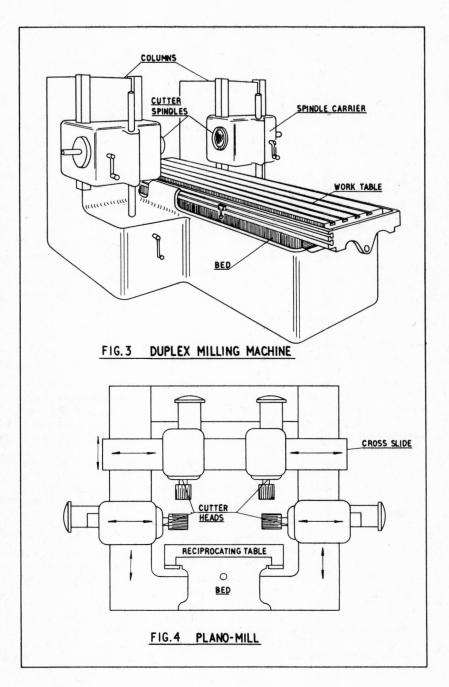

FIG. 3   DUPLEX MILLING MACHINE

FIG. 4   PLANO-MILL

The table traverse is a slow-speed motion providing a variable power feed, the motion being transmitted from electric motor through a gearbox which drives a worm-shaft engaging with a rack attached to the underside of the table.

A plano milling machine possesses several advantages as compared with the planing machine, including the reduction of non-cutting time, wider range of operations in one setting, and increased rate of production.

2. Profile Milling Machines Fig. 5

Vertical-spindle profiling machines are used for machining large batches of production work requiring accurate forms and profiles. Such shapes are determined with the aid of metal formers or templates fixed to the work-table of the machine. A tracer pin or stylus is kept in contact with the template, and its movement is synchronised with that of the cutter head ensuring that the cutter follows the master form throughout the cutting operation. These machines may be broadly classified under two headings:—

(a) Hand-operated: simple machines in which the traverse motions of table and cutter head are manipulated manually, while the tracer pin is spring-loaded.

(b) Automatic: more complicated machines of widely differing design, operated by means of mechanical, electrical, pneumatic, or hydraulic systems. Machines of both single- and multi-spindle type are used in current practice.

3. Thread Milling Machines

Two conventional types:—

(a) *Machines employing a single form cutter* Fig. 6

Thread milling machines designed primarily for the machining of long external threads, e.g. leadscrews of acme thread form, or long worm-shafts. These machines are similar in appearance to a lathe, but a cutter head replaces the lathe saddle. A single form cutter of the required contour is mounted at the rear of the work, and can be inclined to suit the helix angle of the thread required.

Three basic driving motions are involved: one to rotate the cutter at the appropriate speed, one to rotate the work at a slower speed, and a third to provide the longitudinal traverse for the cutter head. The cutter is normally set to the full depth of thread required, thus one traverse of the cutter produces the finished thread.

(b) *Machines employing a multiple-thread cutter* Fig. 7

Thread milling machines used for cutting large numbers of internal and external threads of vee-form and short length. The multi-ribbed cutter, slightly longer in length than thread to be cut, is made of annular rows of teeth perpendicular to the axis of the cutter (not helical as in a tap or hob). This cutter is fed in the required depth, revolving at a suitable speed while the workpiece revolves slowly to give the desired feed. A longitudinal movement equivalent to the lead is given either to the work or cutter.

This method is both speedy and convenient for cutting internal and external threads close up to a shoulder face.

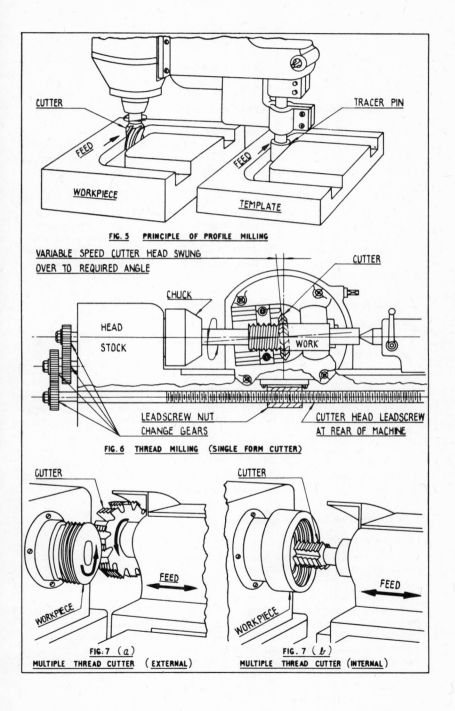

CUTTER

TRACER PIN

FEED

FEED

WORKPIECE

TEMPLATE

FIG. 5   PRINCIPLE OF PROFILE MILLING

VARIABLE SPEED CUTTER HEAD SWUNG
OVER TO REQUIRED ANGLE

CUTTER

CHUCK

HEAD
STOCK

WORK

LEADSCREW NUT
CHANGE GEARS

CUTTER HEAD LEADSCREW
AT REAR OF MACHINE

FIG. 6   THREAD MILLING   (SINGLE FORM CUTTER)

CUTTER

CUTTER

FEED

FEED

WORKPIECE

WORKPIECE

FIG. 7 (a)
MULTIPLE THREAD CUTTER (EXTERNAL)

FIG. 7 (b)
MULTIPLE THREAD CUTTER (INTERNAL)

Milling Cutters

Milling cutters are classified by three methods:—

1. Classification based on relief of cutter teeth

(a) *Profile Cutters*

All types of cutters which are sharpened by grinding the profile of the teeth, the clearance or relief is obtained by grinding a narrow land behind the cutting edge. The rake angle is obtained by grinding the tooth face. Fig. 8.

(b) *Form Relieved Cutters*

All types of cutters with a tooth profile which is produced by a form or master tool in a relieving machine, thus providing an eccentric relief behind the cutting edge. Fig. 9. Such cutters are sharpened by grinding the tooth face only, thus preserving the contour of the original profile. These cutters may be re-sharpened many times and are serviceable until the remaining tooth section is too weak to withstand the cutting load.

2. Classification based on method of holding

(a) *Arbor-Type Cutters* Figs. 11–15

All types of cutters with a centre locating bore for holding on a standard milling arbor. Fig. 10.

(b) *Shank-Type Cutters* Figs. 17–24

Cutters held by means of a solid shank either tapered or parallel. Tapered shanks are located with the aid of reducing sockets which fit into the spindle nose. Parallel shanks are located with the aid of collets held in a chuck arbor, as shown in Fig. 16.

(c) *Facing Cutters* Figs. 26–28

Cutters designed for direct attachment to the spindle nose, or attached to a stub arbor located in the spindle nose. Fig. 25.

3. Classification based on application

(a) *Standard Cutters*

Cutters which conform in shape and dimensions to the approved standards governing cutter manufacture.

(b) *Special Cutters*

Cutters designed and manufactured for special applications. They may or may not conform to the generally accepted dimensional standards. Such cutters are expensive to produce, but may be justified if several milling operations can be combined, thereby producing a complicated form more rapidly.

FIG. 8   PROFILE TYPE MILLING CUTTER :-

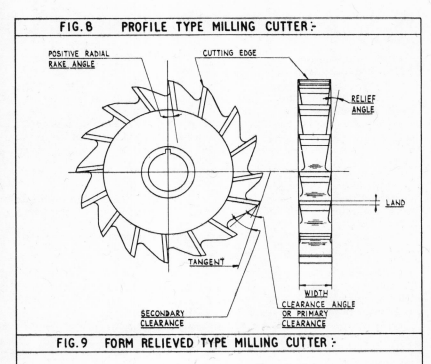

POSITIVE RADIAL RAKE ANGLE

CUTTING EDGE

RELIEF ANGLE

LAND

TANGENT

WIDTH

SECONDARY CLEARANCE

CLEARANCE ANGLE OR PRIMARY CLEARANCE

FIG. 9   FORM RELIEVED TYPE MILLING CUTTER :-

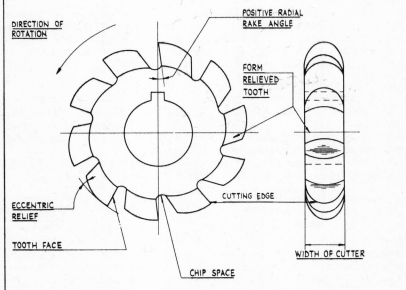

DIRECTION OF ROTATION

POSITIVE RADIAL RAKE ANGLE

FORM RELIEVED TOOTH

ECCENTRIC RELIEF

TOOTH FACE

CUTTING EDGE

CHIP SPACE

WIDTH OF CUTTER

Type of Cutters

1. Plain Milling Cutter (Roller Mill) Fig. 11

Cylindrical cutters made in a variety of diameters and widths, having teeth on the circumferential surface only—helix angles of the teeth between 25–45° depending on application.

Heavy-duty cutters have fewer teeth, which ensures a strong tooth with greater chip space. Used to produce flat surfaces parallel to axis of the cutter. Cutters of this type with helix angles between 45–60° are known as helical-mills.

2. Side-and-Face Cutter Fig. 12

Narrow cylindrical cutters, having teeth of limited length on both side faces in addition to teeth on the periphery. Used for light facing operations and for cutting slots.

Staggered tooth mills with alternate teeth of opposite helix angle are more efficient for cutting deep slots.

3. Metal-Slitting Saws Fig. 13

Thin cylindrical cutters 0·8–5 mm wide, teeth on the periphery only. Side faces relieved slightly to prevent rubbing. Used for cutting-off operations and for the production of deep narrow slots.

Heavier-type slitting saws 6–10 mm wide have staggered teeth.

4. Angle Cutters

(a) *Single Angle* Fig. 14

Cylindrical cutters with teeth on the conical surface and on the large flat side. The normal angle of the cutter is the angle between the large flat side and the conical side. The most commonly used cutters have an angle of 45° or 60°. Used for cutting angular faces, e.g. chamfers, dovetail slots, vee-notches, serrations, and for cutting reamer teeth.

(b) *Double Angle* Fig. 15

Cylindrical cutters with teeth on two conical surfaces forming vee-shaped teeth. Some cutters have equal angles between the conical faces and the plane of intersection of the two cones. Other cutters have unequal angles, and are made with included angles of 45°, 60° or 90°. Used for milling annular grooves, and for milling helical flutes in cutter blanks.

Note. Cutters 1–4 are all standard profile cutters, all arbor type, and used chiefly on the horizontal milling machine.

5. End-Mills

(a) *Standard End-Mills* Fig. 17

Solid-type cutters with teeth on the periphery and end face. The cutter portion is made integral with the shank which may be tapered or parallel. The cylindrical flutes may be straight or helical while the end teeth are radial. Manufactured in standard sizes from 3 mm diameter up to 50 mm diameter. Used for light facing operations, profiling, and for milling slots.

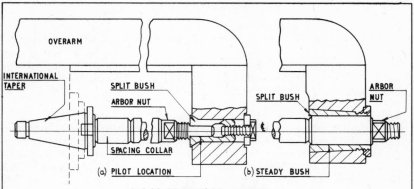

OVERARM

INTERNATIONAL
TAPER

SPLIT BUSH

ARBOR NUT

SPACING COLLAR

SPLIT BUSH

ARBOR
NUT

(a) PILOT LOCATION

(b) STEADY BUSH

FIG.10 STANDARD ARBOR

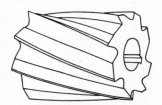

FIG.11 PLAIN MILLING CUTTER (ROLLER MILL)

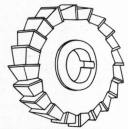

FIG.12 SIDE AND FACE

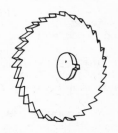

FIG.13 METAL SLITTING SAW

FIG.14 SINGLE ANGLE

FIG.15 DOUBLE ANGLE

(b) *Two-lipped End-Mills* (Slotting Mills) Fig. 18

Solid shank-type cutters with two straight or helical teeth on the circumferential surface, and end teeth cut to the centre. (Note difference between end teeth on standard end-mill.) This type of cutter is designed primarily for milling accurate slots and keyways, and may be fed into the material like a drill and then traversed longitudinally.

6. **Tee-Slot Cutters** Fig. 19

A shank-type cutter with straight or staggered teeth on the circumferential surface and both sides. Used for milling undercuts and for milling the wide groove at the bottom of tee-slots. The narrow portion of the tee-slot is produced with an end-mill or slotting mill; this provides clearance for the reduced portion of the shank of the tee-slot cutter while cutting the wide groove.

7. **Woodruff Key Milling Cutter** Fig. 20

Shank-type cutter designed for milling semi-circular keyways in shafts for Woodruff keys. Cutters up to 50 mm diameter have teeth on the circumferential surface only, the side faces slightly relieved for clearance. (Larger-diameter cutters have side teeth and are designed for arbor mounting.)

Note. Cutters 5–7 are all standard shank-type cutters and are used mainly on the vertical milling machines. Other types of shank-type cutters are shown in Figs. 21–24.

8. **Facing Cutters**

(a) *Shell End-Mill* Fig. 26

A cutter with teeth on the periphery and end face; length of teeth on periphery greater than diameter. A central hole locates the cutter on a stub arbor, and the counter bore allows the head of the retaining screw which holds the cutter in position to clear the end teeth. A slot across the back face locates with driving keys in the arbor ensuring a positive drive. The teeth are usually of helical form, and as these cutters are not reversible on the arbor the hand of helix required must be stated when ordering this type of cutter.

Used for face milling and, since the surface is generated, it provides one of the most accurate methods of producing a flat surface on a milling machine. It is also particularly useful when milling two surfaces at right angles to each other.

(b) *Face-Mill* (Solid Type) Fig. 27

Cutters of larger diameter than the shell end-mill, whose diameter is greater than the tooth length.

(c) *Inserted-Tooth Face-Mill* Fig. 28

The cutter body is made of cast iron or mild steel. Grooves or slots in the body carry the inserted teeth which may be made of high-speed steel, cemented carbide, or stellite. The inserts are rigidly held in position by taper wedges or taper pins, and can be quickly replaced or adjusted to compensate for wear.

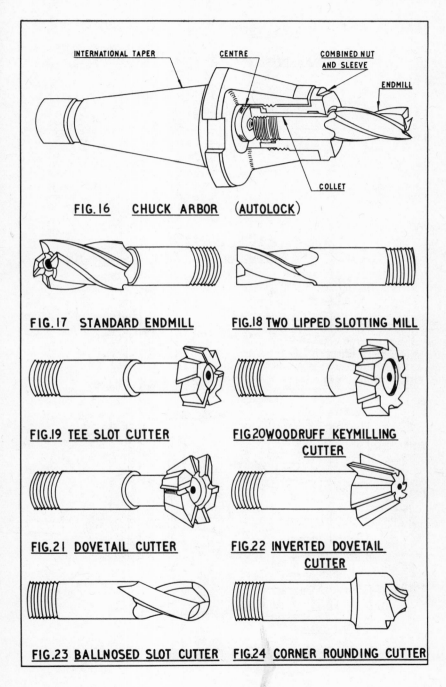

FIG.16   CHUCK ARBOR   (AUTOLOCK)

FIG.17   STANDARD ENDMILL

FIG.18 TWO LIPPED SLOTTING MILL

FIG.19 TEE SLOT CUTTER

FIG.20 WOODRUFF KEYMILLING CUTTER

FIG.21 DOVETAIL CUTTER

FIG.22 INVERTED DOVETAIL CUTTER

FIG.23 BALLNOSED SLOT CUTTER

FIG.24 CORNER ROUNDING CUTTER

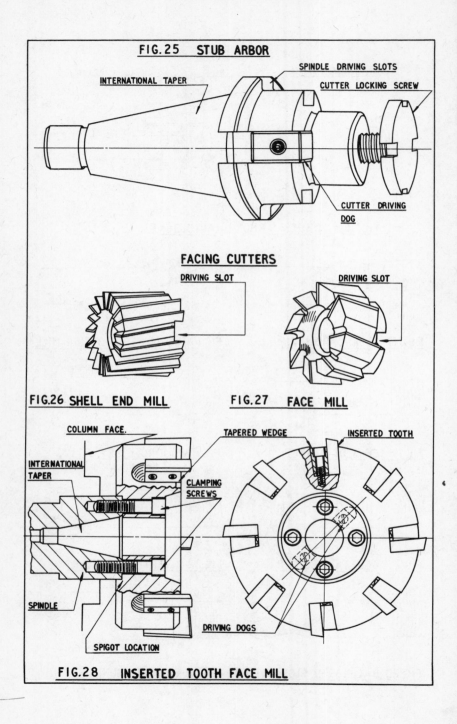

FIG.25   STUB ARBOR

SPINDLE DRIVING SLOTS

CUTTER LOCKING SCREW

INTERNATIONAL TAPER

CUTTER DRIVING DOG

FACING CUTTERS

DRIVING SLOT

DRIVING SLOT

FIG.26 SHELL END MILL

FIG.27   FACE MILL

COLUMN FACE.

TAPERED WEDGE

INSERTED TOOTH

INTERNATIONAL TAPER

CLAMPING SCREWS

SPINDLE

DRIVING DOGS

SPIGOT LOCATION

FIG.28   INSERTED TOOTH FACE MILL

9. Form-Relieved Cutters

(a) *Gear Cutters* Fig. 29

A rotary form-relieved cutter having teeth on the periphery of required form to cut a single tooth space in a gear. Involute gear cutters are made in a range of eight cutters numbered 1–8 for each different module and pressure angle. Ranges for the individual cutters are shown in the table below.

Cutter Number	1	2	3	4	5	6	7	8
Range of Gear Teeth cut	135 to a rack	55 to 134	35 to 54	26 to 34	21 to 25	17 to 20	14 to 16	12 to 13

The range number, pressure angle, and module is clearly stamped on each cutter.

(b) *Sprocket-Wheel Cutters* Fig. 30

A rotary form-relieved cutter having teeth on the periphery of required form to cut a single tooth space in a roller chain sprocket wheel.

A range of three cutters are manufactured for each pitch of chain and roller diameter.

Cutter No. 1 to cut 9 to 12 teeth range.

Cutter No. 2 to cut 13 to 19 teeth range.

Cutter No. 3 to cut 20 and above range.

(c) *Convex and Concave Cutters*

The convex rotary form-relieved cutter is used for milling semi-circular grooves. Fig. 31.

The concave rotary form-relieved cutter is used for milling external radius of semi-circular form. Fig. 32.

Single- and double-sided concave radius cutters are also produced for milling external radii of quarter-circle form. Figs. 33 and 34.

Cutter Teeth

Milling cutters are designed so that the required rake and clearance angles are incorporated in the tooth shape. Each individual tooth in a milling cutter is virtually a single-point tool rotating about a central axis and taking inter-rupted cuts. The rake angle can be measured in two planes: (a) Radial Rake and (b) Axial Rake.

Radial Rake

On both profile and form-relieved cutters the radial rake can be defined as the angle in degrees formed by the tooth face and a radial line drawn from the centre of rotation to the cutting edge as shown in Figs. 8 and 9.

Both these examples show positive rake, i.e. the tooth face is set back from the radial centre line.

FORM RELIEVED CUTTERS

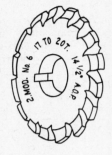

FIG.29 STANDARD GEAR CUTTER

FIG.30 SPROCKET WHEEL CUTTER

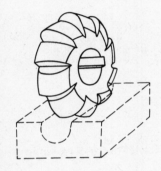

FIG.31 CONVEX CUTTER

FIG.32 CONCAVE CUTTER

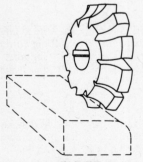

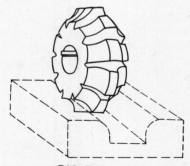

FIG.33
SINGLE SIDED CONCAVE CUTTER

FIG.34
DOUBLE SIDED CONCAVE CUTTER

When the tooth face is in advance of the radial line it is called negative rake. If the tooth face coincides with the radial line it is referred to as zero rake.

The radial rake angle on a milling cutter tooth is equivalent to the front (or top) rake on a single-point turning tool as shown in Fig. 10, Chapter Five.

Axial Rake

On profile cutters with helical flutes an axial rake angle is introduced whose magnitude is related to the value of the helix angle. This axial rake corresponds to the side rake of a single-point turning tool shown in Fig. 10(b), Chapter Five.

With face-milling cutters the teeth on both the face and the periphery are inclined with respect to the radial and axial centre-lines, therefore radial and axial rake angles are introduced as shown in Fig. 27. These two rake angles are comparable with the front and side rakes on the single-point tool, but consideration must be given to direction of cutting with a face-milling cutter when comparing its action with that of a turning tool.

Positive rake angles are normally used on all types of high-speed-steel cutters and efficiency of cutting increases with increase in rake angle, but maximum value permissible is limited by strength of the teeth. The value selected will vary according to the material being cut, e.g. 10° for cast iron and 25–30° for aluminium alloys.

Clearance Angle

To prevent undue interference between the cutter and the work a small clearance is essential, but in all cases this is kept to a minimum value in order to ensure maximum strength at the cutting edge.

On all profile-type cutters the clearance is provided by grinding a small land behind the cutting edge as shown in Fig. 8. This angle is generally referred to as the primary clearance angle, typical values being 3–5° for milling steels, and up to 10° when milling aluminium alloys.

Due to successive re-sharpening of the cutter the width of land gradually increases, therefore a secondary clearance about 3° larger than the primary clearance is ground on the back of the tooth to maintain the original width of land, approximately 0·5–1·5 mm according to diameter of cutter.

Face-milling cutters have teeth on both face and periphery, therefore the clearance angle must be provided as a narrow land along the complete contour of the cutting edge.

In the case of form-relieved-type cutters the clearance is provided by the eccentric relief behind the cutting edge which is produced during manufacture. This type of cutter is re-sharpened by grinding the tooth face only, and the original clearance is maintained throughout its life. Fig. 9, p. 157.

Number of Teeth

No general rule exists regarding the number of teeth in milling cutters, but the modern tendency is towards a coarser-pitch cutter with less teeth, giving a larger chip space and a free flow of the chip, and also a stronger tooth section.

Direction of Rotation and Feed

Up-Cut Milling

The normal or conventional method of milling is known as up-cut milling. The work advances towards the cutter from the side where the teeth are moving upwards. The cutter rotates against the direction of the feed, and the chip thickness is a minimum at the beginning of the cut and a maximum at the end. Fig. 35.

Down-Cut Milling.

The work advances towards the cutter from the side where the teeth are moving downwards. The cutter rotates in the same direction as the feed and the chip thickness is maximum at beginning of cut and minimum at the end. Fig. 36.

This method is sometimes referred to as climb milling and is not recommended unless the machine table is fitted with a backlash eliminator.

Straddle Milling

When milling operations are carried out in production shops it is often desirable to machine more than one surface at the same time. One common form of production milling is that known as straddle milling, i.e. the right- and left-hand parallel faces of a workpiece are milled simultaneously. A pair of side-and-face cutters are mounted on a standard milling arbor with a suitable-width spacing collar or collars between them. A trial cut may be taken, dimension checked, and the width of the collars adjusted if necessary.

Examples of work performed by this method would include the milling of such items as squares, hexagons, tenons, and fork-ends. Two typical examples are shown in Figs. 37(a) and (b).

Gang Milling

A production method of milling intricate forms. A number of cutters of different diameters, lengths, and shapes are mounted on the arbor at the same time, and the workpiece can be brought to the required shape by one pass beneath the cutters.

The diameter of the cutters must be selected in relation to the depth of cut of each individual cutter, so that the arbor clears the work and that the contour produced is within the required dimensions. The spindle revolutions should be related to the cutting speed suitable for the largest-diameter cutter in the gang.

Two typical gang-milling set-ups are shown in Figs. 38(a) and (b). In the latter example note the opposite helix angles on the two plain milling cutters.

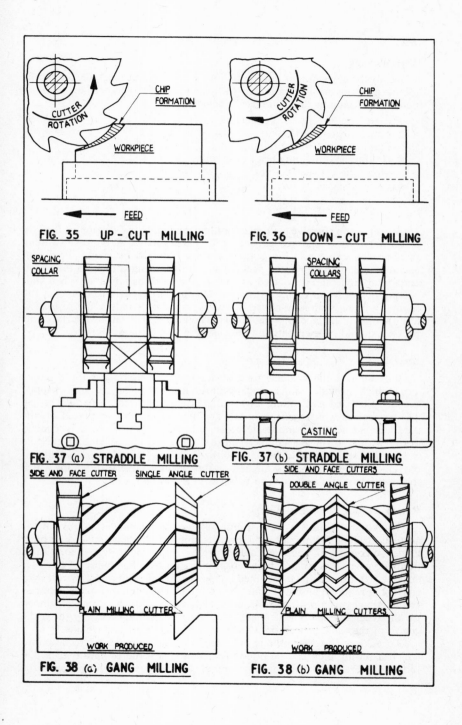

FIG. 35   UP-CUT MILLING

FIG. 36   DOWN-CUT MILLING

CHIP FORMATION

CUTTER ROTATION

WORKPIECE

FEED

SPACING COLLAR

SPACING COLLARS

CASTING

FIG. 37 (a) STRADDLE MILLING

FIG. 37 (b) STRADDLE MILLING

SIDE AND FACE CUTTER   SINGLE ANGLE CUTTER

SIDE AND FACE CUTTERS

DOUBLE ANGLE CUTTER

PLAIN MILLING CUTTER

PLAIN MILLING CUTTERS

WORK PRODUCED

WORK PRODUCED

FIG. 38 (a) GANG MILLING

FIG. 38 (b) GANG MILLING

Work Holding

Due to the intermittent cutting action of the milling machine the work-holding methods must be particularly firm and positive to prevent any possible movement. Many methods are used, including:—

1. Clamping directly to the machine table or angle plate.
2. Using a machine vice.
3. Clamping to a rotary milling table.
4. Holding in a dividing head or dividing chuck.
5. Mounting between centres.
6. Using a special fixture.

Clamping

A simple and effective method of holding many jobs is by clamping directly to the table or to the vertical face of an angle plate. A typical clamping arrangement is shown in Fig. 39(a) utilising a standard flat clamp. To obtain maximum clamping force the packing should be arranged to keep the clamp horizontal, and the bolt placed as near to the work as possible. When supporting the work on parallel strips the clamp must be arranged so that the clamping force is directly above the work support to reduce the distortion to a minimum. If the clamp has to make contact with a finished surface soft packing should be used between the clamp face and the workpiece.

Machine Vice Fig. 39(b)

Probably the most widely used device for work holding is the machine vice, which provides quick and accurate location. The work is gripped between the fixed and sliding jaws and is often supported on parallel strips. The workpiece which must be clean and free from burrs is placed on the parallels and held with moderate pressure between the jaws, and is 'bedded down' with a soft-faced hammer before final tightening. Whenever possible the cutting action should be against the fixed jaw to reduce possibility of movement. The vice may be aligned on the machine table with tenons which locate the table tee-slots, or can be set with a dial indicator.

Rotary Milling Table Fig. 39(c)

The rotary table is a most useful milling attachment, especially on the vertical machine for milling radii, profiles, and drilling holes spaced on pitch circles. It consists of a circular table or platen graduated in degrees around its periphery, which is rotated by a worm operated by a handwheel. For closer spacing a graduated dial is mounted on the worm shaft, and where repetition of spacing is required an index plate can be fitted. The work is usually clamped to the table by means of tee-slots, or is held in a vice which in turn is clamped on the rotary table. When milling radii or profiles it is necessary to set the centre of the table concentric with the main spindle of the machine.

To achieve this the table is provided with an accurate centre hole into which a setting plug can be fitted. The plug is set true by means of a dial indicator carried in the machine spindle which is rotated by hand, the

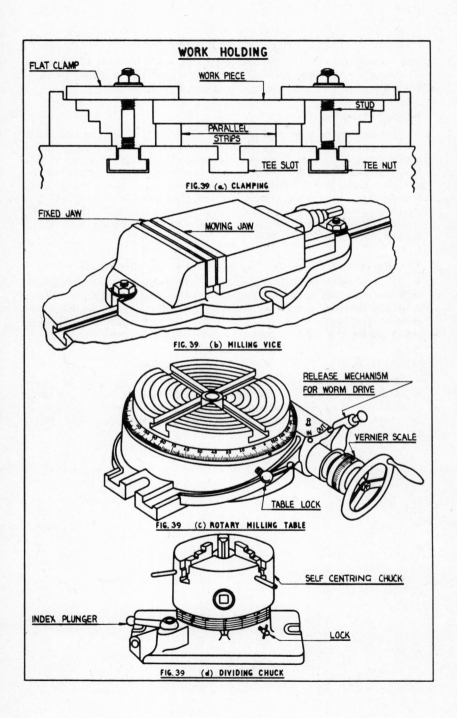

WORK HOLDING

FLAT CLAMP

WORK PIECE

STUD

PARALLEL STRIPS

TEE SLOT　　**TEE NUT**

FIG. 39 (a) CLAMPING

FIXED JAW　　**MOVING JAW**

FIG. 39 (b) MILLING VICE

RELEASE MECHANISM FOR WORM DRIVE

VERNIER SCALE

TABLE LOCK

FIG. 39 (c) ROTARY MILLING TABLE

SELF CENTRING CHUCK

INDEX PLUNGER

LOCK

FIG. 39 (d) DIVIDING CHUCK

necessary adjustments being made on the machine table and saddle screws. The work is then clamped so that the centre of the required radius is directly below the spindle axis and hence on the centre of the table.

Dividing Chuck Fig. 39(d)

The dividing or table chuck consists of a three-jaw self-centring chuck with an attached index plate, which in conjunction with a plunger allows a wide range of circular divisions to be obtained. This unit is mounted on a base plate which can be bolted directly to the machine table. Many components which require indexing, e.g. bolt heads, etc., can be conveniently held in these chucks. The compact design gives a holding device which is extremely rigid and free from vibration. Quite apart from the indexing feature they also provide a useful means of holding circular work which requires milling on the end faces.

Mounting between centres (See Fig. 43, Universal Dividing Head)

This method of location is useful when concentricity of the milling with previous turning is essential. The work is supported between the dividing head and tailstock centres with jacks located beneath the work to give additional support and to reduce vibration. A carrier attached to the work and engaging with the dividing-head catch-plate provides the drive.

Milling Fixtures

When large numbers of duplicate parts have to be milled a special fixture is usually employed. These fixtures locate and clamp the work and often incorporate setting pieces for setting the position of the cutter. If the number of components is large enough to justify the additional expense the clamps may be cam or air operated.

The Universal Dividing Head

A Universal dividing head is a precision attachment frequently employed on milling machines to increase the range of work that may be carried out. This attachment has three main functions:—

1. To hold and support the workpiece during the milling operation.
2. To provide a convenient means of obtaining accurate circular division or angular spacing, e.g. milling gear teeth, serrations, or splines.
3. To provide rotary motion to the workpiece simultaneously with its longitudinal travel, an essential when performing helical milling operations.

The main details of a Cincinnati universal dividing head are shown in Figs. 40 and 41.

The head is usually held on the right-hand end of the milling machine table, located by means of two tenons attached to the base, which fit into the tee-slots of the machine table ensuring accurate alignment. The head is held in position by two bolts also located in the tee-slots.

The main casting, which is hollow, houses the main spindle which carries a 40-tooth worm wheel. A second spindle located at right angles to the main spindle carries a single-threaded worm which engages with the 40-tooth worm wheel (40:1 gear-ratio standard for all dividing heads).

This worm shaft also locates a spur gear which meshes with an identical gear carried on the index-crank spindle. The latter controls the manual operation of the head; any movement of the index-crank drives the pair of spur gears, turning the worm shaft, and in turn the worm wheel imparting rotary motion to the workpiece.

The index-crank handle is slotted, providing the adjustment necessary to allow the spring-loaded plunger to engage in any one of the various circles of holes on the division plate.

The main spindle is hollow with a tapered bore for locating a work centre, and is externally screwed to carry the driving plate or chuck. When work is to be held between centres a tailstock is provided and is located and bolted in the same tee-slot as the dividing head. When work is held in the chuck or faceplate the head may be rotated so that its main spindle can be inclined at any required angle between the horizontal and vertical.

Indexing

1. Direct Indexing Fig. 40

A simple form of division plate known as the front index plate is attached to the main spindle nose into which a spring-loaded index pin locates. The required rotary movement of workpiece is obtained by withdrawing the index pin and turning the spindle by hand to the desired position and re-locating the index pin in the appropriate hole in the index plate.

Before commencing a direct indexing operation the worm shaft must be disengaged from the worm wheel. (Fig. 41 shows the eccentric which disengages the worm.)

When using this method of indexing the number of possible divisions is limited to the three-hole circles available on the front index plate. (Cincinnati head 24, 30, 36 holes in front index plate.)

2. Indirect Indexing Fig. 41

When using this method of indexing the worm is permanently engaged with the worm wheel, and the workpiece is rotated by means of the index-crank. The side index plate carries a large number of circles of holes on each face, therefore the range of divisions is much greater than in direct indexing.

Cincinnati head: 1st Side—24, 25, 28, 30, 34, 37, 38, 39, 41, 42, 43.
                   2nd Side—46, 47, 49, 51, 53, 54, 57, 58, 59, 62, 66.

Since the standard worm-gear drive in the universal dividing head is 40:1 it will require 40 turns of the index-crank to turn the main spindle and the workpiece it carries through one complete revolution, i.e. 360°.

The side index plate will accommodate the fractional part of one turn of the index-crank.

Thus to obtain any particular number of divisions:—

Let $N=$ Number of divisions required

Then turns of index-crank $= \dfrac{40}{N}$

Example 1. Find index-crank setting for 6 equally spaced divisions.

$$\text{Index setting} = \frac{40}{N} = \frac{40}{6} = 6\tfrac{2}{3}$$

i.e. <u>6 complete turns + 20 holes in the 30-hole circle</u>

Example 2. Find the index-crank setting for 13 equally spaced divisions.

$$\text{Index setting} = \frac{40}{N} = \frac{40}{13} = 3\tfrac{1}{13}$$

i.e. <u>3 complete turns + 3 holes in 39-hole circle</u>

Example 3. Find index-crank setting for 31 equally spaced divisions.

$$\text{Index setting} = \frac{40}{N} = \frac{40}{31} = 1\tfrac{9}{31}$$

i.e. <u>1 complete turn + 18 holes in 62-hole circle</u>

Example 4. Find index-crank setting for 72 equally spaced divisions.

$$\text{Index setting} = \frac{40}{N} = \frac{40}{72} = \frac{5}{9}$$

i.e. <u>30 holes in 54-hole circle</u>

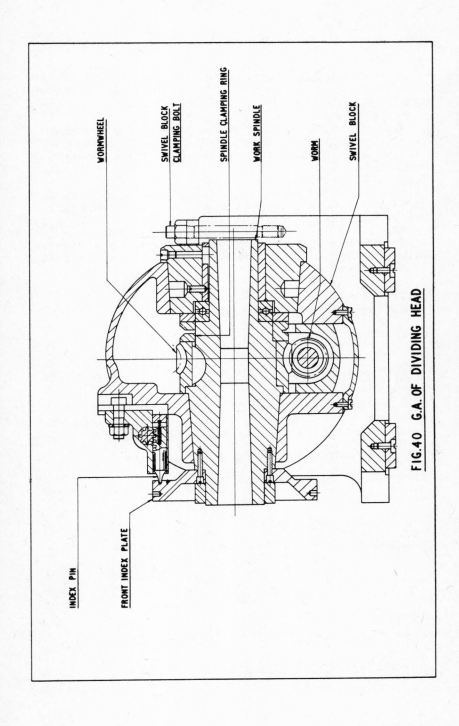

WORMWHEEL

SWIVEL BLOCK
CLAMPING BOLT

SPINDLE CLAMPING RING

WORK SPINDLE

WORM

SWIVEL BLOCK

INDEX PIN

FRONT INDEX PLATE

FIG.40 G.A. OF DIVIDING HEAD

Sector-Arms Fig. 41

To accomodate the fractional part of the index-crank movement a pair of sector-arms is attached to the side index plate. This fitment eliminates the need of counting the required number of spaces each time the head is indexed to the next position.

The two arms may be spread apart and then locked to incorporate the required number of holes. When setting the sector it is customary to locate the index pin in the appropriate hole circle, bring the left arm against the outside of the pin, and then adjust the right-hand arm to include the required number of holes established by calculation.

It should be noted that the hole in which the pin locates is counted as zero, i.e. number of holes between the two sector arms is always one more than the number calculated.

When indexing to the next position the index pin is moved up to the right-hand arm; with the pin in this new position the sector is swivelled round to the right until the left arm strikes the pin, so leaving the sector in position for the next indexing.

Angular Spacing

If 40 turns of index-crank = 1 revolution = 360°

Then 1 turn of index-crank $= \dfrac{360}{40} = 9°$

∴ index setting necessary to obtain any required angle will be

$$\dfrac{\text{Angle required (\textit{degrees})}}{9} \quad \text{or} \quad \dfrac{\text{Angle required (\textit{minutes})}}{540}$$

Example 1. Find index-crank setting for 27° (Cincinnati head).

$$\text{Index setting} = \frac{27}{9}$$

i.e. <u>3 complete turns of crank</u>

Example 2. Find index-crank setting for 39°.

$$\text{Index setting} = \frac{39}{9} = 4\tfrac{3}{9} = 4\tfrac{1}{3}$$

i.e. <u>4 complete turns + 10 holes in 30-hole circle</u>

Example 3. Find index-crank setting for 7° 30′.

$$\text{Index setting} = \frac{7°\ 30'}{9} = \frac{7\tfrac{1}{2}}{9} = \frac{15}{18} = \frac{5}{6} = \frac{20}{24}$$

i.e. <u>20 holes in 24-hole circle</u>

Example 4. Find index-crank setting for 61° 40′.

$$\text{Index setting} = \frac{61°\ 40'}{9} = \frac{61\tfrac{2}{3}}{9} = 6\tfrac{7\tfrac{2}{3}}{9} = 6\tfrac{23}{27} = 6\tfrac{46}{54}$$

i.e. <u>6 complete turns + 46 holes in 54-hole circle.</u>

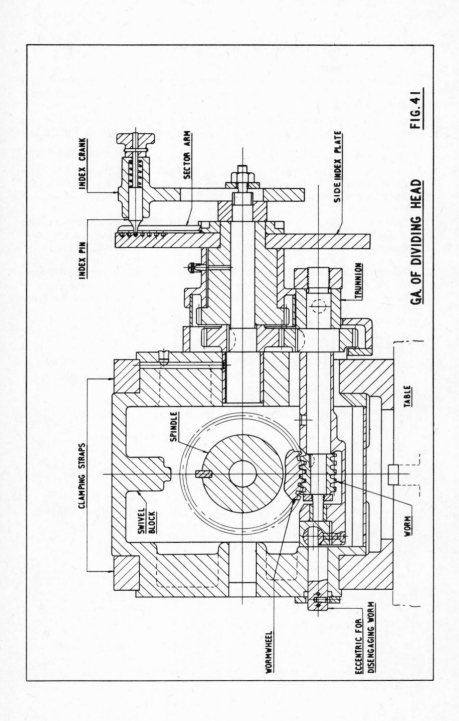

INDEX CRANK

INDEX PIN

SECTOR ARM

SIDE INDEX PLATE

TRUNNION

CLAMPING STRAPS

SPINDLE

SWIVEL BLOCK

TABLE

WORM

WORMWHEEL

ECCENTRIC FOR DISENGAGING WORM

GA. OF DIVIDING HEAD   FIG. 41

3. Differential Indexing

Divisions outside the range of standard index plates can be obtained on a Cincinnati head with the aid of high-number index plates or by utilising a wide-range divider.

On many dividing heads, divisions unobtainable by indirect indexing using standard index plates can be obtained by a system of differential indexing. Fig. 42 illustrates the principle of differential indexing.

An extension drive shaft is located in the rear end of the main spindle of the dividing head; this drives a train of gearing, which in turn drives a pair of bevel gears and two spur gears providing a rotary motion to the side index plate.

The index plate is unlocked and is therefore free to revolve in a clockwise or anti-clockwise direction, depending on the number of gears in the gear-train arrangement. (One additional gear will reverse direction.)

When the index-crank is moved through a known setting the main spindle revolves via the worm and worm wheel an equivalent amount, and simultaneously the index plate is moved via the gear-train either in the same or opposite direction to that of the index-crank. The sole function of the gear-train is to advance or retard the movement of the index plate.

Standard gears supplied with a Victoria head:—
     24, 24, 28, 32, 40, 48, 56, 64, 72, 86, 100.

Standard index plate with following hole circles:—
     15, 16, 17, 18, 19, 20, 21, 23, 27, 29, 31, 33, 37, 39, 41, 43, 47, 49.

Calculations to find gear ratio for a required number of divisions:—

Let N_1 = Number of divisions required

Let N_2 = Number of divisions actually indexed
     (either slightly greater or less than divisions required)

Let R   = Gear ratio required

Then $R = \left[\dfrac{N_1 - N_2}{N_2} \right] \times 40$

Example 1.   Determine a differential indexing for 63 equal divisions.

     Let $N_1 = 63$

     Let $N_2 = 60$ (obtainable on standard index plate)

         N_2 is less than required number therefore index plate must be retarded

$$R = \left[\frac{N_1 - N_2}{N_2} \right] \times 40 = \left[\frac{63 - 60}{60} \right] \times 40$$

$$R \qquad = \frac{3 \times 40}{60} = \frac{120}{60}$$

$$= \frac{2}{1} = \frac{48}{24} = \frac{\text{Driver}}{\text{Driven}}$$

Indexing for 60 divisions $= \dfrac{40}{60} = \dfrac{2}{3}$

$$= 22 \text{ holes in 33-hole circle, with above gearing}$$

Actual movement of work $= 1/63$ revolution

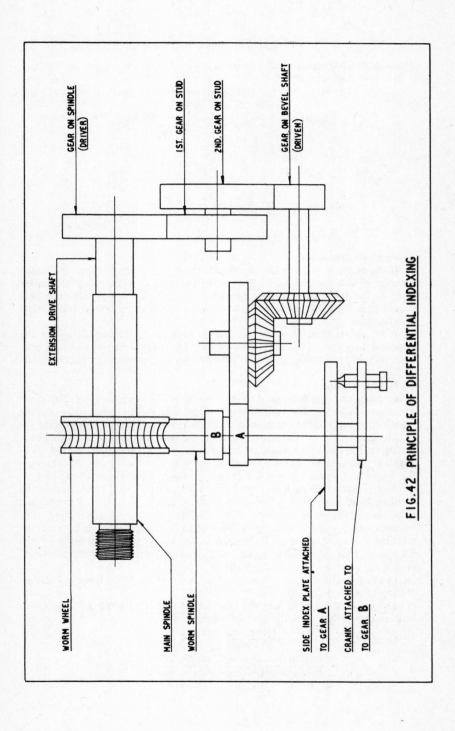

GEAR ON SPINDLE (DRIVER)

1ST. GEAR ON STUD

2ND. GEAR ON STUD

GEAR ON BEVEL SHAFT (DRIVEN)

EXTENSION DRIVE SHAFT

WORM WHEEL

MAIN SPINDLE

WORM SPINDLE

SIDE INDEX PLATE ATTACHED TO GEAR **A**

CRANK ATTACHED TO GEAR **B**

B

A

FIG. 42 PRINCIPLE OF DIFFERENTIAL INDEXING

Example 2. Determine a differential indexing for 99 equal divisions.

Let $N_1 = 99$

Let $N_2 = 100$ (greater than required number: therefore index plate must be advanced)

$$R = \left[\frac{N_1 - N_2}{N_2}\right] \times 40 = \left[\frac{99 - 100}{100}\right] \times 40$$

$$= \frac{40}{100} = \frac{4}{10} = \frac{4 \times 1}{5 \times 2}$$

$$= \frac{32 \times 28}{40 \times 56} = \frac{\text{Driving Gears}}{\text{Driven Gears}}$$

Indexing for 100 divisions $= \frac{40}{100} = \frac{4}{10}$

$= 8$ holes in 20-hole circle

With the above gearing actual movement of work $= 1/99$ revolution

Number of Idler Gears

If the number of divisions actually indexed (N_2) is greater than the actual number of divisions required (N_1), then the gearing must drive the index plate in the same direction as the crank movement. This is achieved in a simple gear train by using one idler gear, and with compound train using no idler gear.

If N_2 is less than N_1 then the gearing must drive the index plate in the opposite direction to the crank movement. This is achieved in a simple gear train by using two idler gears, and with compound train using one idler gear.

4. Helical Milling

In order to cut a helix on a milling machine the workpiece must be given simultaneous longitudinal and rotary motion. This can be achieved by gearing the dividing head to the machine-table leadscrew as shown in Figs. 43 and 44.

The gear train from the leadscrew drives the bevel shaft of the dividing head; this drives the side index plate, and providing the spring-loaded plunger is engaged in a hole in the index plate it will revolve the index crank, and through the worm and worm wheel the workpiece. (Index plate stop withdrawn.)

A standard machine leadscrew has a 6 mm pitch, and if connected to the dividing head with gears of equal number of teeth, i.e. 1:1 gear ratio, then it would require 40 revolutions of the leadscrew to drive the dividing head through one complete revolution. Also these 40 revolutions will cause the machine table to advance a distance equal to 40 times the pitch of the leadscrew. This longitudinal movement is known as 'the lead of the machine', or is referred to as 'the natural lead'.

i.e. Lead of machine $= 40 \times 6$ mm $= 240$ mm, and this is the basis for helical-milling gear-train calculations.

The formula for obtaining the gear ratio for cutting a required helix of a lead greater or less than the lead of machine is

$$\text{Gear ratio} = \frac{\text{Lead of Helix required (mm)}}{\text{Lead of Machine (240 mm)}}$$

$$= \frac{\text{Product of Driven Gears} = A \times C}{\text{Product of Driving Gears} = B \times D} \text{ (Fig. 43)}$$

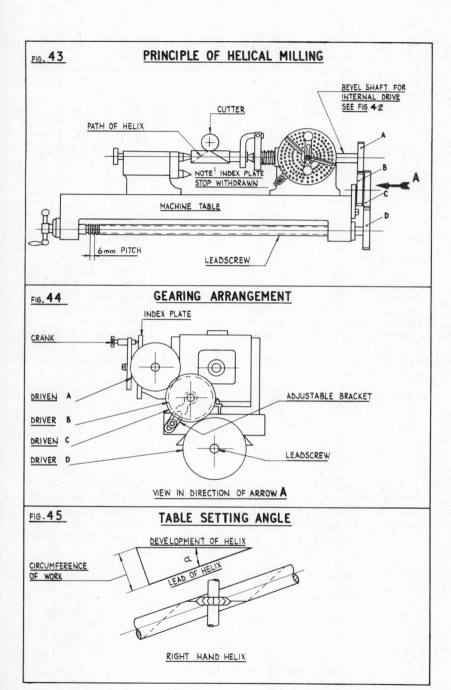

FIG. 43 — PRINCIPLE OF HELICAL MILLING

BEVEL SHAFT FOR INTERNAL DRIVE SEE FIG. 42

CUTTER

PATH OF HELIX

A

B

A

C

D

NOTE! INDEX PLATE STOP WITHDRAWN

MACHINE TABLE

6mm PITCH

LEADSCREW

FIG. 44 — GEARING ARRANGEMENT

INDEX PLATE

CRANK

DRIVEN A

DRIVER B

DRIVEN C

DRIVER D

ADJUSTABLE BRACKET

LEADSCREW

VIEW IN DIRECTION OF ARROW **A**

FIG. 45 — TABLE SETTING ANGLE

DEVELOPMENT OF HELIX

α

CIRCUMFERENCE OF WORK

LEAD OF HELIX

RIGHT HAND HELIX

Example 1. Find a gear ratio suitable for cutting a helix of 320 mm lead on a standard milling machine (Victoria head).

$$\text{Gear ratio} = \frac{\text{Lead of Helix required}}{\text{Lead of Machine}} = \frac{320}{240} = \frac{4 \times 8}{6 \times 4}$$

$$= \frac{32 \times 56}{48 \times 28} = \frac{\text{Product of Driven Gears}}{\text{Product of Driving Gears}}$$

Example 2. Find a gear ratio suitable for cutting a helix of 400 mm lead on a standard milling machine (Victoria head).

$$\text{Gear ratio} = \frac{\text{Lead of Helix required}}{\text{Lead of Machine}} = \frac{400}{240} = \frac{5}{3}$$

$$= \frac{5 \times 8}{6 \times 4} = \frac{40 \times 64}{48 \times 32} = \frac{\text{Product of Driven Gears}}{\text{Product of Driving Gears}}$$

Note.—An additional intermediate gear will change the hand of the helix.

Helix Angle

In order to avoid undue interference between the cutter and the work-piece the universal milling machine table is swivelled to the angle of the helix being cut. For a right-hand helix, the right end of the table is swivelled towards the column, the maximum movement being approximately 45°. If the helix angle is greater than 45° it will involve the use of a vertical-head attachment, the cutter being swivelled and the table remaining in its normal position.

Fig. 45 shows the relationship between lead, circumference, and helix angle, and from this we get

$$\text{Tan} \propto = \frac{\text{Circumference of Workpiece (mm)}}{\text{Lead of Helix required (mm)}}$$

$$= \frac{\pi D}{\text{Lead}}$$

$$\therefore \text{Lead} = \frac{\pi D}{\tan \propto}$$

When cutting helical grooves of appreciable depth, it is usual to use the mean diameter as a basis for calculating the helix angle. When cutting gear teeth the helix angle is usually calculated on the pitch circle diameter.

Example 3. Calculate the gear ratio and table setting suitable for cutting 7 helical flutes in a 80 mm diameter cutter blank, depth of flute 5 mm and lead is 720 mm (Victoria head).

$$\text{Gear ratio} = \frac{\text{Lead of Helix required}}{\text{Lead of Machine}} = \frac{720}{240} = \frac{72 \times 64}{48 \times 32}$$

Mean diameter of blank $= 80 - 5 = 75$ mm

Tangent of helix angle $= \dfrac{\pi \times \text{Mean Diameter}}{\text{Lead}}$

$$= \frac{22 \times 75}{7 \times 720} = 0 \cdot 3274$$

$\therefore$ Helix angle and table setting $= 18° \ 8'$

CHAPTER SEVEN

GRINDING MACHINES

Towards the end of the nineteenth century, manufactured abrasives were first introduced, and with subsequent development and improvement they were soon adopted as an additional cutting agent on machine tools. Prior to the introduction of abrasive grinding wheels the cutting agents were single-point steel tools, and multi-tooth steel cutters.

During the last sixty years a large range of widely differing types of machine tools have been designed and developed under the general heading of Grinding Machines.

Definition

A grinding machine may be simply defined as any type of machine tool which utilises an abrasive grinding wheel as its cutting agent.

Functions of a Grinding Machine

1. *To remove surplus material*

The removal of surplus stock is common to all types of grinding operations. The amount to be removed varies from one type of machine to another, but the surface finish required will usually determine the rate of stock removal. Often both roughing and finishing operations can be performed by the same grinding wheel by changing the rate of stock removal.

In many cases the initial machining is carried out on turning machines or milling machines and the finishing operations performed on a grinding machine.

2. *To generate size*

The removal of sufficient stock to bring the workpiece within the prescribed limits of size for a given dimension.

3. *To obtain a desired quality of surface finish*

In many grinding operations a high grade of surface finish is essential combined with close dimensional accuracy, e.g. final grinding operation on a crankshaft.

In other types of work a high-class finish may be required although size is relatively unimportant, e.g. final grinding operation on a master surface-plate.

4. *To machine hardened components*

When components are made from materials of such hardness that they cannot be turned or milled, and in cases where parts are hardened by heat-treatment, the grinding process is the only satisfactory method of machining to the required size and finish.

The Abrasive Grinding Wheel

Grinding is a cutting process comparable with milling, but the multi-tooth milling cutter is replaced by a rotating abrasive grinding wheel possessing a very large number of small cutting edges. Fig. 1.

The abrasive wheel is composed of a large number of extremely hard particles called abrasive grain which are embedded in a suitable bonding material. The choice of type of abrasive grain, its size, and the type of bond material will depend on the nature of the grinding operation and the properties of the material being ground.

Abrasive Grain

1. Natural Abrasives

Hard natural abrasives include emery, sandstone, and corundum. These materials were originally used for the manufacture of grinding wheels, but have been largely discontinued owing to the presence of impurities and lack of uniformity in cutting action.

2. Manufactured Abrasives

These are products of the electric furnace, thus their quality and cutting characteristics can be carefully controlled to meet specific requirements. The two main types are:—

(a) Aluminium Oxide.
(b) Silicon Carbide.

Aluminium Oxide

Aluminium oxide abrasive is prepared in an electric-arc furnace by the fusion of bauxite, a clay-like substance which is the purest form of aluminium oxide found in nature in commercial quantities.

A mixture of bauxite, ground coke, and iron borings is fed into the furnace and is fused at high temperature. When the resultant product is allowed to cool and solidify it forms a crystalline abrasive. Typical trade names include:—

'Aloxite', manufactured by Carborundum Company.
'Alundum', manufactured by Norton Company.

Silicon Carbide

Silicon carbide abrasive is produced in the high temperature of resistance-type electric furnaces by the chemical reaction of silica sand and carbon. A mixture of silica sand and finely ground coke, to which are added varying quantities of sawdust and common salt is built up around an electrical conductor. When the current is passed through the conductor and a temperature of approximately 2750°C is reached, a vapour is given off which deposits silicon-carbide crystals around the conductor. After the furnace has been in operation for about 36 hours it is allowed to cool, and the silicon carbide is removed from the conductor or 'core' in the form of large masses of loosely adhering crystals, which still need crushing, refining, and grading for size.

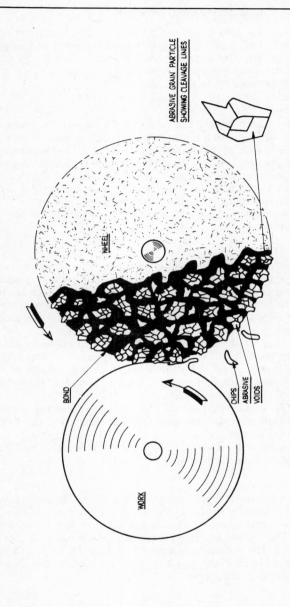

ABRASIVE GRAIN PARTICLE
SHOWING CLEAVAGE LINES

WHEEL

BOND

CHIPS
ABRASIVE
VOIDS

WORK

THE STRUCTURE & ABRASIVE ACTION OF A GRINDING WHEEL

FIG. 1

This type of abrasive is used chiefly for grinding the low-tensile-strength materials, e.g. chilled iron, most of the non-ferrous materials and alloys, and non-metallic materials. Typical trade names include:—

'Carborundum', manufactured by Carborundum Company.

'Crystolon', manufactured by Norton Company.

Abrasive Grain Sizes

After the abrasive materials have been crushed and treated, the grains or grits are graded for size by sifting the particles through screens of various sizes, providing a wide range of different grain sizes to meet the requirements of various types of grinding wheels. Wire-mesh screens containing a given number of openings or 'meshes' per centimetre are used for grading the coarse range of grits, and silk screens are used for the medium-size grits. The very fine grits are separated by hydraulic methods.

The full range of commercial grain sizes are shown in the section dealing with wheel specifications, p. 186.

Bond Materials

The bond or binder is the material used to support the abrasive grains while they do the cutting, and to hold them in the form of a grinding wheel. The amount of bond material will determine the 'Grade' of wheel, i.e. the ability of the bond to retain the grains or, alternatively, to release them when the wheel is subjected to the grinding stresses which tend to tear the grains out of the wheel face.

Grinding wheels are classified as soft, medium, or hard grade according to the strength of the bond. A soft grade will readily release the blunt grains, while the hard grade will retain them for a longer period. Letters of the alphabet from A, very soft, to Z, very hard, denote the range of different grades.

Again it should be stressed that the relative terms, hardness and softness of a wheel, refer to the strength and tenacity of the bond and not to the hardness value of the abrasive grains.

Four main types of bond material are used for the manufacture of both aluminium oxide and silicon carbide wheels:—

Vitrified Bond (V)

The vitrified bond is made from fusible ceramic clays. These are mixed with the abrasive in a semi-dry condition and the mixture is moulded into the desired wheel shape under pressure. The shaped wheel is then baked for a prolonged period. The vitrified bonding process is used for up to 80% of all wheels manufactured. The porosity and strength of these wheels gives a high stock removal, and an open structure which does not readily clog. A wide range of different grades is obtainable.

Resinoid Bond (B)

This bond is made from synthetic resins. The powdered resin mixed with abrasive grains is placed in metal moulds under pressure. Heat is applied, which hardens the bond to give the required strength.

Such wheels can be run at higher speeds than vitrified bond wheels; used for thin cut-off wheels as required in foundries and welding shops, or on work requiring very fine finish.

Shellac Bond (E)

Flake shellac and the required amount of abrasive are mixed in a heated mixing machine, which coats the abrasive grains with the melted shellac bond. The appropriate amount of this mixture is then placed in heated steel moulds and consolidated either by a steel roller, as for thin wheels up to 3 mm thickness, or by hydraulic pressure for the thicker wheels.

Shellac-bonded wheels give a very high-grade-surface finish and have a cool cutting action, and are therefore used on such work as camshaft and roll grinding. These wheels are not suitable for heavy-duty grinding.

Rubber Bond (R)

Abrasive grains are repeatedly rolled into vulcanised rubber sheet until a uniform mix of the required abrasive content is obtained. The sheet is then passed through rolls to obtain the desired thickness. Wheels of various diameters are then cut from the sheet, and are finally heated in ovens to vulcanise the rubber while held in moulds under pressure.

Rubber bond is the strongest of all bond materials and is used chiefly for thin cut-off wheels where minimum burr is important, and where high-quality finish is required.

Structure of a Grinding Wheel

The structure of a grinding wheel depends upon the size of the abrasive grain and its spacing. Manufacturers can control the relationship of the abrasive grain and bonding material to produce wheels of open or dense structure. Open structure provides greater chip clearance and prevents the chips from clogging or loading the wheel face.

Wheel Specification. B.S. 4481, Part I: 1969

The Abrasive Industries Association adopt a standard marking system in accordance with I.S.O. Recommendation R525, which provides a method of clearly specifying the characteristics of any particular abrasive grinding wheel. Each marking is arranged as in the following sequence:—

1. Nature of Abrasive.　　　　4. Structure.
2. Size of Grain.　　　　　　5. Type of Bond.
3. Grade.　　　　　　　　　6. Manufacturer's record.

1	Nature of Abrasive	A=Aluminium Oxide　C=Silicon Carbide			
2	Grain Size	Coarse	Medium	Fine	Very Fine
		8	30	70	220
		10	36	80	240
		12	46	90	280
		14	60	100	320
		16	54	120	400
		20		150	500
		24		180	600
3	Grade	Soft　　　　　　　　　Medium A B C D E F G H I J K L M N O P Q R S T U V Hard W X Y Z			
4	Structure	Spacing from closest to most open 0　1　2　3　4　5　6　7　8　9　10　11　12　13　14　etc.			
5	Bond	V = Vitrified　　　　R = Rubber B = Resinoid　　　　S = Silicate E = Shellac　　　　　Mg = Magnesia			

Example:　Wheel specification A.46.M.5.V.
　　　　　　A = Aluminium oxide abrasive
　　　　46 = Medium grain size
　　　　M = Medium grade
　　　　　5 = Fairly dense structure
　　　　V = Vitrified bond material.

Guide to selection of wheels

The following factors must be considered when selecting the proper grinding wheel for a given job:—

Constant Factors:—

1. Type of material to be ground.
2. Accuracy and finish required.
3. Area of contact between wheel and work.
4. Nature of grinding operation.

Variable Factors:—

1. Wheel speed.
2. Rate of feed or grinding pressure.
3. Condition of grinding machine.

Choice of abrasive (largely determined by material to be ground):—

Aluminium oxide—steels and steel alloys.
Silicon carbide—soft iron and non-ferrous materials.

Choice of Grain Sizes:—

36–80 for commercial roughing and finishing.
80–400 for high-quality finishes.

Coarse Grain—for soft ductile materials.
for high rate of stock removal.
Fine Grain— for low rate of stock removal.
Form grinding.
When grinding hardened work.
(Larger number of cutting points.)

Choice of Grade:—

M–S for commercial grinding of soft steels.
I–P for commercial grinding of hard steels.
The smaller the area of contact the harder the grade required.
Soft grades for high stock removal.
Harder grades for form grinding.

Choice of Structure: —

Standard structure for commercial grinding.
Dense structure for small wheels and work.
Open structure for hard materials.
Open to standard structures for high stock removal.
Dense structure for form grinding.

Choice of Bond Materials:—

Largely governed by dimensions and speed of wheel.
Thin cut-off wheels—rubber.
                        resinoid.
                        shellac.
Solid wheels of large dimensions—vitrified.
Speed—vitrified up to 1950 metres per minute;
            above 1950 m/min: resinoid, rubber, or shellac.
Precision Grinding —normally vitrified.
Snagging or Fettling—resinoid or rubber.
High-quality finish —shellac.

Guide for Wheel Speeds:—

Cylindrical Grinding —1650–1950 m/min.
Internal Grinding   — 600–1200 m/min.
Surface Grinding   —1200–1500 m/min.
Snagging and Fettling—2700–3600 m/min.

Guide for Work Speeds:—

Cylindrical Grinding—18–30 m/min.
Internal Grinding   —15–30 m/min.
Surface Grinding   —10–150 m/min.
                    (Depending on type of machine.)

Abrasive Wheel Regulations 1970

Speeds of Abrasive Wheels:—

1. An abrasive wheel larger than 55 mm (2·165 in) in diameter must be clearly marked, either on its wheel or washer, with the maximum permissible speed in revolutions per minute.

2. No abrasive wheel of 55 mm (2·165 in) or less in diameter shall be taken into use unless a notice showing the maximum permissible speed in rev/min. as specified by the manufacturer is permanently fixed in each workshop where such wheels are used. In the case of mounted wheels or points permanently mounted on a quill or mandrel the notice shall also show the permissible overhang at that speed.
Note. (The manufacturers intend to produce such notices and they are negotiating amongst themselves to standardize given speeds for different diameters.)

3. No abrasive wheel shall be operated at a speed in excess of that marked on the wheel or washer, or as shown on the notice. However, a wheel may have its speed increased as the diameter is reduced by wear, provided that it is not run at a speed in excess of that laid down for that reduced diameter.
    (The notices, when produced, will show this information on wheel speeds.)

The Basic Grinding Operations

The basic types of grinding operations can be broadly classified under three main headings:—

1 Cylindrical Grinding; 2 Internal Grinding; 3 Surface Grinding.

Each in turn can be sub-divided according to the type of grinding machine selected to perform any particular operation. Details of a few of these grinding machines will be dealt with later.

1. Cylindrical Grinding incorporates the grinding of external diameters of any type of cylindrical workpiece. Typical pieces would include:—

   (a) Plain parallel shafts and spindles.
   (b) Spindles having two or more different diameters.
   (c) Tapered shafts and spindles.

   Such pieces are often previously machined to within $0 \cdot 25 - 0 \cdot 5$ mm over size, and are then cylindrically ground to the required dimensional accuracy and surface finish. Alternatively the piece in the form of rolled bar, forging, or casting may be ground to its final dimensions without any preliminary machining.

2. Internal Grinding as its name implies is the grinding of internal surfaces or holes (inside diameter). These holes are initially produced by some other type of machining process, e.g. drilling, turning, or boring, and left slightly smaller in diameter than final dimension; hence the amount of material to be removed by internal grinding is comparatively small, but the final size and finish of these holes is most important. Typical examples of internal work would include:—

   (a) Straight-through holes.
   (b) Blind holes.
   (c) Tapered holes.
   (d) Formed holes.

3. Surface Grinding—the grinding of plane or flat surfaces. In some cases this is a finishing operation only, with a small amount of metal removal; in other cases large amounts of metal are removed quite rapidly and with far greater accuracy than is possible by planing or milling. Typical examples would include:—

   (a) Grinding the faces of forgings or castings.
   (b) Gauge making, grinding parallel faces, angular faces, kissing shoulder faces.
   (c) Grinding faces of circular pieces, e.g. piston rings, gear blanks, and ball races.
   (d) Grinding press-tool parts and die-blanks.

Movements of Wheel and Work

The relationship between grinding wheel and workpiece movements for the basic grinding operations is shown in diagrammatic form on p. 191.

Cylindrical Grinding (Centre type, i.e. work held between fixed centres)

Fig. 2(a) shows the relative position of wheel and work for external grinding. Both revolve in the same direction, but the surfaces in contact move in opposite directions. The wheel revolves at high speed, approximately 1800 metres per minute; the work revolves at about 18 metres per minute. When the length of workpiece being ground is greater than the width of the wheel, a reciprocating traverse movement is given to the work, Fig. 2(b); this is known as longitudinal traverse. At the end of each traverse the wheel is fed in towards the work by a small amount, 0·005–0·025 mm; this movement is referred to as in-feed, and it controls reduction of work diameter.

If wheel width exceeds the length of work to be ground, longitudinal traverse is not required; instead the wheel is fed slowly into the work while the latter is oscillated a very slight amount to equalise the wheel wear. This method is known as plunge-cut grinding.

Internal Grinding (Revolving workpiece)

Fig. 3(a) shows the relative position of wheel and work for internal grinding. The contact surfaces are moving in opposite directions. The relatively small diameter wheel (of necessity smaller than hole to be ground) at a high speed up to 1200 metres per minute, the work at a comparatively low speed up to 30 metres per minute. Fig. 3(b) indicates the longitudinal traverse; while the in-feed operates at the end of each traverse stroke as in the external process. The much larger arc of contact between wheel and work can be readily seen in Fig. 3(a) when compared with Fig. 2(a).

Surface Grinding

(a) Horizontal-spindle machine employing the edge of a disc wheel. Fig. 5(a) illustrates this principle: wheel revolving at high speed up to 1500 metres per minute, work reciprocating at slow speed 10·5–30 metres per minute. The cross-feed is shown in Fig. 5(b); this will never exceed one-half of the wheel width per stroke even when rough grinding. The in-feed controls the depth of cut.

(b) Vertical-spindle machine employing the face of a cup or segmental wheel, while the work reciprocates as shown in Fig. 6(a). Often the diameter of the wheel is sufficient to cover the width of the work; in that case no cross-feed is required. The in-feed controls depth of cut.

(c) Horizontal-spindle machine with revolving work-table commonly referred to as a Ring Grinder. Fig. 7(a) shows the rotating wheel and revolving work, while Fig. 7(b) shows the cross-feed. The wheel speed, work speed, and in-feed will be similar to those stated in (a).

Cylindrical Grinding (Centreless type, i.e. work not held between fixed centres)

Fig. 4(a) illustrates the principle of centreless grinding. The main elements are the grinding wheel, a control wheel, and a static work-rest blade; all three support the work during the grinding operation. Fig. 4(b) shows the 'through-feed' method of feeding the work. The centreless grinding machine is explained later in the text.

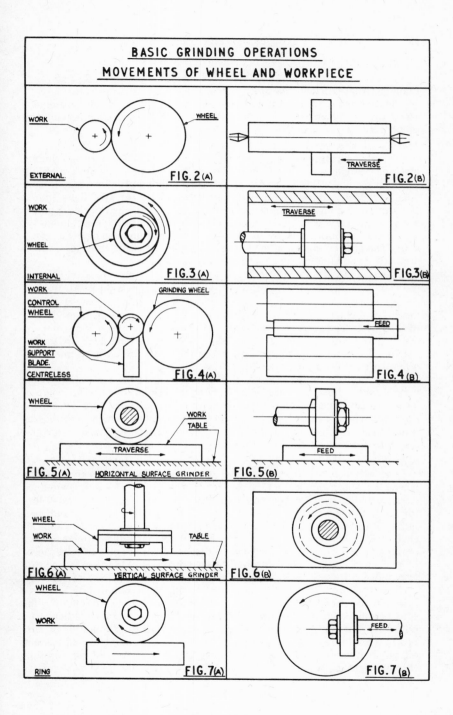

BASIC GRINDING OPERATIONS
MOVEMENTS OF WHEEL AND WORKPIECE

WORK — WHEEL
EXTERNAL. FIG. 2 (A)

TRAVERSE
FIG. 2 (B)

WORK
WHEEL
INTERNAL FIG. 3 (A)

TRAVERSE
FIG. 3 (B)

WORK
CONTROL WHEEL
GRINDING WHEEL
WORK SUPPORT BLADE.
CENTRELESS FIG. 4 (A)

FEED
FIG. 4 (B)

WHEEL
WORK TABLE
TRAVERSE
FIG. 5 (A) HORIZONTAL SURFACE GRINDER

FEED
FIG. 5 (B)

WHEEL
WORK
TABLE
FIG. 6 (A) VERTICAL SURFACE GRINDER

FIG. 6 (B)

WHEEL
WORK
RING FIG. 7 (A)

FEED
FIG. 7 (B)

Types of Grinding Machines

Plain External Grinding Machine (Centre types)

Fig. 8 shows the main features common to all external grinding machines. These vary in dimensions, but their capacity is given as maximum swing and length between dead centres.

Machine Base or Body

The base construction is a most important feature of any type of grinding machine—usually a heavy cast-iron one-piece box-section casting, the weight being correctly distributed to assure permanent alignment and freedom from vibration. This casting is heavily ribbed throughout to give the required strength and rigidity. The upper face is accurately machined, forming guideways for the table which is mounted on vee and flat ways. These guideways are adequately lubricated by spring-loaded rollers running in pocket reservoirs. The base of small and medium-size machines rests on three lugs, which are used for maintaining the alignment of the machine.

Work-Table

The table is made in two sections, the lower portion locating and traversing on the guideways of the machine base, the upper portion carrying the workhead, tailstock, and steadies. This upper section is pivoted at its centre and may be swivelled relative to the lower half, providing a method of aligning the centres, and also providing the necessary adjustment required to set the machine for taper grinding. At one end of the table a screw adjustment and a graduated scale are provided for setting purposes.

A hydraulic cylinder attached to the underside of the table controls the variable-speed traverse action which is both smooth and silent. The length of stroke is governed by trip dogs which can be set at any pre-determined position. These engage with a traverse-lever control which reverses the direction of the traverse at the end of each working stroke. The traverse speed can be varied from $0 \cdot 15$ to 6 metres per minute.

Wheelhead

The wheelhead is a self-contained unit which incorporates the grinding wheel, the wheel spindle, and the electric driving motor. This unit is mounted on a cross-slide which moves perpendicular to the table providing the in-feed for the grinding wheel. The in-feed movement is controlled by a handwheel fitted with a large graduated dial; a fine adjustment is also provided, and this enables the wheelhead to be advanced by $0 \cdot 0025$ mm for each increment of movement. A dead stop is provided so that the total amount of feed can be limited, ensuring accurate control of the final diameter of workpiece. The stop also makes provision for grinding repetition work to close limits of accuracy.

The drive from the electric motor to the spindle is obtained by multi-vee belts. The hardened and ground alloy-steel spindle is running in self-adjusting split bearings. Oil pressure ensures that the running clearance is kept to a minimum and that it remains constant under all operating conditions. These bearings are lubricated by a constant supply of filtered oil, delivered from an oil pump housed in the main wheelhead sump. The flow of oil is visible through sight glasses.

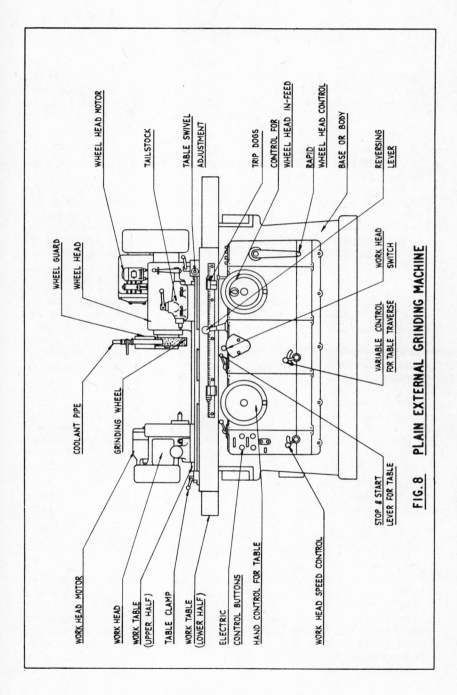

WHEEL HEAD MOTOR

WHEEL GUARD

WHEEL HEAD

TAILSTOCK

TABLE SWIVEL
ADJUSTMENT

TRIP DOGS

CONTROL FOR
WHEEL HEAD IN-FEED

RAPID
WHEEL HEAD CONTROL

BASE OR BODY

REVERSING
LEVER

COOLANT PIPE

GRINDING WHEEL

WORK HEAD
SWITCH

VARIABLE CONTROL
FOR TABLE TRAVERSE

STOP & START
LEVER FOR TABLE

WORK HEAD MOTOR

WORK HEAD

WORK TABLE
(UPPER HALF)

TABLE CLAMP

WORK TABLE
(LOWER HALF)

ELECTRIC
CONTROL BUTTONS

HAND CONTROL FOR TABLE

WORK HEAD SPEED CONTROL

FIG. 8   PLAIN EXTERNAL GRINDING MACHINE

G

Tailstock

The tailstock unit which carries one of the dead centres is located at the right-hand end of the table. This unit can be moved along the table and then securely locked in the required position to suit length of workpiece. The tailstock is fitted with a hardened and ground-steel spindle which is spring-loaded to allow for the axial expansion of the workpiece during the grinding operation.

Workhead

The workhead is also a self-contained unit carried at the opposite end of the table to the tailstock.

The plain external machine usually has a fixed workhead, i.e. no facilities for swivelling relative to the table. The workhead spindle locates a dead centre, the workpiece being rotated by a driving plate which supports a driving pin and this in turn drives the carrier attached to the workpiece. The drive is from the workhead electric motor, and provision is made for varying the work speed with either a variable-speed motor or stepped pulleys and belts.

Coolant Tank

An ample supply of coolant is necessary for all external grinding operations—approximately 27 litres per minute. This coolant is usually a mixture of soft water and soluble cutting oil (1 part oil to 50 parts water), and is supplied to the work by means of an electric-suds pump mounted in a small tank. Coolant is fed from the main tank into the pump tank, and when it returns with the swarf into the main tank it is filtered before entering the pump tank again.

Universal Grinding Machine

Although the plain external-grinding machine is a much more robust machine than the universal type it is far less versatile, and many additional cylindrical grinding operations can be performed on the universal machine. The basic design of a universal is similar to the plain external with the following additional features:—

(a) *Swivel Wheelhead*

The wheelhead unit is mounted on a main cross-slide carried on a swivel base graduated in degrees; this enables the grinding wheel to be set and fed in at an angle relative to the workpiece. A secondary swivel base integral with the main slide allows the wheel to be set perpendicular to the work while the main slide is fed in at the required angle, as shown in Fig. 9.

(b) *Swivel Workhead* Fig. 10

The body of the workhead is arranged to swivel up to 90° each side of the zero setting. Graduations marked around the base give approximate settings. The workhead spindle may be locked for dead-centre grinding as on the plain external machine, the work carried between centres and driven by the driving plate and pin. Alternatively the spindle may be live (revolving) and the work held by means of a chuck, face-plate, collets, special fixture, or be located directly in the tapered spindle nose.

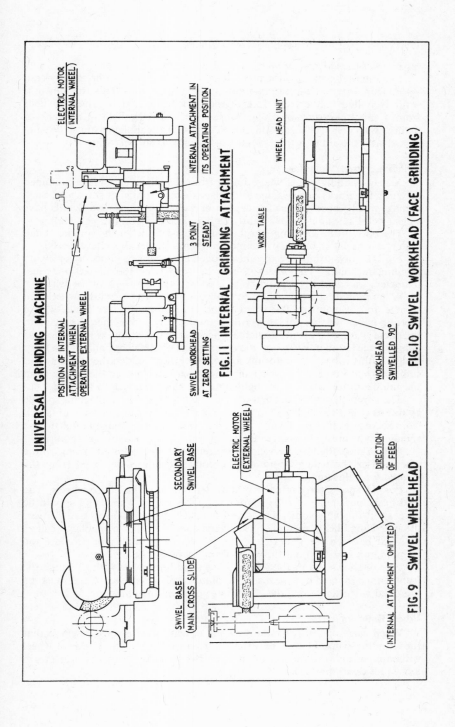

UNIVERSAL GRINDING MACHINE

ELECTRIC MOTOR (INTERNAL WHEEL)

INTERNAL ATTACHMENT IN ITS OPERATING POSITION

POSITION OF INTERNAL ATTACHMENT WHEN OPERATING EXTERNAL WHEEL

3 POINT STEADY

SWIVEL WORKHEAD AT ZERO SETTING

FIG. 11 INTERNAL GRINDING ATTACHMENT

WHEEL HEAD UNIT

WORK TABLE

WORKHEAD SWIVELLED 90°

FIG. 10 SWIVEL WORKHEAD (FACE GRINDING)

SECONDARY SWIVEL BASE

ELECTRIC MOTOR (EXTERNAL WHEEL)

SWIVEL BASE (MAIN CROSS SLIDE)

DIRECTION OF FEED

(INTERNAL ATTACHMENT OMITTED)

FIG. 9 SWIVEL WHEELHEAD

(c) *Internal-Grinding Attachment* Fig. 11

The internal-grinding attachment enables the machine to be rapidly converted from external work to internal-grinding operations. This attachment is securely bolted to the front face of the wheelhead, and is driven by belts from a small electric motor. The workpiece is usually held in a chuck or fixture, with live-workhead-spindle drive. Long components must be supported with the aid of a three-point work steady as shown in Fig. 11.

Grinding Wheel Mounting

A new grinding wheel when drawn from the stores should be examined carefully for cracks or flaws due to damage during storage or transport. Such damage might cause serious accident at operating speed. Sound wheels have a clear bell-like ring if tapped lightly with a piece of wood (never metal).

The bore of the grinding wheel should be a free fit on the spindle (small diameter wheels) or on the wheel mount flanges (larger diameter wheels).

Fig. 12 shows the type of wheel collet or mount as used on precision grinding machines. The wheel is held between two steel flanges of equal diameter; this diameter should be at least half the diameter of the wheel.

When mounting a new wheel the collet is withdrawn from the wheelhead spindle and dismantled. The wheel is located against the rear flange with a blotting-paper washer or thin rubber washer between them (maximum thickness 0·6 mm). Ensure that the wheel bears uniformly around the rear flange, place another washer on the outside face of the wheel, and fit the front flange. If this is bearing uniformly against the wheel tighten the retaining nut sufficiently to prevent the wheel slipping when transmitting the power from the spindle to the wheel. Over-tightening will cause damage to the wheel.

The complete unit, collet and wheel, is then located on the machine spindle by means of the tapered bore in the rear flange. A positive drive is obtained from the key in the spindle and a retaining nut securely holds the unit to the spindle. (Nut must always tighten in opposite direction to wheel rotation.)

At this stage the balance weights are removed for the initial 'truing' of the wheel; after the truing operation the complete unit is removed from the spindle for balancing.

Fig. 13 shows the normal method of mounting small-bore wheels. The lead bush must not protrude beyond the faces of the wheel, and should be an easy fit on the spindle. The wheel is held between two recessed flanges, the rear flange being securely fixed to the spindle. Paper or rubber washers are used between the flanges and the wheel. The spindle nut provides the clamping pressure to hold the wheel firmly between the flanges.

Fig. 14 shows the method of holding large-bore wheels. In this case the front flange is held by means of a number of set-screws. Care must be exercised when tightening these screws to give uniform pressure.

Wheel Balancing

When carrying out precision grinding operations it is most essential that the grinding wheel should be carefully balanced. An out-of-balance wheel will hammer the workpiece causing regular-spaced chatter-marks which form a chequer-board pattern.

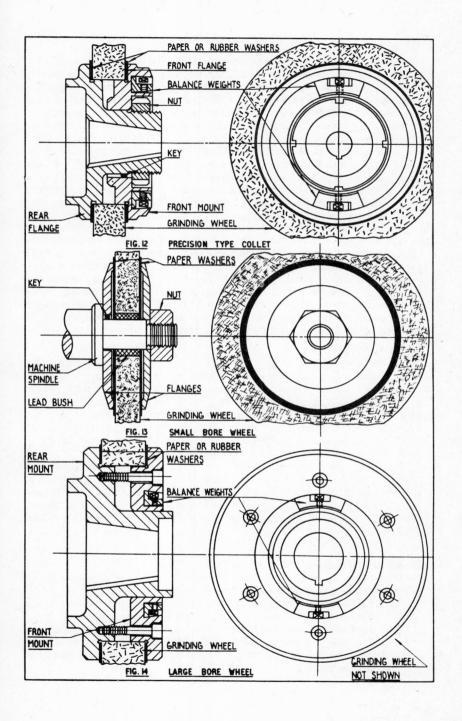

PAPER OR RUBBER WASHERS
FRONT FLANGE
BALANCE WEIGHTS
NUT
KEY
FRONT MOUNT
GRINDING WHEEL
REAR FLANGE

FIG. 12   PRECISION TYPE COLLET

PAPER WASHERS
NUT
KEY
MACHINE SPINDLE
LEAD BUSH
FLANGES
GRINDING WHEEL

FIG. 13   SMALL BORE WHEEL

REAR MOUNT
PAPER OR RUBBER WASHERS
BALANCE WEIGHTS
FRONT MOUNT
GRINDING WHEEL

FIG. 14   LARGE BORE WHEEL

GRINDING WHEEL NOT SHOWN

Fig. 12 illustrates a typical wheel collet. Initially the balance weights are removed, the new wheel is mounted, and trued up with the diamond truing tool. The wheel should be run for several minutes to remove all coolant absorbed during the truing operation. The wheel and collet is then removed as a complete unit from the wheelhead spindle and is statically balanced.

Fig. 15 shows a typical wheel-balancing stand. The wheel and collet are mounted on a special balancing spindle supported on the parallel ways—either knife-edges or rollers. When the wheel is oscillated it will come to rest with the heavy side down. To obtain accurate balance the ways must be level and parallel, and the balancing spindle must be located at right angles to them.

Fig. 16 shows an alternative balancing device. The balancing spindle is supported in the vees formed by two pairs of overlapping discs. The levelling is less important with this equipment.

When the heavy position of the wheel has been established, mark the top or light side with a chalk mark. The two balance weights are replaced in the wheel collet and are set on the light side equal distances from the chalk mark towards the horizontal centre-line, as shown in Fig. 16. The wheel is again oscillated and heavy point located. The two balance weights are adjusted to suit. These operations are repeated until the wheel is in balance. When balancing very large wheels more than two balance weights may be required.

After the balancing operation the wheel assembly is remounted on the machine spindle, and is finally trued before grinding commences.

Wheel Truing and Dressing

In the first chapter on machine-tool processes it was established that turning tools and multi-tooth milling cutters need re-sharpening periodically in order to maintain a good cutting edge and to give efficient cutting action. In the same way a grinding wheel, which is but another form of cutting tool with many more cutting edges, also requires periodic truing or dressing. These operations vitally effect the performance of any grinding wheel, and unless the wheel runs perfectly true and presents a clean sharp surface to the work, it is impossible to produce a good finish on the work.

Truing may be defined as an operation performed on a grinding wheel in order to produce specific shapes, e.g. outside diameter concentric with machine spindle, side faces true and parallel, or special shapes including angles, radii, and thread forms. Dressing may be defined as an operation which changes the cutting surface of the wheel, but may not cause the wheel to run true. This operation may be carried out with a star-type dresser, abrasive stick, or with an abrasive wheel dresser.

Diamond Truing Tools

Wheels used for precision grinding are usually trued and dressed with one of the main types of diamond truing tools:—

1. Single-point diamond. One diamond securely held in a suitable holder with sufficient of the stone exposed to act as a cutting edge.

2. Multi-diamond tool (five in line). Five diamonds set in line in a single holder. The first partially exposed, and when this diamond is completely used the metal matrix is turned or ground away sufficiently to expose the second.

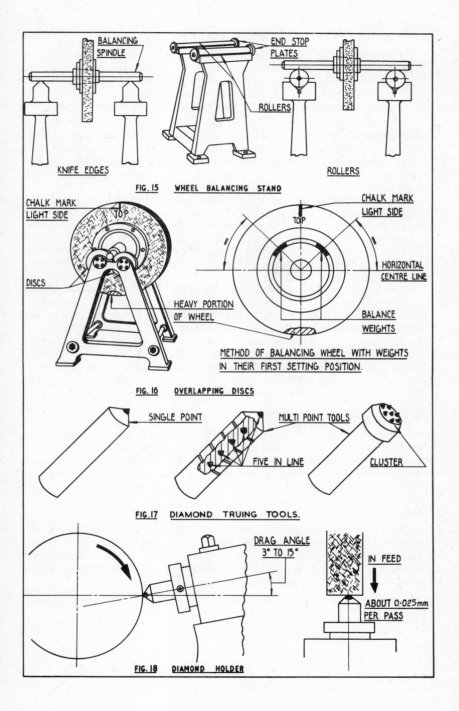

BALANCING SPINDLE

END STOP PLATES

ROLLERS

KNIFE EDGES

ROLLERS

FIG. 15   WHEEL BALANCING STAND

CHALK MARK LIGHT SIDE

TOP

DISCS

CHALK MARK LIGHT SIDE

TOP

HORIZONTAL CENTRE LINE

HEAVY PORTION OF WHEEL

BALANCE WEIGHTS

METHOD OF BALANCING WHEEL WITH WEIGHTS IN THEIR FIRST SETTING POSITION.

FIG. 16   OVERLAPPING DISCS

SINGLE POINT

MULTI POINT TOOLS

FIVE IN LINE

CLUSTER

FIG.17   DIAMOND   TRUING   TOOLS.

DRAG ANGLE 3° TO 15°

IN FEED

ABOUT 0·025mm PER PASS

FIG. 18   DIAMOND   HOLDER

3. Multi-point or cluster diamond tool. A series of small diamonds set in the face of the tool, arranged so as to give the best contact between the diamonds and wheel face. This arrangement relieves the loading on each individual diamond as compared with the single-point tool. Fig. 17. shows an example of each type of diamond truing tool mentioned.

The most widely used type of industrial diamond for this purpose are African brown bort, grey bort, and ballas stones, the latter being more expensive. These diamonds are classified according to quality, shape, and mass. The most suitable mass depends on wheel diameter, width of wheel face, type of abrasive, grade, grit size, and bond. Masses vary from 0·5 to 5 carats (0·1 to 1 gram).

The diamond truing tool must be securely held in the bracket on the tailstock, or in a universal holder mounted on the machine table. In the former case the wheel can be trued without removing the workpiece from the centres. The point of the diamond tool is set on the centre-line of the wheel, and is inclined at an angle of 3–15° from the point of contact, ensuring that the wheel face is always moving away from the diamond, preventing any tendency of chatter or gouging. Fig. 18.

The wheel is run at its normal working speed and when the diamond tool is almost in contact with the wheel face the coolant is applied, the traverse is started, and the wheel is fed in 0·025 mm at the end of each pass. When very fine finishes are required the rate of traverse and in-feed will be reduced.

Periodically the diamond tool is turned in the bracket so that a sharp point is always presented to the wheel. The diamond will eventually wear down flush with its seating; at this stage it is useless, but it can be re-set so that further facets are made available. Re-setting is normally carried out by the company who supplied the original diamond tool.

Wheel Loading

When the small metal chips removed from the work become embedded in the face of the grinding wheel the cutting rate of the grains is decreased, a condition referred to as loaded wheel face. This condition may be caused by incorrect speeds or feed rates, or by using a wheel unsuitable for the material being ground.

Wheel Glazing

When the abrasive grains have become dull and are worn down to the bond holding them, the wheel face has a shiny or glazed appearance, and ceases to cut efficiently, rubbing the work rather than cutting. This condition is known as glazed wheel, and may be caused by using a wheel too hard or too fine grit size, or by unsatisfactory truing or dressing.

Internal-Grinding Machine

Internal-grinding operations may be carried out on a universal grinding machine with the aid of the internal attachment, but such operations can be performed more effectively on a machine specifically designed for the purpose, namely the internal-grinding machine. These can be classified under four main headings:—

1. *Plain Internal-Grinding Machine*

On which the workpiece is rotated by a live workhead spindle, and the in-feed is operated by hand or mechanically at the end of each table stroke.

2. *Automatic Internal-Grinding Machine*

Similar in basic design to the plain machine, but apart from loading and unloading the work, all the grinding operations including the dressing of the wheel and the gauging of the hole, are carried out on an automatic cycle. Such machines will give a far greater output than the manually operated machines.

3. *Planetary-Motion Internal-Grinding Machine*

Machines on which the work is held stationary. The wheel spindle not only revolves on its axis, but also travels in a circular orbit about the axis of the job. Such machines are used to grind work that cannot be rotated on a live spindle owing to its size, shape, or mass.

4. *Centreless Internal-Grinding Machine*

The work is located by its outside diameter between live rollers which cause it to revolve at the appropriate speed while the wheelhead spindle traverses the length of the hole. This method of location simplifies setting and ensures that the bore is ground concentric with the outside diameter. Distortion is also reduced to a minimum.

Plain Internal Machine

The main details of a standard plain machine are shown in Fig. 19.

Machine Body

A rigid cast-iron box-section casting, similar in design to the body of the external machine.

Work-Table

A two-piece work-table. The lower section locates on the guideways of the body, is actuated hydraulically, and can be pre-set to suit length of traverse stroke required for any particular workpiece. Direction of traverse is controlled by a reverse lever manually or automatically operated by adjustable trip-dogs mounted on the front of the table. The upper section of the table which carries the workhead can be swivelled about its centre relative to the lower section, providing sufficient adjustment to obtain parallelism in the hole being ground.

Workhead

The workhead houses the live spindle which drives the work-holding device and this could be a chuck, face-plate, or special fixture. The workhead is driven by its own electric motor, and provision is made for obtaining a range of speeds to suit different-diameter workpieces.

The standard-type of spindle nose is the improved screw-type with two spigot locations very similar to that used on certain centre-lathes, as shown in Fig. 6(a), p. 115. In other cases the flanged spindle is used; the chuck or face-plate is then located by a spigot and is bolted to the flange.

The base of the workhead incorporates a turn-table graduated in degrees, and this provides the movement required for setting components having tapered holes.

Wheelhead

The wheelhead unit which includes grinding wheel, its spindle, and driving motor is carried on a cross-slide supported by a bridge piece securely attached to the machine body, and is therefore supported quite independently from the work-table. The in-feed of the internal-grinding wheel is controlled by a graduated handwheel which operates the cross-slide leadscrew. To eliminate the effects of backlash a counter weight is incorporated. Various types and sizes of grinding-wheel spindles which are housed in a special bracket can be quickly mounted on the cross-slide. Three main types are in general use: 1. The Adaptor Type, as its name implies, a spindle with interchangeable adaptors or quills to suit various size holes. 2. Solid Type, with grinding wheel mounted directly on the end of spindle. 3. Tube Type, the spindle supported by a bearing mounted immediately behind the grinding wheel, which gives greater rigidity and less deflection than the other types.

All three types of spindle are driven by a flat endless belt with facilities for tension adjustment.

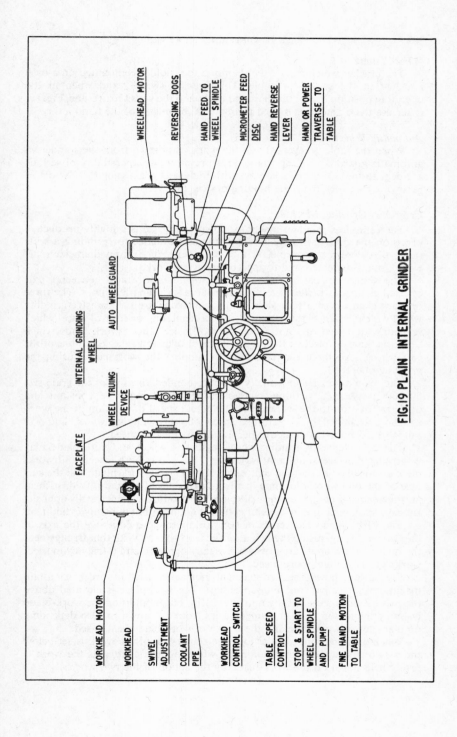

WHEELHEAD MOTOR

REVERSING DOGS

HAND FEED TO WHEEL SPINDLE

MICROMETER FEED DISC

HAND REVERSE LEVER

HAND OR POWER TRAVERSE TO TABLE

INTERNAL GRINDING WHEEL

AUTO WHEELGUARD

FACEPLATE

WHEEL TRUING DEVICE

WORKHEAD MOTOR

WORKHEAD

SWIVEL ADJUSTMENT

COOLANT PIPE

WORKHEAD CONTROL SWITCH

TABLE SPEED CONTROL

STOP & START TO WHEEL SPINDLE AND PUMP

FINE HAND MOTION TO TABLE

FIG.19 PLAIN INTERNAL GRINDER

Wheel Truing

The bracket which carries the diamond-tool holder is mounted on a base attached to the swivel-top table. This bracket swivels, and when in the operating position brings the diamond tool on to the wheel centre-line. Fig. 19. After use the diamond is moved through 90° by means of the hand lever.

Automatic Wheel Guard

When the table is reversed and the work withdrawn from the spindle an automatic guard covers the wheel, thus preventing the possibility of serious accident to the operator by contact with the wheel when gauging the hole or removing the work from the holding device. Fig. 19.

Centreless Grinding Machine

The centreless grinding machine shown in Fig. 20 is a highly productive precision machine used extensively in modern practice for grinding a wide range of cylindrical workpieces, including work of a given diameter (barwork), multi-diameter, and formed or spherical work.

The term centreless indicates that the work is not rotated between a pair of fixed centres as is the case in plain external-grinding machines. The three primary elements of a centreless grinding machine are the abrasive grinding wheel which performs the actual cutting, a regulating or control wheel which regulates the speed of rotation of the workpiece, and a work blade which supports the workpiece at the required height relative to the centre-line of the two wheels. All three elements help to support the workpiece during the grinding operation.

The regulating wheel is usually a rubber-bonded abrasive of the grain size 80–100, possessing frictional characteristics which impart a constant and uniform rotation to the workpiece. The actual speed of rotation of the work will be determined by the surface speed of the regulating wheel, and will range from about 15–75 metres per minute peripheral speed.

The three elements, grinding wheel, regulating wheel, and work-blade, may be arranged in several different ways. Fig. 21(a) shows both wheels and workpiece arranged on a common centre-line. The flat-top work blade and the surface of the two wheels forming in effect three sides of a square. With such an arrangement a high spot on the workpiece will produce a diametrically opposite concave spot, resulting in work of constant diameter but not truly cylindrical.

Fig. 21(b) shows the centre of the workpiece elevated above the axis of the two wheels by raising the height of the work-blade. With this arrangement the high and low spots are not diametrically opposite and a truly cylindrical workpiece is gradually produced.

Fig. 21(c) shows the arrangement normally used in order to attain maximum corrective rounding-up action. The workpiece is elevated above the axis of the wheels as shown in Fig. 21(b), but in addition the work-blade has an angular top face; the angle varies from 30° down to zero depending on diameter of workpiece and the length of work-blade being used.

When grinding long slender jobs the centre-line of the work is set below the axis of the wheels; this eliminates whipping and chatter as the work is firmly held down on the work-blade by the action of the two wheels.

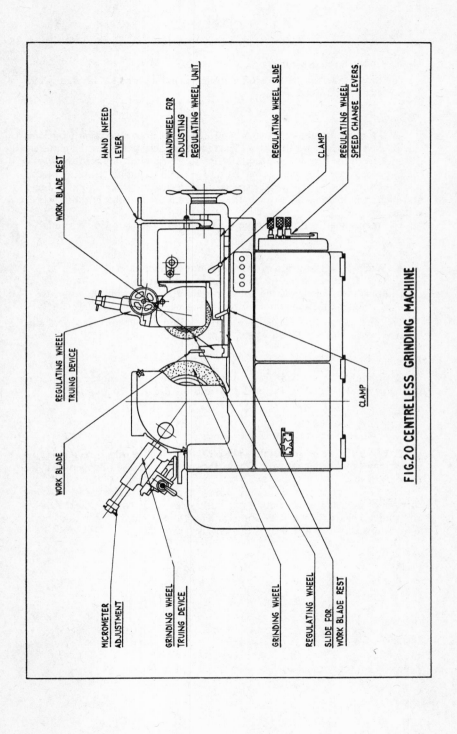

WORK BLADE REST

HAND INFEED LEVER

HANDWHEEL FOR ADJUSTING REGULATING WHEEL UNIT

REGULATING WHEEL SLIDE

CLAMP

REGULATING WHEEL SPEED CHANGE LEVERS.

REGULATING WHEEL TRUING DEVICE

WORK BLADE

CLAMP

MICROMETER ADJUSTMENT

GRINDING WHEEL TRUING DEVICE

GRINDING WHEEL

REGULATING WHEEL

SLIDE FOR WORK BLADE REST

FIG.20 CENTRELESS GRINDING MACHINE

Methods of Centreless Grinding

The three principal methods of centreless grinding are: 1. Through-Feed; 2. In-Feed; 3. End-Feed.

Through-Feed Figs. 22(a) and 22(b)

As the name suggests the work is ground as it passes through from one side of the two wheels to the other. The regulating wheel is set at the required distance from the grinding wheel, and this together with the height of work-blade governs the diameter being ground. The longitudinal traverse of the work is controlled by the surface speed of the regulating wheel, and the angle at which it is inclined relative to the horizontal axis of the grinding-wheel spindle.

The theoretical feed rate can be obtained from the following formula:—

$$F = \frac{\pi d.N.\sin\alpha}{1000}$$

When F = Feed rate of work in metres per minute.

d = Diameter of regulating wheel in millimetres.

N = Speed of regulating wheel in revolutions per minute.

α = Angle of inclination of regulating wheel.

This theoretical formula is based on the assumption that there is no slip between work and regulating wheel, in practice not more than 2%.

Example

Calculate the theoretical feed rate in metres/min. when using a 250 mm diameter regulating wheel inclined at 6° and revolving at 70 rev/min.

$$F = \frac{\pi \times 250 \times 70 \sin 6°}{1000} = \frac{22 \times 250 \times 70 \times 0.1045}{7 \times 1000}$$
$$\simeq 5.75 \text{ metres/min.}$$

To offset the wear which takes place on the grinding wheel the regulating wheel may be re-adjusted to maintain the original relationship between the three elements.

The work-blade rest or fixture which carries the work-blade also incorporates adjustable work-guides at both sides of the wheel; these can be adjusted to ensure the work is kept parallel with the space between the wheels as it enters, and also as it leaves the wheels.

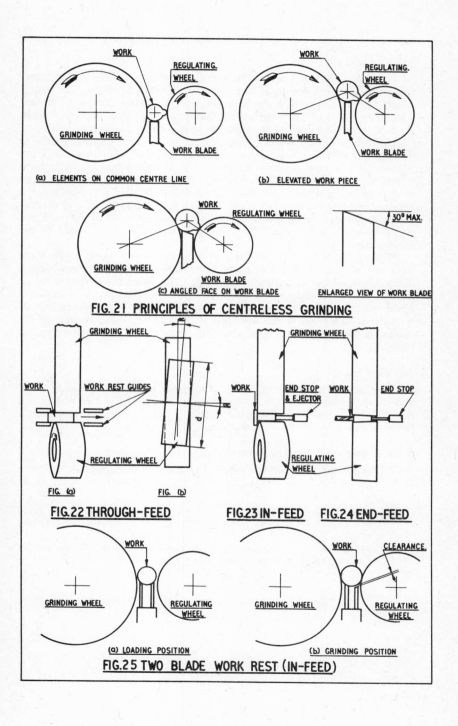

(a) ELEMENTS ON COMMON CENTRE LINE

(b) ELEVATED WORK PIECE

(c) ANGLED FACE ON WORK BLADE

ENLARGED VIEW OF WORK BLADE

30° MAX.

FIG. 21 PRINCIPLES OF CENTRELESS GRINDING

FIG. (a)

FIG. (b)

FIG. 22 THROUGH-FEED

FIG. 23 IN-FEED

FIG. 24 END-FEED

(a) LOADING POSITION

(b) GRINDING POSITION

FIG. 25 TWO BLADE WORK REST (IN-FEED)

In-Feed Fig. 23

The in-feed method is similar to plunge-cut or form grinding on a centre-type machine, and is employed for grinding work which has a shoulder, flange, or some section larger than that being ground—length of section to be ground limited by width of grinding wheel. The regulating wheel is given a slight angle of inclination 1/4–1/2° to keep the work against the end stop.

The in-feed work-blade is mounted on a slide which is clamped rigidly to the slide carrying the regulating wheel, therefore both regulating wheel and work-blade rest maintain a fixed relationship. When loading the component it rests in the vee formed by the top edge of the work-blade and the surface of the regulating wheel; the wheel slide is then advanced a pre-determined amount bringing the work in contact with the grinding wheel and so producing the desired dimension. The slide is then reversed and the work ejected either manually or automatically, and another component placed in the loading position.

When using the in-feed method for large and heavy work, a two-blade work rest is used, and this is mounted on the lower slide, whose movement is independent of the regulating-wheel slide. The work-blade rest is set in relation to the grinding wheel; the workpiece is loaded on the two work-blades; as the regulating wheel is advanced it brings the workpiece in contact with the grinding wheel and also lifts it clear of the blade nearest to the regulating wheel. Fig. 25(a) shows the loading position, Fig. 25(b) the grinding position.

End-Feed Fig. 24

This method is used for grinding taper work only. Both grinding wheel and regulating wheel are dressed to the required shape. The two wheels and the work-blade are set in fixed relationship to each other; the workpiece is fed in from the front to a fixed end stop.

Main advantages of Centreless Machines

1. Loading time very small compared with centre-type grinding.
2. No axial thrust imposed on the work, therefore long brittle work easily ground.
3. Less grinding stock required.
4. Work rigidly supported, therefore no deflection during the grinding operation.
5. Large quantities of small components can be automatically ground by use of magazine, gravity chute, or hopper feeding attachments.

Truing the Wheels

Both the grinding and regulating wheels have individual truing devices. The one supplied for the grinding wheel is hydraulically operated, while that of the regulating wheel is hand operated. The grinding wheel used in centreless machines will need truing or dressing for the same reasons as those given when we considered the centre-type-machine wheels, e.g. to balance the wheels, to obtain a desired standard of surface finish, to eliminate effects of loading or glazing, etc. The standard grinding-wheel truing device is designed for truing the wheel for grinding straight parts, and an additional device is required for truing the wheel for work involving profile contours.

The regulating-wheel truing device is only used to true the wheel when initially setting the machine, or to remove damage marks caused by rough work or carelessness. The regulating wheel must be trued in a manner that will ensure that the work when passing between the wheels makes contact with the entire width of wheel face, therefore the truing device must be swivelled to an angle equal to the angle of inclination of the regulating-wheel spindle. Another factor to be taken into account when setting the diamond holder is the height of the work above or below the centre of the wheels. The maximum regulating-wheel speed is used when truing.

Work-Blades

The contact surface of the work-blade may be made of cast iron, high-speed steel, or sintered carbide.

Cast-iron blades are used for soft work to prevent the possibility of scoring, and 'pick-up' between work and blade.

High-speed steel is suitable for non-ferrous materials and for small diameter parts.

Cemented carbide blades have good wearing properties, and are often used for hardened components and non-metallic materials.

The magnitude of the angle of the top face of the blade will be largely governed by the width of grinding-wheel face and diameter of work being ground. The maximum angle, 30°, would be reduced as the length of blade, width of wheel, or work diameter increases.

The length of blade is proportional to the width of grinding wheel, and the thickness is determined by the diameter of the work.

Surface-Grinding Machines

Horizontal Spindle (with reciprocating work-table)

A small-type surface-grinding machine which is both versatile and sensitive, used chiefly for light precision work such as tools and gauges; it is therefore found frequently in tool-rooms and experimental shops, but also used extensively in many production departments.

A typical modern example is shown in Fig. 26, the capacity being 500 mm longitudinal table traverse, 180 mm cross traverse, and a grinding wheel 200 mm diameter × 20 mm width.

The main details of construction include:—

Body

A strong hollow casting which forms the main base of the machine. The lower right-hand section contains the oil pump for the hydraulic system, and also acts as the oil reservoir. The pump is driven by multi-link belts from a 750 W electric motor located in a separate compartment in the left-hand section, ensuring protection from oil or dust.

Vee guideways are machined on the top face to locate the cross-saddle. Attached to the rear face of the body are long guideways of dovetail form which ensure accurate vertical movement of the column carrying the wheelhead.

Cross-Saddle

The cross-saddle provides the cross-traverse movement for the table, and is located by inverted vee slideways. As these slideways are relatively short they are subjected to extreme wear, therefore hardened steel inserts are sometimes fitted to both body and cross-saddle. A handwheel attached to the cross-feed screw is graduated and movement of 0·025 mm can be obtained. When a fine-feed attachment is fitted much smaller increments can be obtained. When the automatic cross-feed is in operation the cross-slide is hydraulically operated with each reversal of the table.

Guideways, usually one flat and one vee machined in the upper face of the cross-saddle, locate the work-table.

Work-Table

The longitudinal power traverse of the work-table is operated hydraulically, providing a stepless variable speed range up to 18 metres per minute. The length of traverse stroke is controlled by two adjustable dogs carried in a tee-slot in the front edge of the table. As the table approaches the end of its stroke the appropriate dog makes contact with a roller carried on the reversing lever, the dog continues to override the roller, the lever is reversed, and the table travels in the opposite direction. Such an arrangement provides a smooth reversal at all table speeds. The left-hand dog has a hinged contact piece which enables the table to be run-out to the limit of its travel for checking or loading purposes without disturbing the stroke-length setting.

The table can also be traversed by hand with the aid of the appropriate hand wheel which brings into operation a rack-and-pinion movement. Operation of the power traverse automatically disengages the hand control.

The table slideways are lubricated by means of spring-loaded oil rollers located in oil pockets in the cross-saddle guideways. Oil grooves machined in the guideways assist in the distribution of the lubricant.

The working surface of the table (450×150 mm) is ground in position, and tee-slots enable the workpiece or the work-holding device to be clamped to the table.

Work may be held by several different methods:—

(a) Held by means of a rectangular magnetic chuck.

(b) Held in a vice.

(c) Clamped to the table direct.

(d) Clamped to an angle plate (angle plate clamped to table).

(e) Held in a special fixture.

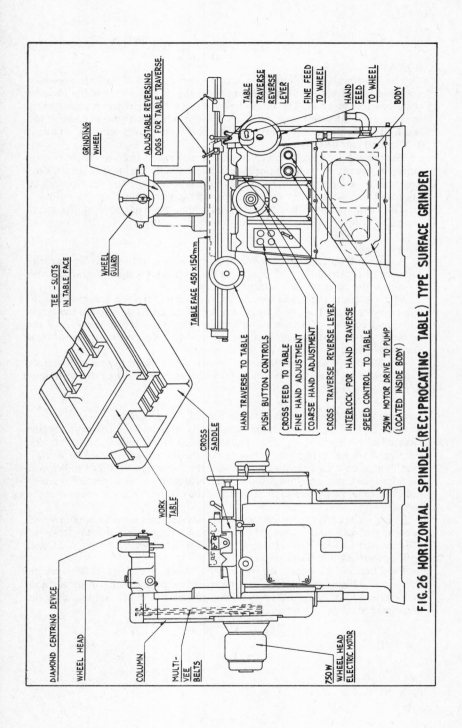

DIAMOND CENTRING DEVICE

WHEEL HEAD

COLUMN

MULTI-
VEE
BELTS

750 W
WHEEL HEAD
ELECTRIC MOTOR

TEE -SLOTS
IN TABLE FACE

WHEEL
GUARD

TABLE FACE 450 x 150 mm

GRINDING
WHEEL

ADJUSTABLE REVERSING
DOGS FOR TABLE TRAVERSE.

TABLE
TRAVERSE
REVERSE
LEVER

FINE FEED
TO WHEEL

HAND
FEED
TO WHEEL

BODY

CROSS
SADDLE

WORK
TABLE

HAND TRAVERSE TO TABLE

PUSH BUTTON CONTROLS

CROSS FEED TO TABLE
FINE HAND ADJUSTMENT
COARSE HAND ADJUSTMENT

CROSS TRAVERSE REVERSE LEVER

INTERLOCK FOR HAND TRAVERSE

SPEED CONTROL TO TABLE

750W MOTOR DRIVE TO PUMP
(LOCATED INSIDE BODY)

FIG. 26 HORIZONTAL SPINDLE-(RECIPROCATING TABLE) TYPE SURFACE GRINDER

Wheelhead and Column

The wheelhead is mounted as a unit on the top face of the column which is a rigid box-shaped casting, moving vertically in the dovetailed guideways at the rear of the body. The down-feed for the grinding wheel is operated by an accurate feed screw controlled by a hand wheel with both coarse- and fine-feed movements. By means of the fine feed, movements as small as 0·0025 mm can be obtained.

The wheelhead spindle is driven at constant speed from a 750 W electric motor by means of multi-vee belts which are totally enclosed. The nitralloy steel spindle is supported on bearings of special design, giving the rigidity and freedom from vibration so essential for precision grinding.

The grinding wheel is adequately guarded; the front face of the guard carries the centring device for the diamond truing tool.

Wheel Truing

A diamond tool can be held in a bracket which is located on the magnetic chuck or alternatively bolted directly to the table, and is then centralised with the aid of the centring device mentioned previously.

When shaping the wheel for more complicated forms, a crushing attachment may be used. The crushing attachment is mounted directly on the worktable, and consists of a freely rotating hardened-steel crushing roller of the required form which is pressed into the wheel. The crushing pressure is always in the same plane as the grinding pressure.

The grinding wheel must be rotated slowly for crushing purposes, therefore a supplementary drive to the grinding wheel is required if using this technique to form the wheel.

Horizontal Spindle (with rotary table) Fig. 27. Ring Grinder

This type of surface-grinding machine is used mainly for grinding the faces of circular work, e.g. gear blanks, piston rings, milling-cutter blanks, etc., the work revolving under the edge of the traversing wheel. The work is usually held on a circular magnetic chuck revolving in a fixed position, while the wheelhead, mounted on a slide, reciprocates over the work; the travel is sufficient to allow the wheel to move from the centre to the outside rim of the chuck.

The spindle carrying the chuck can be elevated by means of a hand wheel operating a rack and pinion; the machine illustrated has a total travel of 130 mm when using a new grinding wheel. The hand wheel is graduated, and both coarse and fine feeds are obtainable.

Facilities are provided for tilting the chuck about its cross axis, or alternatively tilting the wheelhead slide to enable concave or convex surfaces to be ground. When grinding parallel surfaces the chuck spindle and the wheelhead slide will be set at zero settings.

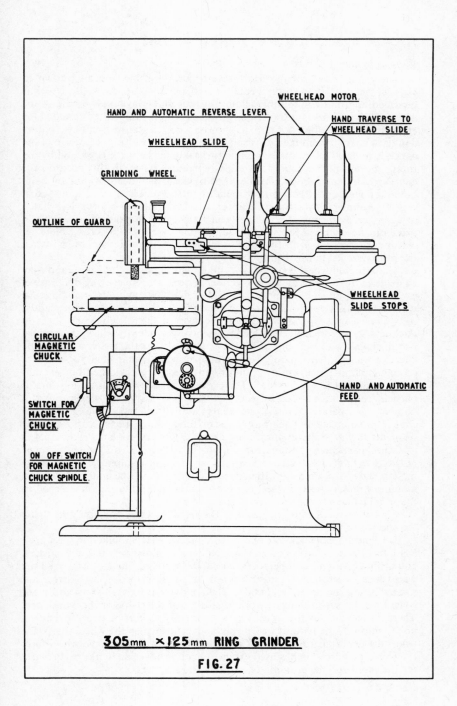

HAND AND AUTOMATIC REVERSE LEVER

WHEELHEAD MOTOR

HAND TRAVERSE TO WHEELHEAD SLIDE

WHEELHEAD SLIDE

GRINDING WHEEL

OUTLINE OF GUARD

WHEELHEAD SLIDE STOPS

CIRCULAR MAGNETIC CHUCK.

SWITCH FOR MAGNETIC CHUCK.

HAND AND AUTOMATIC FEED

ON OFF SWITCH FOR MAGNETIC CHUCK SPINDLE.

305mm ×125mm RING GRINDER

FIG. 27

Vertical Spindle (with rotary table) Fig. 28

The main details of a vertical-spindle-grinding machine are shown in Fig. 28. The work is held on a rotary magnetic chuck. In turn, this chuck is mounted on a horizontal table sliding on flat guideways on the base of the machine. The horizontal traverse is power operated, and is used to move the chuck from the loading position, as shown in Fig. 28, to the grinding position and back again for unloading. When in the grinding position the centre of the chuck is under the face of the grinding wheel, and the work is ground by the rotary motion of the chuck, the table remaining static. In this position the chuck rotates continuously, while the wheelhead is fed downward by hand or power feed until the work is reduced to the required thickness. Actual size is determined by setting the automatic-feed stop from a previous batch of work, or by means of a calliper attachment which measures the work in place on the chuck. After initially setting the calliper to a setting block, it will indicate on a dial in hundredths of a millimetre the amount by which the pieces exceed finished size.

The grinding wheel is a hollow cylinder cutting on its end face, and may be made in three forms: 1. Plain Cylinder Wheel; a complete ring of abrasive, e.g. 450 mm outside diameter, by 125 mm thick, and 380 mm internal diameter, usually reinforced around the outside diameter with wire bands; these are easily stripped off by the operator as the wheel wears down in thickness. 2. Sectored Wheel, which is essentially a cylinder wheel of increased rim thickness with vee-shaped notches moulded into the outer surface. The effect of these notches is to give approximately the same length of abrasive on any circumference, ensuring that grains are not overworked on one diameter and wasted on another. This type of wheel is cool cutting and is particularly suitable for broad surfaces. 3. Segmental Wheel, consisting of a number of separate abrasive segments securely clamped into a segment chuck, the complete unit being mounted on the spindle. The spaces between the segments facilitate the clearance of chips and flow of coolant, which makes this wheel particularly suitable for grinding broad surfaces and rough castings.

Both cylinder and sectored wheels are set with sulphur, which in its molten state is poured into the space between the wheel and the cast-iron mounting ring. After the wheel has been set the mounting ring is attached to the spindle face-plate by means of several retaining screws.

Coolant is supplied to the inside of the grinding wheel and also directly on the surface of the work.

The wheel dresser consists of a vertical bronze shaft mounted in the wheelhead, having at its lower end an arm holding a group of toothed-steel cutters, and at its upper end an operating handle for swinging the cutters across the wheel face. Micrometer adjustment for height is provided by a hand nut located above the operating handle. The relative motions of wheel and work generate a flat surface on the work regardless of the shape of the wheel face. Therefore, as long as the wheel wears sufficiently to keep it sharp it requires no attention. If the natural wear is not sufficient to keep the wheel sharp, the wheel dresser will provide a quick and safe way of dressing the wheel face.

This type of machine is used extensively on production work, particularly for the rapid surface grinding of castings and forgings.

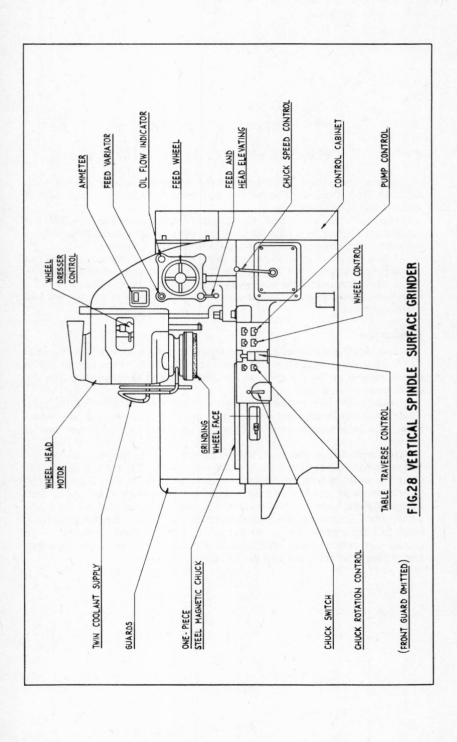

FIG.28 VERTICAL SPINDLE SURFACE GRINDER

WHEEL HEAD MOTOR

WHEEL DRESSER CONTROL

AMMETER

FEED VARIATOR

OIL FLOW INDICATOR

FEED WHEEL

FEED AND HEAD ELEVATING

CHUCK SPEED CONTROL

CONTROL CABINET

PUMP CONTROL

WHEEL CONTROL

TWIN COOLANT SUPPLY

GUARDS

ONE-PIECE STEEL MAGNETIC CHUCK

GRINDING WHEEL FACE

CHUCK SWITCH

CHUCK ROTATION CONTROL

TABLE TRAVERSE CONTROL

(FRONT GUARD OMITTED)

CHAPTER EIGHT

THE SHAPING MACHINE

The shaping machine is used mainly for machining plane or flat surfaces, although with the aid of special attachments both concave and convex surfaces can be produced.

Single-point tools are used, the surface being generated by combining a straight cut applied by a reciprocating tool with the transverse movement of the work. These basic movements are shown in Fig. 1, Chapter Four.

Milling machines have taken over much of the work formerly carried out on shaping machines, but despite this, owing to the comparative simplicity of the work setting and the cheapness of the cutting tools, a shaper is still a most useful and economic machine tool for certain types of production and tool-room work.

Construction

Most shaping machines are of the crank type as shown in Figs. 1 and 3. The main drive is through a crank housed in the body of the machine. The ram is located in the top slideways of the body and is reciprocated by the crank mechanism shown in Fig. 3.

Single-point tools are held in the tool holder at the front of the ram. These tools can be adjusted by means of the tool slide attached to a swivel base; such an arrangement allows both vertical and angular movements of the tool.

The saddle which slides on the vertical slideways at the front end of the body provides the vertical adjustment for the work. The table slides on the front face of the saddle, providing the transverse movement for the work. The table movement is controlled by a screw equipped with a graduated dial. Frequently machines are also equipped with a graduated dial on the screw which controls the vertical movement of the saddle. Power feeds are normally fitted to both transverse and vertical movements, the feed operating at the end of each return stroke. The amount of feed per stroke can be varied to suit the material being cut and the finish required.

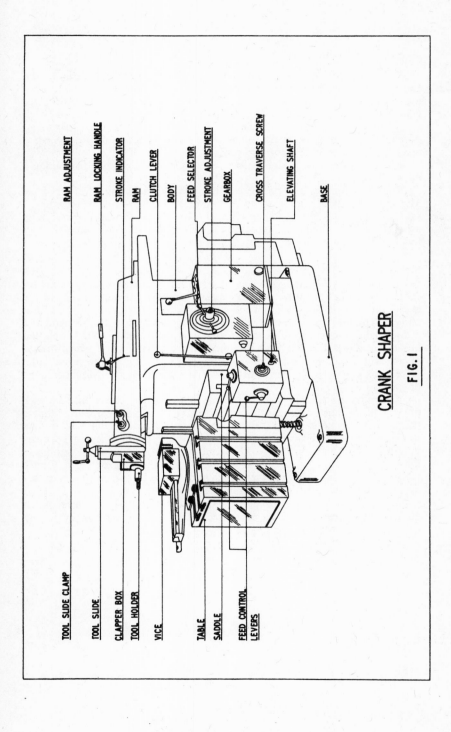

TOOL SLIDE CLAMP

TOOL SLIDE

CLAPPER BOX

TOOL HOLDER

VICE

TABLE

SADDLE

FEED CONTROL
LEVERS

RAM ADJUSTMENT

RAM LOCKING HANDLE

STROKE INDICATOR

RAM

CLUTCH LEVER

BODY

FEED SELECTOR

STROKE ADJUSTMENT

GEARBOX

CROSS TRAVERSE SCREW

ELEVATING SHAFT

BASE

CRANK SHAPER

FIG. I

Clapper Box Fig. 2

The tool holder or post is attached to the tool slide by means of the clapper box. This box, being hinged, prevents undue rubbing of the tool on the return stroke. Its design provides a limited amount of angular movement which is independent of the swivel base attached to the tool slide, and such an arrangement facilitates the machining of both vertical and angular faces. A relief strip or stop is fitted to reduce the swinging action of the box when using long strokes at high cutting speeds.

Fig. 2(a) shows the normal setting of the clapper box when machining a flat surface.

Fig. 2(b) shows the clapper box setting when machining a vertical face. The angular setting ensures adequate tool relief on the return stroke.

Fig. 2(c) shows the tool slide set at the appropriate angle for machining an angular face, while the clapper box is swivelled to give the necessary tool relief on the return stroke.

Quick-Return Mechanism

In order to reduce the time wasted during the return non-cutting stroke, shaping machines are fitted with a quick-return mechanism, usually of the crank and slotted-link design. This is shown diagrammatically in Figs. 3(a) and (b). The ram is driven by a slotted link which pivots at its lower end and is attached to the ram by a loose connecting link at its upper end. The slotted link engages with the crank pin mounted on the driving wheel which rotates at constant speed and causes the link to oscillate and the ram to reciprocate. A gearbox controls the speed of the driving pinion, thus providing a range of speeds for the ram.

Assuming the driving wheel is rotating in a clockwise direction, then with the ram at the start of the cutting stroke the centre-line of the slotted link is tangential with the path of the crank pin shown at point 2 on diagram. As the wheel rotates the ram moves forward until the link again becomes tangential, shown at point 10. Further rotation of the driving wheel withdraws the ram to its starting position at point 2. Hence the rotation from point 2 to 10 in this example, 240°, is the cutting stroke, and that from 10 to 2 in this example, 120°, is the return stroke, giving a 2:1 ratio.

As the length of the stroke is increased or decreased the ratio of the cutting time to the return time varies (see chain-dotted line in Fig. 3(b)).

Therefore ratio of $\dfrac{\text{Cutting Time}}{\text{Return Time}} = \dfrac{360 - \phi}{\phi}$

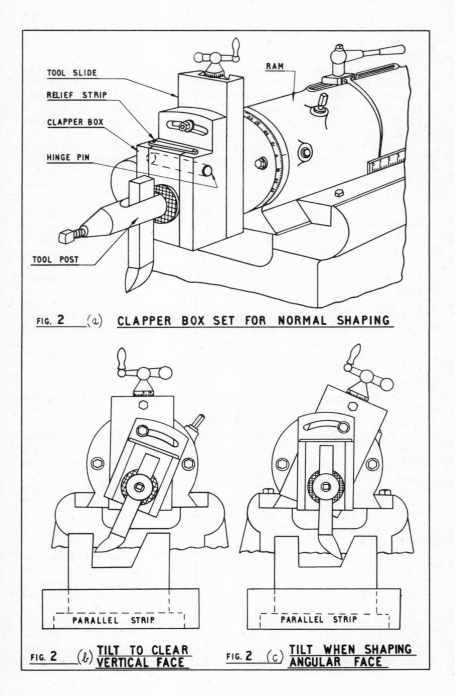

TOOL SLIDE

RELIEF STRIP

CLAPPER BOX

HINGE PIN

RAM

TOOL POST

FIG. 2 (a) CLAPPER BOX SET FOR NORMAL SHAPING

PARALLEL STRIP

PARALLEL STRIP

FIG. 2 (b) TILT TO CLEAR VERTICAL FACE

FIG. 2 (c) TILT WHEN SHAPING ANGULAR FACE

Stroke Adjustment

The stroke can be adjusted both for length and position. Length of stroke is varied by moving the crank pin radially on the driving wheel, thereby increasing or decreasing the oscillation of the link. This movement is effected by a hand crank on the square-ended stroke-adjustment shaft, shown in Fig. 1, which operates through bevel gears and a screwed spindle passing through the crank-pin carrying-block.

Stroke position is changed by moving the ram in relation to the driving mechanism. This is carried out by releasing the ram locking handle, shown in Fig. 1, and moving the ram in the required direction by turning the ram-adjustment shaft, Fig. 1; the locking handle is then re-clamped before starting the machine.

Cutting Speed

As already stated, the ram is driven by a crank pin, and its speed varies throughout the stroke. By reference to Fig. 3(a) it can be seen that an angular displacement of the crank pin from point 2 to 3 produces a simultaneous linear movement of the ram from $2^{\setminus}$ to $3^{\setminus}$, while the same angular movement from point 5 to 6 results in a much larger ram displacement; in short, the ram speed is a minimum at the start and finish of the stroke, and a maximum at the centre of the stroke. Due to this no definite figure for cutting speed can be fixed, but a chart on the machine gives a guide to cutting speeds in metres per minute for given lengths of stroke and cycles per minute.

Example given on page 106, Chapter Four.

Work Holding

Much of the work carried out on the shaper can be held in the vice. The shaper vice is of robust construction and is usually equipped with a swivel base which is most useful for a variety of jobs.

Work which due to size or shape cannot be held in a vice is usually clamped to the machine table. The table has tee-slots machined in its upper and side faces to accommodate holding bolts, and often has a vertical vee-groove on the side face to locate circular bars which require machining on their end face.

Due to the intermittent cutting action, the work must be held very securely, therefore the clamping is most important. End stops are frequently used to prevent work from sliding on the table.

Tools and Tool Holding

The standard tools used on the shaping machine are similar to those used on the centre lathe (see Fig. 8, Chapter Five), although ideally the shank depth should be greater to withstand the increased cutting forces. Nose radii are increased on finishing tools to give an improved surface finish; in some cases the finishing tools have a broad flat face. The tool should be held as far up in the tool holder as possible to give maximum support, and to prevent the tool springing under the initial impact of the cut. Normally a workpiece should be roughly machined all over before commencing to finish machine any particular face.

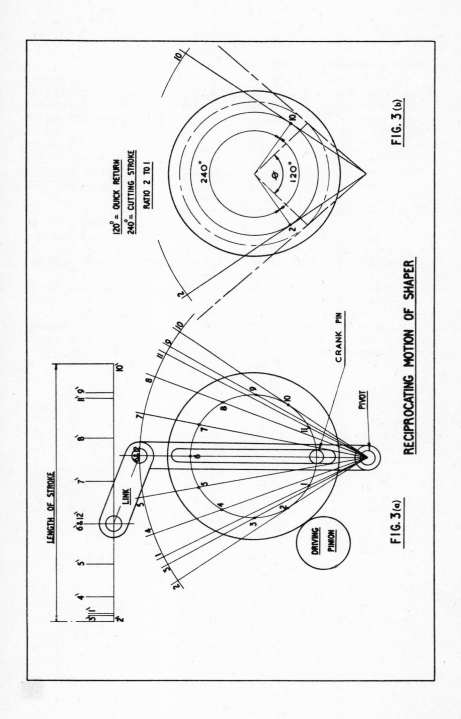

FIG. 3 (b)

120° = QUICK RETURN
240° = CUTTING STROKE

RATIO 2 TO 1

240°

120°

Ø

10

10

2

2

CRANK PIN

PIVOT

DRIVING
PINION

LINK

LENGTH OF STROKE

FIG. 3(a)

RECIPROCATING MOTION OF SHAPER

Example—Shaping a Lapping Plate

The lapping plate shown in Fig. 4(a) is a typical example of a shaping job. The material is cast iron supplied in the form of a rough casting. The plate requires machining on all surfaces, and in addition two series of grooves are to be cut in the top face. These grooves are at 90° to each other, and at 45° to the edges of the plate.

Operations

1. Set jaws of machine vice at right angles to ram axis by means of graduations on swivel base. (If greater accuracy is required a dial indicator may be used.)
2. Support plate on parallel strips and hold in vice, one edge of plate extending just beyond the jaws. Fig. 4(b). Shape face No. 1 using straight roughing tool, clapper box set as in Fig. 4(b). Shape side face No. 2 using a cranked tool, clapper box set as in Fig. 4(c).
3. Reverse plate in vice; repeat operation 2 in respect of face No. 3 and edge No. 4, machining the block to thickness and length.
4. Hold plate in vice by gripping edges No. 2 and 4; shape edge No. 5.
5. Reverse material in vice; repeat operation 4, shaping edge No. 6, bringing the plate to width.
6. Swing vice through 45°; using form tool cut one series of diagonal grooves. The spacing of the grooves is controlled by using the table index, and their depth by using the tool slide index. Fig. 4(d).
7. Swing vice through 90° and cut second series of grooves.

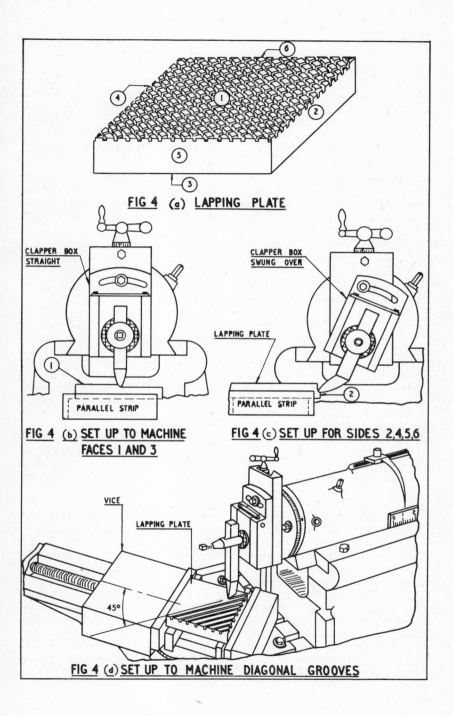

FIG 4 (a) LAPPING PLATE

CLAPPER BOX STRAIGHT

CLAPPER BOX SWUNG OVER

LAPPING PLATE

PARALLEL STRIP

PARALLEL STRIP

FIG 4 (b) SET UP TO MACHINE FACES 1 AND 3

FIG 4 (c) SET UP FOR SIDES 2,4,5,6

VICE

LAPPING PLATE

45°

FIG 4 (d) SET UP TO MACHINE DIAGONAL GROOVES

CHAPTER NINE

DRILLING AND DRILLING MACHINES

Drilling is one of the most important and widely used machining operations and a wide range of machines is manufactured for its performance. The machines will in addition to drilling carry out a variety of ancillary operations, i.e. reaming, tapping, counterboring, etc. Such machines can be broadly divided under three headings:—

1. Pillar or Vertical Drilling Machines (single and multi-spindle).
2. Radial Drilling Machines.
3. Sensitive Drilling Machines.

The selection of a machine for a particular application depends largely upon hole and work size.

Pillar or Vertical Drilling Machines

The pillar drilling machine shown in Fig. 2 is one of a wide range of machines built to this general design. It consists of a vertical pillar or column to which is attached the drill spindle and work-table. The spindle is bored to a suitable-size morse taper for the location of taper shank drills or a drill chuck, and is driven by an electric motor through a gearbox giving a range of speeds to suit drills within the capacity of the machine.

A hand lever provides manual control of the spindle and power feed is usually available for such operations as reaming, hole depth being controlled by an adjustable stop. The machine table has tee-slots cut in its upper surface for the clamping of work, vices, and other work-holding devices. The table is elevated by means of a hand crank.

The hole positions are commonly indicated by marking-out, the work being moved and re-clamped in position for each hole. This method is suitable for small numbers of components or where no great accuracy is required, but on production work a drilling jig is usually employed. Such a jig locates and clamps the work and also incorporates hardened-steel drill bushes which guide the drill. Except when drilling very small holes it is always advisable to clamp the jig firmly to the table.

The multi-spindle machines consist of a series of pillar drills mounted over a common table, thus eliminating the constant tool changing associated with the single-spindle machine. The drills and other tools required are mounted in the various spindles and the work is moved from one spindle to the next until the operations are completed. A separate drive is available for each spindle, and the cutting speeds of each are initially set to suit the tool located in them.

224

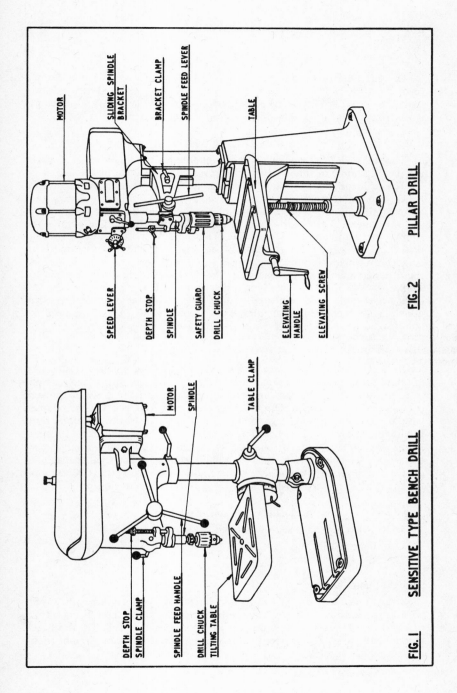

MOTOR

SLIDING SPINDLE
BRACKET

BRACKET CLAMP

SPINDLE FEED LEVER

TABLE

SPEED LEVER

DEPTH STOP

SPINDLE

SAFETY GUARD

DRILL CHUCK

ELEVATING
HANDLE

ELEVATING SCREW

FIG. 2   PILLAR DRILL

MOTOR

SPINDLE

TABLE CLAMP

DEPTH STOP

SPINDLE CLAMP

SPINDLE FEED HANDLE

DRILL CHUCK

TILTING TABLE

FIG. I   SENSITIVE TYPE BENCH DRILL

H

Turret Drilling Machines

On this type of machine the drills and other tools are mounted on a revolving turret which can be quickly and accurately indexed into position under the spindle. This arrangement reduces the time necessary to move the work from one spindle to another and also saves floor space.

Radial Drilling Machines

The radial drilling machine is most suitable for the larger class of work; a typical example of this type of drilling machine is shown in Fig. 3(a).

The drill spindle is mounted in a saddle adjustable along the radial arm which can be rotated about and elevated on the vertical column, thus allowing the spindle to cover any point on the machine bed and eliminating any movement of the work. Gearboxes enclosed in the saddle control the spindle speed and automatic-feed rate. The spindle can also be fed by means of a hand lever, or through a handwheel which provides a very fine feed. Provision is made for machine tapping and also for boring holes beyond the drilling capacity of the machine. Tee-slots are machined in the bed for clamping work, and for clamping either a box-table as shown in Fig. 3(a) or a swivel-table as shown in Fig. 3(b). The swivel-table is a most useful attachment which enables angular holes to be drilled without the need for complicated set-ups.

Sensitive Drilling Machines

Sensitive drilling machines which are of light and simple construction are used for the drilling of small holes where it is essential that the machine operator shall 'feel' the passage of the drill through the work to prevent excessive drill breakages. The machine shown in Fig. 1 is bench mounted with a maximum drill capacity of 13 mm. It is fitted with a swivelling table for angular holes, and in addition the table can be swung clear to allow larger work to be clamped to the bed. The spindle is driven by a small electric motor and vee belts, and is fitted with hand feed only. The smaller machines of this design are capable of very high spindle speeds (up to 10000 rev/min) for the drilling of very small holes as required in instrument work.

Drill Types and Location

Twist drills are made with two types of shank:—

1. Straight Shank. Fig. 7.
2. Morse Taper Shank. Fig. 9.

Straight-Shank Drills

Straight-shank drills in the metric series are now available in a very wide range of sizes, from 0·32 mm to 16 mm in diameter, there being a total of 191 drills in the series. This range is in accordance with B.S. 328 and I.S.O. recommendations. The former drill gauge and letter series of straight-shank drills are now obsolete.

FIG.3(a) RADIAL DRILLING MACHINE

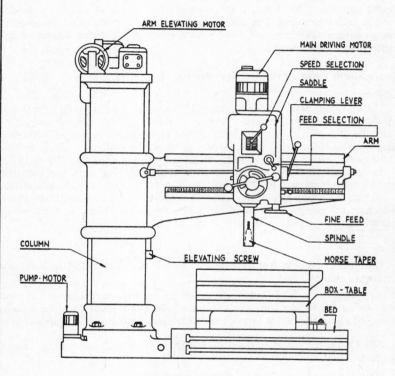

ARM ELEVATING MOTOR

MAIN DRIVING MOTOR

SPEED SELECTION

SADDLE

CLAMPING LEVER

FEED SELECTION

ARM

FINE FEED

SPINDLE

MORSE TAPER

COLUMN

PUMP·MOTOR

ELEVATING SCREW

BOX - TABLE

BED

FIG.3(b) SWIVEL TABLE

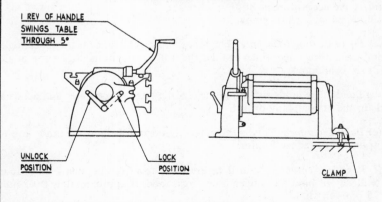

I REV OF HANDLE
SWINGS TABLE
THROUGH 5°

UNLOCK
POSITION

LOCK
POSITION

CLAMP

Straight-shank drills are held in a drill chuck, shown in Fig. 5, which grips the shank between three self-centring jaws. The jaws are opened or closed by rotating the knurled or grooved outer ring and a key is provided for the final tightening. The chuck may be screwed to the machine spindle, but more generally they are fitted with a taper shank which locates in the taper bore of the spindle.

Taper-Shank Drills—Principal Features Fig. 4

Shank

Taper-shank drills are manufactured in standard sizes ranging from 3 mm to 100 mm diameter, but special sizes are obtainable both smaller and larger than the standard range. The size of the taper shank increases with drill size, ranging from No. 1 to No. 6 Morse taper, the drilling machine spindle being bored with a taper to suit its maximum drilling capacity. The drive for these drills comes from the intimate contact and 'binding' action of the male and female tapers and is only positive when both tapers are clean and free from burrs. A sharp jerk of the drill or a light tap with a soft-faced hammer is sufficient to engage the drill firmly. The shank includes the tang which facilitates the removal of the drill from the machine spindle.

Body

The body extends from the shank to the drill point and includes the following elements:—

(a) *Point Angle.* The angle included by the cutting edges, usually 118°, but may be varied to suit different materials. The point angle must be equally disposed about the centre-line of the drill, otherwise the drill will cut oversize.

(b) *Flutes.* Flutes run the full length of the body and have several functions:—

    (i) Form cutting edges.
    (ii) Provide necessary rake angle.
    (iii) Give access for the cutting lubricant.
    (iv) Facilitate swarf removal.

(c) *Lip or Cutting Clearance.* The lip or cutting clearance is the relief angle behind the cutting edge which enables the drill to cut. In most cases an angle of 10–12° is adopted.

(d) *Lands.* The lands run along the leading edge of the flutes and act as a guide in the hole already drilled.

(e) *Body Clearance.* This is the cut-away portion behind the lands and is incorporated to reduce friction.

(f) *Length Clearance.* A drill tapers back towards the shank to reduce the tendency of binding in deep holes. This taper is approximately 0·02 mm per 25 mm length.

STANDARD TAPER SHANK TWIST DRILL

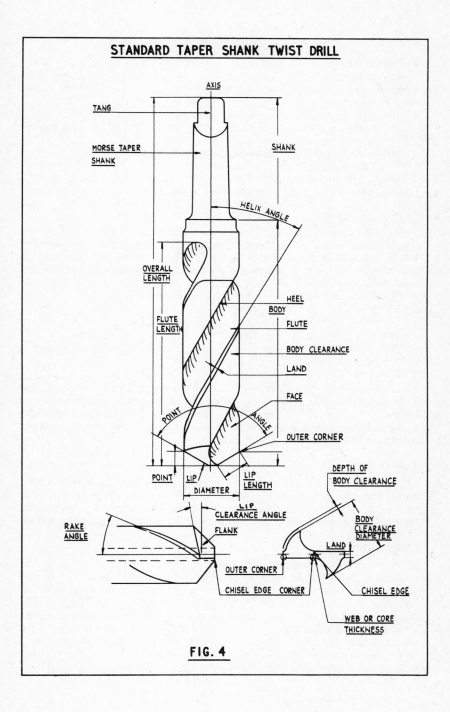

FIG. 4

Drill Grinding

If a drill is to produce a good hole it is essential that the point be in good condition and correctly ground When grinding a drill the following points must be observed.—

   (i) Drill points must not be damaged by overheating.
   (ii) Point angle must be correct for the material being cut, and equally disposed about centre-line.
   (iii) Length of the two cutting edges must be equal.
   (iv) Clearance angle must be maintained.

While it is possible to make a drill cut by free-hand grinding, a drill-grinding machine or fixture must be used if good results are to be obtained.

Drill Sockets or Sleeves

To hold a drill having a No. 1 Morse taper shank in a drilling-machine spindle bored with a No. 3 Morse taper, it is necessary to use one or more of the drill sockets or sleeves shown in Fig. 6. These are accurately ground on the internal and external tapers and are made in various combinations; the most usual include:—

No. 1 Morse Internal	—	No. 2 Morse External
No. 2 „ „	—	No. 3 „ „
No. 3 „ „	—	No. 4 „ „
No. 4 „ „	—	No. 5 „ „
No. 5 „ „	—	No. 6 „ „

Drill Removal

Drills are ejected by using a tapered drift shown in position in Fig. 6. The drift passes through the slot in the drilling-machine spindle or sleeve and acts against the tang cut on the end of the shank. Care must be taken to ensure that the drill spindle is at rest before inserting the drift, and that it is not put in motion before the drift is withdrawn.

Core Drills Fig. 10

The core drill has more than two flutes, hence more than two cutting edges; they will not originate a hole as they do not come to a point, but as they have a larger web section they are stronger and therefore more suitable for enlarging cored holes in castings than the standard two-fluted-type drill.

Centre Drills Fig. 8

A centre drill is used on the drilling machine to assist in lining up the machine spindle with the marking-out lines and to ensure a good start for the twist drill. It consists of a parallel portion of small diameter followed immediately by a tapered portion. The angle of the taper is 60° included, and is primarily for use in forming centre holes which will be used for subsequent grinding operations. Its use in this capacity is related more frequently to the centre lathe rather than the drilling machine. When using a centre drill prior to drilling a hole the impression should be made just deep enough to accommodate the centre of the drill point to prevent it from wandering.

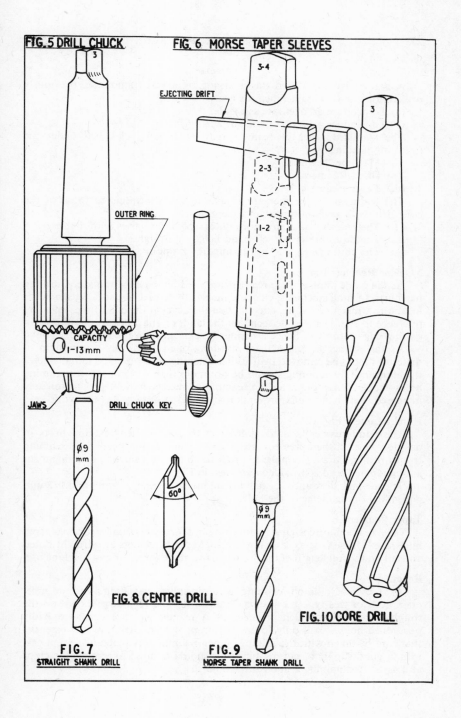

FIG. 5 DRILL CHUCK

FIG. 6 MORSE TAPER SLEEVES

3

3-4

EJECTING DRIFT

2-3

1-2

3

OUTER RING

CAPACITY
1-13 mm

JAWS

DRILL CHUCK KEY

Ø9
mm

60°

Ø9
mm

FIG. 8 CENTRE DRILL

FIG. 10 CORE DRILL

FIG. 7
STRAIGHT SHANK DRILL

FIG. 9
MORSE TAPER SHANK DRILL

Reamers

A reamer is a tool used for enlarging by a small amount a previously drilled hole, and its main functions are:—

(a) To produce an accurate size hole.

(b) To produce a hole of good surface finish.

The standard types of reamers may be broadly classified under the following headings:—

    (i) Machine Reamers.

    (ii) Hand Reamers.

    (iii) Taper Reamers.

The features of a reamer are similar in many respects to those of the twist drill with several important exceptions:—

    (i) The reamer has many more flutes. (Number varies with diameter.)

    (ii) The flutes are either left-hand helix, or straight.

    (iii) The cutting edges do not terminate in a point.

Machine Reamers Fig. 11

As the name implies these reamers are used on machine tools, e.g. drilling machines, turning machines, etc., and invariably have a Morse taper shank for location. A machine reamer cuts only on the bevel at the end of the flutes. By reference to Fig. 11 it can be seen that the lands on the flutes are circular so no cutting edge is formed, hence a reamer is re-ground on the bevel edges only.

As the reamer is designed for finishing operations only a minimum of material should be removed by it. When reaming holes up to 25 mm diameter the allowance for reaming should be not more than 0·4 mm. When reaming holes above 25 mm diameter the reaming allowance may be proportionately increased. Left-hand helix prevents reamer being drawn into the work.

Hand Reamers Fig. 12

The hand reamer is used mainly by the fitter when reaming holes in position, e.g. bushes pressed into mating components need final reaming to ensure an accurate size hole. In order to obtain easy starting and alignment a long tapered lead is provided as shown in Fig. 12.

The normal allowance for hand reaming is between 0·1 mm and 0·2 mm depending on diameter of the hole.

Taper Reamers

Taper reamers are designed for finishing and correcting small errors in tapered holes, e.g. Morse tapers, taper pin holes, etc. Such reamers are straight fluted and cut on the full length of the flute, and are made for hand and machine use.

Reaming

As previously stated reaming is a finishing operation, and in most operations of this type the results obtained depend to a large extent on the roughing operation which precedes it. A reamer will not correct a badly positioned hole, it will only follow the original hole, therefore it is essential that care be taken with the drilling. When reaming any material, except cast iron, a good supply of cutting lubricant should be used to remove the chips and assist in obtaining a good surface finish.

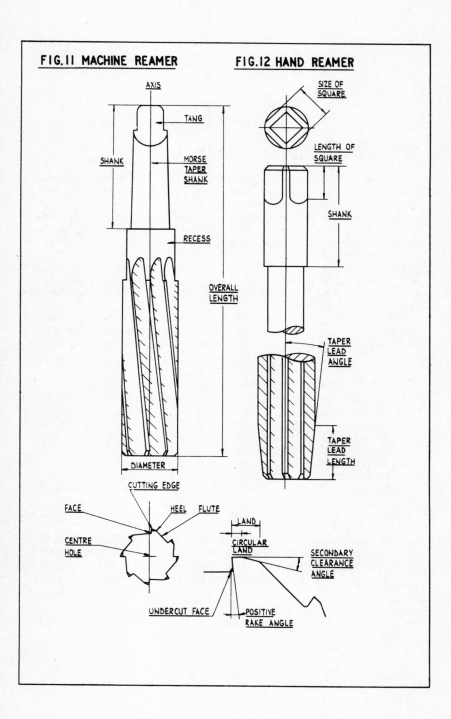

FIG.11 MACHINE REAMER FIG.12 HAND REAMER

SAND CASTING

The sand casting process is the oldest method of making an intricately shaped component in metal, yet still extensively used today, often proving to be the cheapest method of production.

Basically a sand casting is produced by pouring molten metal into a non-permanent sand mould prepared with the aid of a suitable pattern. When the metal cools and solidifies the casting is extracted by breaking away the mould, hence a new mould is required for each casting. Sand castings can be made from a variety of materials; the most commonly used include cast iron, brass and other copper alloys, aluminium and magnesium alloys. Castings in steel are very limited because of their high melting temperatures and related contraction problems.

During recent years many sand foundries have been fully mechanised, transforming what was previously a crude art into a controlled science. Despite this, however, the basic principles of the process remain unchanged.

The Basic Stages in Sand Casting

1. A finished component drawing is sent to the pattern shop providing all essential information, e.g. casting shape, dimensions, material, surfaces requiring machining, etc. After careful analysis of the drawing the pattern-maker in conjunction with foundry personnel will decide the best technique of moulding the casting.
2. Making the pattern and core boxes.
3. Making the sand mould and appropriate sand cores.
4. Preparation of the molten metal, transporting it to the mould, and pouring it into the mould.
5. Fettling the casting, i.e. cleaning and dressing the casting after its removal from the mould.
6. Inspection of the casting, including visual examination, checking dimensions, and tracing visible defects. Crack detection methods, e.g. chalk test or dye tests. X-Ray examination to reveal any internal flaws. Pressure-testing castings which have to withstand pressures.

Pattern Making

Patterns for small repetition work are frequently made in metal, but the bulk of patterns are made in wood which although not as durable as metal is relatively cheap, of light weight, more easily worked, and easier to modify if this should be required.

The two types of wood used for making patterns are yellow pine and mahogany, the latter being more expensive but also more durable. These patterns make only a limited number of castings, possibly fifty to a hundred, after which they need repair or replacing.

The pattern is a replica of the required casting, but all its dimensions are made slightly larger than those of the casting to allow for the contraction which takes place when the hot metal solidifies in the mould. Accordingly the pattern maker employs a special rule known as a contraction rule, but since the contraction allowance varies with different materials, he will select the rule appropriate for the material from which the casting is to be made. The normal contraction allowances are cast iron 8 mm per metre, brass 15 mm per metre, aluminium 13 mm per metre.

Machining allowances must also be incorporated in the pattern dimensions on all surfaces which will require subsequent machining. It is essential that the pattern be constructed in such a manner that it can be withdrawn without causing damage to the mould impression, therefore a slight taper or 'draught' is provided on pattern faces where necessary. Many patterns are made in sections with additional loose pieces for bosses, etc. Dowel pins register the various sections.

B.S. 467 gives recommendations regarding the colour scheme to be used when marking patterns. The finished pattern is usually given a coat of shellac varnish, providing a smooth finish and safeguarding it against the effects of moisture in the mould.

Sand Moulds

1. *Open Sand Moulds*

An open sand mould is the simplest form of mould—merely a depression formed in a level bed of sand in the foundry floor into which molten metal is poured and allowed to solidify. Open sand moulds are only used for making very simple castings requiring no great accuracy on the upper face, as this will be quite rough. Typical examples might include castings for manhole covers or drain grids.

2. *Closed Sand Moulds*

Most sand moulds are made in metal moulding boxes or flasks; a simple two-part box mould is shown in Fig. 1(c). The bottom box is known as the drag, and the top box as the cope. These two boxes are registered by locating pins which fit into lugs on each side of the box. During the actual pouring the two boxes are locked together by means of keys which are driven into slots in the locating pins as shown in Fig. 2(g). The large boxes have transverse webs or ribs which strengthen the box, and also help to 'key' the sand of the mould.

3. *Green Sand Mould*

Green sand mould is the name given to a mould which is made from sand in its natural or 'green' state, i.e. damp, still containing moisture. Green sand moulds are commonly used for small and medium-sized ferrous and non-ferrous castings.

4. *Dry Sand Mould*

Dry sand mould refers to a mould which is artificially dried before the molten metal is poured into it. The small moulds may be dried in an oven, while the large moulds made on the shop floor are skin-dried by coke braziers or by gas torches. These moulds are much stronger than green sand moulds and are generally used for the larger and more complicated castings. Less steam is given off during pouring so reducing the possibility of blowholes in the final casting.

Types of Sand

1. Facing Sand

A fine grade of sand consistent for grain size, highly refractory, and specially mixed for the purpose of withstanding the action of the molten metal. This type of sand is used against the face of the pattern, and will therefore form the surface of the mould and finally govern the surface finish of the casting.

2. Parting Sand

Parting sand is used to preserve the joint face between the cope and the drag and prevents the two lots of sand from adhering to each other. It consists of a mixture of burnt sand and bone dust which does not become damp or sticky.

3. Moulding Sand

The moulding sand or 'floor sand' is the main body of sand which is used to fill in the mould at the back of the thin facing layer. The two types of moulding sand are:—

(a) *Natural Sand*, i.e. sand containing the silica grains and clay bond as found, therefore varying in grain size and clay content. Main sources of supply are Erith, Mansfield, Belfast, and Clyde.

(b) *Synthetic Sand*, i.e. sand composed of washed and graded silica grains, with the desired type and amount of clay bond added.

Good moulding sand must be:—

(i) *Cohesive*, i.e. ability to retain shape of impression after the removal of the pattern and during pouring and solidifying.
(ii) *Refractory*, i.e. withstand the heat of the molten metal without fusing.
(iii) *Permeable*, i.e. porous enough to allow gases evolved during pouring to escape.
(iv) *Strong*, i.e. strong enough to support the weight of hot metal and necessary sand cores.

The important qualities in the sand are:—

(a) Size and shape of the silica grains; this affects the porosity of the mould.

(b) Moisture content; adequate moisture is necessary to give a good bond, but excess moisture lowers porosity, and blowholes in the casting may result. Too little moisture makes the mould liable to crumble and thus difficult to finish. Moisture content should be about 4–8%.

(c) Amount and type of clay bond; an average figure being between 2 and 6%. The clay should be fine particle clay, e.g. colloidal clay or fuller's earth.

Making a Two-part Mould (Solid Casting)

Fig 1(a) shows the pattern for making a very simple solid casting possessing no holes or undercut sections, but having a flat face which coincides with the largest cross-section This casting could be conveniently made by the following sequence of operations:—

1 The flat face of the pattern is placed on a turnover board and a suitable size moulding box (drag) is placed over it as shown in Fig. 1(b) Smooth facing sand is sprinkled over the pattern; a quantity of moulding sand is then added and is rammed tightly around the pattern Additional moulding sand is added and the ramming repeated until the drag is full The surface of the sand is then trimmed off (strickled) level with the edges of the box This ramming operation requires both skill and experience; if the sand is too loose a bad impression is obtained; if too tight the gases generated when the metal is poured cannot escape, resulting in a defective casting

2 The drag is inverted and the joint surface is sprinkled with parting sand The top box (cope) is placed in position above the drag and the two boxes are registered by locating pins as shown in Fig. 1(c). The cope is now rammed with moulding sand. Two conical wooden plugs form the downgate and riser channels. See additional note on Gates and Risers. After ramming the cope, it should be vented to allow an escape for the hot gases. Vents are made by pushing a small diameter wire down through the sand until it nearly reaches the pattern.

3. The two boxes are separated and the pattern loosened in the impression by rapping. Fig. 1(d). To assist rapping a metal spike may be stuck into the pattern or a screwed rod inserted in the special bush provided in the face of the pattern. After rapping the pattern is carefully withdrawn from the mould. A feed-gate is cut by hand in the joint face of the drag. If molten metal were fed directly into the mould cavity its surface would be damaged. The mould is now painted with blackwash or dusted with plumbago to protect the mould surface and to give a smooth skin on the casting. The conical wooden plugs are removed from the cope, which is replaced in position on the drag and firmly secured by the locating pins and locking keys. A pouring bush is placed over the downgate channel and the completed mould is now ready to receive the molten metal as shown in Fig. 1(e).

4. The molten metal is poured into the mould and allowed to solidify. When cool the two boxes are separated and the casting as shown in Fig. 1(f) is removed.

The casting is now fettled before inspection; if satisfactory it is sent to the machine shop.

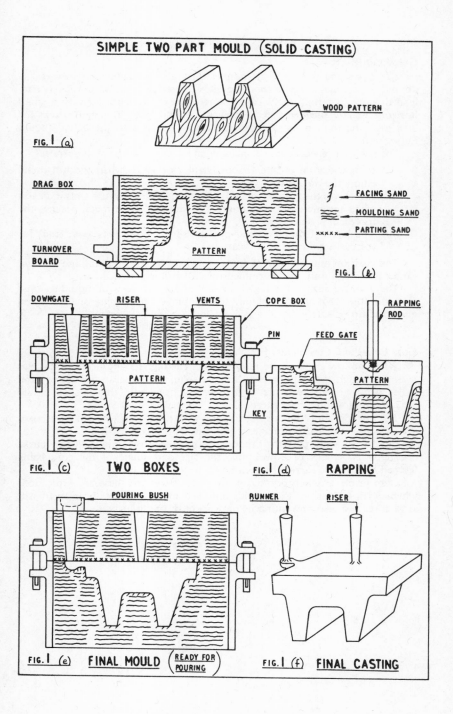

SIMPLE TWO PART MOULD (SOLID CASTING)

WOOD PATTERN

FIG. 1 (a)

DRAG BOX

FACING SAND

MOULDING SAND

PARTING SAND

TURNOVER BOARD

PATTERN

FIG. 1 (b)

DOWNGATE   RISER   VENTS   COPE BOX   RAPPING ROD

PIN   FEED GATE

PATTERN   PATTERN

KEY

FIG. 1 (c)   TWO BOXES   FIG. 1 (d)   RAPPING

POURING BUSH   RUNNER   RISER

FIG. 1 (e)   FINAL MOULD (READY FOR POURING)   FIG. 1 (f)   FINAL CASTING

Gates and Risers

The downgate is a vertical channel through which the molten metal is poured, sometimes called a 'pouring gate', 'vertical gate', or 'sprue'. It may lead directly into the mould cavity, but usually it is connected by a small horizontal channel called a 'feed gate' (horizontal gate). This gate checks the inrush of the molten metal, thus preventing damage to the actual mould impression.

The riser is a vertical channel included in the mould for several purposes:—

(i) It provides an escape for air, steam, or gases when the hot metal enters the mould cavity.

(ii) It receives the surplus metal from the mould cavity and thus indicates when the mould is full. Pouring is stopped when metal reaches the top of the riser.

(iii) The head of molten metal in the riser or risers acts as a 'feed' for the casting during solidification.

The position and number of gates and risers to ensure obtaining a sound sand casting can only be determined by skill and experience.

The pouring bushes are made of metal and are lined with moulding sand shaped in the form of a funnel, and this simplifies the pouring operation and gives additional safety.

Core Boxes and Core Prints Fig. 2(c)

When hollow castings are required, i.e. castings having holes or cavities in their design, the pattern is still made solid, and separate bodies of sand called 'sand cores' are made, and these are fitted into the finished mould after the removal of the pattern.

The appropriate sand cores are made with the aid of wooden core boxes produced by the pattern-maker from similar timber to that used for the making of the solid pattern. Frequently the core box is made in two parts, registered by means of dowel pins, the size and shape of the core being formed by a recess carried in each half.

Core prints are incorporated in the pattern design; these are projections which form recesses in the mould, thus providing accurate location for the sand core, and also preventing its movement during pouring.

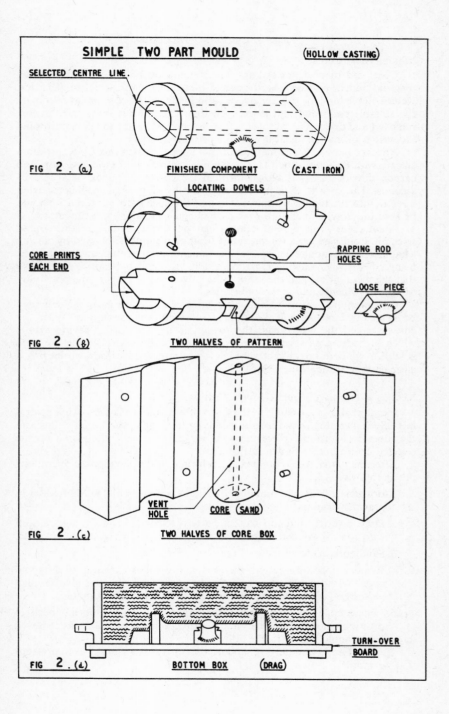

SIMPLE TWO PART MOULD

(HOLLOW CASTING)

SELECTED CENTRE LINE.

FIG 2 . (a)   FINISHED COMPONENT   (CAST IRON)

LOCATING DOWELS

CORE PRINTS EACH END

RAPPING ROD HOLES

LOOSE PIECE

FIG 2 . (b)   TWO HALVES OF PATTERN

VENT HOLE

CORE (SAND)

FIG 2 . (c)   TWO HALVES OF CORE BOX

TURN-OVER BOARD

FIG 2 . (d)   BOTTOM BOX   (DRAG)

Making Sand Cores

Cores are made from ordinary moulding sand with additional binding material added, or from clay-free sand (sea-sand) with special binders, e.g. water-soluble binders, oil binders, or resin binders. The core box is filled with the suitable core sand and is rammed tight. The box is split, and the core removed and dried in an oven. It is then strong and hard enough to withstand the weight of molten metal it will support in the mould.

Another more modern method of making cores is to mix $2\frac{1}{2}$–3% sodium silicate with dry core sand. This mixture is rammed up in the core box, and carbon dioxide (CO_2) is blown through the core for approximately 20–25 seconds. The core is then hard enough for handling and may be inserted directly into the mould without baking. If the core is to be stored it should be kept in a low-temperature oven as a safeguard against moisture attack.

Small cores require reinforcing with rods or wire to give the desired strength. Long slender cores may need additional support achieved by placing 'chaplets' in the mould. These chaplets remain in the casting, any projections being cut off when casting is fettled. Stalks of chaplets should be rough so that the metal grips, and they should be galvanised to prevent the possibility of rusting which could cause blowholes.

Cores require venting to allow the gases generated to escape. Vents may be formed by embedding waxed string in core during ramming-up. When the core is baked the wax melts; the string can be withdrawn leaving a hole which provides a passage for the exit of gases. Alternatively while the core is still in the core box a vent wire can be inserted and withdrawn leaving a clear passage through the core.

Making a Two-part Mould (Hollow Casting)

Fig. 2(a) shows a casting in the form of a flanged cylinder with a central boss. Such a casting would require a split pattern and a core box. To illustrate the function of a loose piece the pattern has been deliberately split on the selected centre-line as shown in Fig. 2(b).

After the pattern and core box are delivered to the foundry the operations are as follows:—

1. Bottom half of pattern, Fig. 2(d), rammed-up in drag. Method as in previous example.

2. Drag inverted and top half of pattern located. Fit cope and ram-up with conical wooden plugs in position, as shown in Fig. 2(e). Vent cope.

3. Sand core made with aid of core box. Fig. 2(c).

4. Remove cope, rap pattern sections, and withdraw from both drag and cope. Withdraw loose piece from drag; cut feed-gate as shown in plan view Fig. 2(f). Insert core in the core-print locations in mould.

5. Locate cope on drag, and lock in position. Place pouring bush in position; mould now ready for pouring. Fig. 2(g). Casting as removed from mould shown in Fig. 2(h).

   Note. Facing and parting sand used in operations 1 and 2 as in previous example.

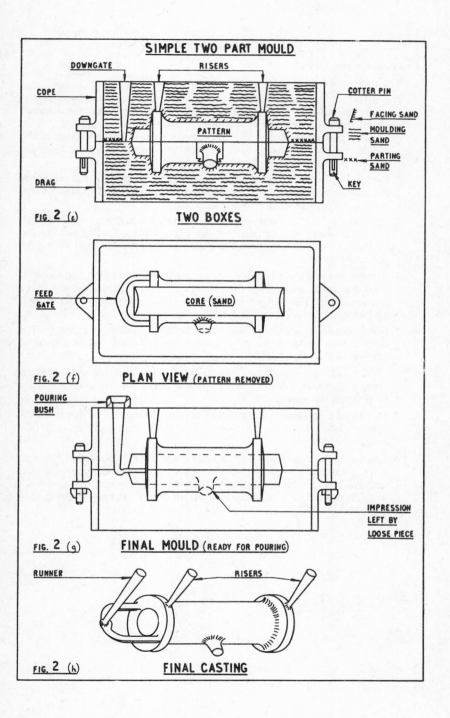

SIMPLE TWO PART MOULD

DOWNGATE   RISERS

COPE

COTTER PIN

FACING SAND

MOULDING SAND

PARTING SAND

PATTERN

DRAG

KEY

FIG. 2 (e)   TWO BOXES

FEED GATE

CORE (SAND)

FIG. 2 (f)   PLAN VIEW (PATTERN REMOVED)

POURING BUSH

IMPRESSION LEFT BY LOOSE PIECE

FIG. 2 (g)   FINAL MOULD (READY FOR POURING)

RUNNER   RISERS

FIG. 2 (h)   FINAL CASTING

Common Casting Defects

The most common casting defects include the following:—

1. Blowholes; these are cavities in the casting that may not be apparent when the casting is visually examined. Often blowholes are detected when metal is removed by machining, e.g. facing or boring.
   Blowholes may be due to several causes, e.g. insufficient venting of the mould preventing escape of trapped gas and steam, excessive moisture content in the mould, or faulty composition of the metal.

2. Porosity; porous sections may prevent the casting being liquid or pressure proof, resulting in its rejection. Porosity is due to faulty composition of the metal or inclusions of dirt.

3. Sponginess; the problem of spongy metal is usually associated with heavy sections in a casting that have been inadequately fed during pouring. Often this problem can be solved by an additional riser over the heavy section.

4. Scabbiness; scabs are rough spots on the casting caused by portions of sand that break away from the mould cavity and adhere to the surface of the casting. The two main causes are faulty ramming of the mould, and incorrect pouring of the metal.

5. Hard Spots, which cause serious difficulties during machining of a casting, may be due to incorrect composition of the metal, or too rapid cooling of thin sections.

6. Cold Shuts are caused when two streams of metal in the mould fail to completely unite, and may be due to pouring at too low a temperature or pouring too slowly.

7. Displaced Cores; any movement of the core in the mould due to slackness or poor locations will result in a faulty casting, having a thin section on one side.

8. Cracks; these may develop in castings if the metal is poured at too high a temperature or into too hard a mould. The most common cause is uneven rates of cooling, especially at intersections where thin and thick sections meet. The uneven cooling sets up internal stresses in the casting and these if of sufficient magnitude will cause fracture.

CHAPTER ELEVEN

DIE CASTING

Die casting is a method of producing castings from a few grams to 50 kg in mass, by pouring or injecting molten metal into a metal mould or die. The two basic methods are:—

1. *Gravity Die Casting*

Molten metal poured by gravity feed into a permanent metal mould.

2. *Pressure Die Casting*

Molten metal forced or injected into a permanent metal mould under pressure which varies between $0 \cdot 7$–175 MN/m^2 (7–1750 bars) according to the type of alloy being cast and type of casting unit employed.

Die casting is essentially a process for large-quantity production: the metal moulds are expensive to make, and in the pressure die-casting process a special casting machine is required. If the quantities of castings required justify the initial costs involved these methods may give a much cheaper and more accurate product than the sand casting process. The minimum number of castings to make the process an economic one is seldom less than 500 for the gravity process, and 2000 or more for the pressure process, but many factors must be taken into account when trying to establish an accurate minimum figure for any specific casting.

Gravity Die Casting Process Fig. 1

Molten metal at the correct temperature is poured from a ladle under gravity feed into a split metal die usually made from cast iron which possesses the following advantages:—

1. It resists the erosive action of high-melting-point alloys.
2. It is relatively cheap.
3. It can be sand cast to approximate size and shape.
4. It is fairly easy to machine to final dimensions.

These dies are usually made in two halves with a vertical parting face, and hinged to facilitate opening, core drawing, and ejection of casting, factors which promote higher output rates. Runner and riser channels are used as in sand casting to provide a head of metal to feed the casting during solidification. The shape and angle of inclination of these runner channels is selected to minimise turbulence; in some cases the dies are tilted by suitable trunions at commencement of pouring and gradually brought back to the horizontal as the cavity fills. Pouring is normally confined to a single entry to reduce the possibility of entrapped air through the convergence of two or more streams of molten metal. The main factor determining the rate of production is the time required to cool the runner and risers.

Dies are usually coated by painting or spraying with a refractory material, e.g. french chalk, graphite, or powdered asbestos; this protects the die surface from erosive action of the hot metal and also prevents the chilling effect.

Pre-heating of the die surfaces is carried out with the aid of a gas torch before commencing a run of castings; after a number of castings have been poured the dies can be maintained at the desired temperatures by heat from the molten metal itself. In some cases additional heating may be necessary in order to maintain correct die temperature; when casting larger components it may be necessary to cool the dies between pouring to prevent over-heating.

Venting is provided by the riser opening and by shallow grooves cut in the die faces.

Advantages of Gravity Die Casting

1. Gravity die castings are generally superior in structure and strength to both sand castings and pressure die castings.
2. Thick wall sections can be produced free from porosity, hence the method is suitable for highly stressed components.
3. Wide range of castings in both size and mass (maximum mass 55 kg).
4. Wider range of aluminium alloys can be used.
5. Sand cores may be used in addition to metal cores.
6. Gravity die casting is quicker and more consistent than sand casting.
7. Surface finish and dimensional accuracy better than sand castings but not as good as pressure die casting.
8. Castings can be heat-treated.

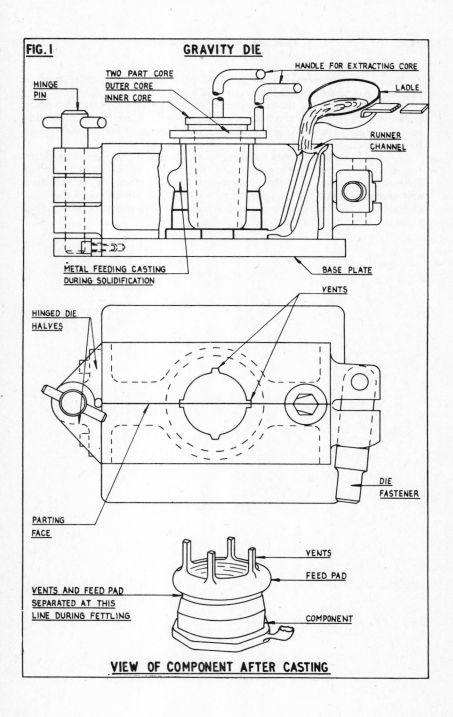

FIG. I

GRAVITY DIE

HANDLE FOR EXTRACTING CORE

TWO PART CORE
OUTER CORE
INNER CORE

HINGE
PIN

LADLE

RUNNER
CHANNEL

METAL FEEDING CASTING
DURING SOLIDIFICATION

BASE PLATE

VENTS

HINGED DIE
HALVES

DIE
FASTENER

PARTING
FACE

VENTS

FEED PAD

VENTS AND FEED PAD
SEPARATED AT THIS
LINE DURING FETTLING

COMPONENT

VIEW OF COMPONENT AFTER CASTING

Collapsible Metal Cores

When a component has complicated or undercut sections it may be necessary to use collapsible metal cores.

Fig. 2(a) illustrates the principle as applied to an internal combustion engine piston, the core comprising of three pieces. After solidification the centre wedge is removed, giving the necessary clearance for the side pieces to be withdrawn. Fig. 2(b).

A more complicated core might consist of seven or eight separate pieces for removal purposes They facilitate the production of many undercut sections, but should be avoided where possible on account of the high tool and operation costs. Fig. 3 illustrates how a change in design could eliminate the need for a collapsible core, and yet provide a component satisfactory from the functional aspect.

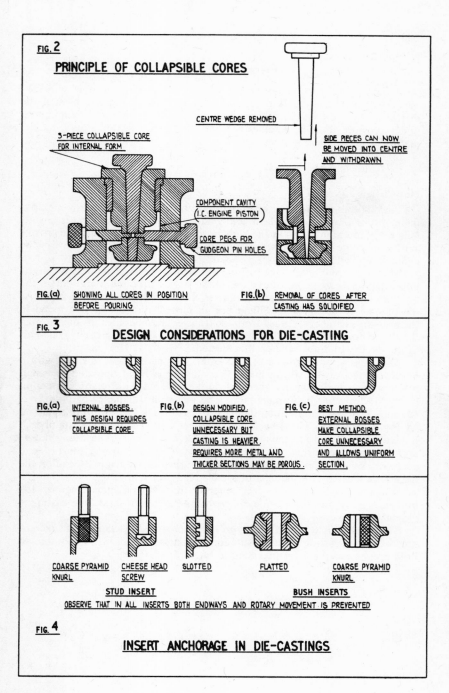

FIG. 2

PRINCIPLE OF COLLAPSIBLE CORES

CENTRE WEDGE REMOVED

3-PIECE COLLAPSIBLE CORE
FOR INTERNAL FORM

SIDE PIECES CAN NOW
BE MOVED INTO CENTRE
AND WITHDRAWN

COMPONENT CAVITY
(I.C. ENGINE PISTON)

CORE PEGS FOR
GUDGEON PIN HOLES

FIG.(a)   SHOWING ALL CORES IN POSITION
BEFORE POURING

FIG.(b)   REMOVAL OF CORES AFTER
CASTING HAS SOLIDIFIED

FIG. 3

DESIGN CONSIDERATIONS FOR DIE-CASTING

FIG.(a)   INTERNAL BOSSES.
THIS DESIGN REQUIRES
COLLAPSIBLE CORE.

FIG.(b)   DESIGN MODIFIED.
COLLAPSIBLE CORE
UNNECESSARY BUT
CASTING IS HEAVIER.
REQUIRES MORE METAL AND
THICKER SECTIONS MAY BE POROUS.

FIG. (c)   BEST METHOD.
EXTERNAL BOSSES
MAKE COLLAPSIBLE
CORE UNNECESSARY
AND ALLOWS UNIFORM
SECTION.

COARSE PYRAMID
KNURL

CHEESE HEAD
SCREW

SLOTTED

FLATTED

COARSE PYRAMID
KNURL

STUD INSERT

BUSH INSERTS

OBSERVE THAT IN ALL INSERTS BOTH ENDWAYS AND ROTARY MOVEMENT IS PREVENTED

FIG. 4

INSERT ANCHORAGE IN DIE-CASTINGS

Pressure Die Casting

A die casting machine consists essentially of an injection unit with self-contained metal-melting facilities and a press for opening and closing the dies. The injection system fills the dies with molten metal and maintains it under pressure until it solidifies. As the die opens ejection pins eject the casting. The two basic systems are:—

(a) Hot-chamber process.

(b) Cold-chamber process.

Hot-Chamber Process

Fig. 5 shows a typical hot-chamber injection unit suitable for low-melting-temperature alloys, e.g. tin, lead, and zinc-base alloys. This system is unsuitable for aluminium alloys as the higher melting temperatures and the erosive action upon the ferrous pressure unit quickly result in a seizure between the cylinder and plunger.

Molten metal is held in the melting pot heated by gas or oil jets. When the injector plunger is raised above the filling port C, molten metal enters the pressure chamber A and fills the transfer chamber B to a common level. As the plunger D descends the filling port is closed, and the molten metal in the pressure chamber is forced from the transfer chamber into the die through the filling nozzle E. After the metal has solidified in the die cavity, one-half of the die is withdrawn and casting ejected.

The melting pot is made of cast iron, and the cylinder is fitted with a hardened-steel heat-resisting liner. The plunger is hand operated on small machines and hydraulically operated on large machines. Pressures range up to 14 MN/m² (140 bars) maximum. The maximum diameter of plunger is 100 mm, hence a limitation on the mass of castings possible with this system.

Fig. 6 shows the 'Gooseneck' hot-chamber unit. The pressure chamber A is pivoted at B and is oscillated by a crank mechanism. The filling nozzle dips beneath the surface of the molten metal, thus charging the pressure chamber. When the pressure chamber is returned to its original position the die nozzle locates with the inlet of the die ready for filling.

When air pressure is applied directly into the pressure chamber the molten metal is forced into the die cavity. After solidification the casting is ejected and the cycle is repeated.

This method is confined mainly to the zinc-base alloys, and is not recommended when casting requires subsequent machining, or when required to hold pressure as these castings tend to be porous.

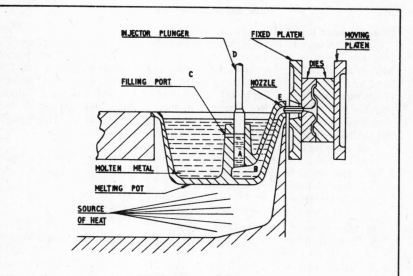

INJECTOR PLUNGER

FIXED PLATEN

MOVING PLATEN

D

FILLING PORT

C

DIES

NOZZLE

E

A

B

MOLTEN METAL

MELTING POT

SOURCE OF HEAT

FIG. 5

HOT CHAMBER PRESSURE DIE-CASTING MACHINE

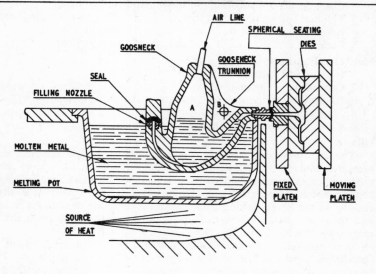

AIR LINE

SPHERICAL SEATING

GOOSNECK

DIES

GOOSENECK TRUNNION

SEAL

FILLING NOZZLE

A

B

MOLTEN METAL

MELTING POT

FIXED PLATEN

MOVING PLATEN

SOURCE OF HEAT

HOT CHAMBER 'GOOSENECK' PRESSURE DIE-CASTING MACHINE

FIG. 6

Cold-Chamber Process Fig. 7

In this process the metal is melted in an independent graphite-lined melting pot. The injection cylinder A is attached to the die through a fixed platen. Molten metal sufficient for one casting plus excess for the runner is ladled by hand and poured through pouring slot B; the hydraulically operated plunger C advances and forces the metal into the die cavity and maintains it under pressure until it solidifies. The die is then opened and plunger further advanced to clear the runner slug from the injection cylinder. This process has the following advantages over the hot-chamber process:—

   (i) Pressure chamber not suspended in molten metal.

  (ii) Higher pressures are permissible (15 to 150 MN/m^2, 150–1500 bars).

 (iii) Hot metal only in momentary contact with injection cylinder therefore not contaminated with iron.

 (iv) Particularly suitable for the aluminium alloys.

  (v) Castings of good mechanical properties produced.

Main Advantages of Pressure Die Casting

1. Castings dimensionally accurate, and machining is minimised or completely eliminated.
2. High-production rates giving a cheap component. Fully automatic machines may give an output of 1000 shots per hour when casting lead and zinc alloys. Typical figures for general work 50–200 shots per hour.
3. Permanent mould.
4. Components are consistent in quality and surface finish.
5. Thinner wall sections than those possible with gravity or sand castings.
6. Inserts, bushes, and studs may be cast in position. Fig. 4.
7. Lettering etc., gear teeth, and threads readily produced.

Main Disadvantages

1. Initial cost of the die.
2. Cost of die maintenance.
3. Range of casting materials is limited (no ferrous metals).
4. Maximum size and mass of casting is limited.
5. Cores must be made in metal.

Dies

The dies must be massively constructed to withstand the high casting pressures. The material is usually alloy steel, hardened and tempered chrome-tungsten, or chrome-molybdenum, to withstand the alternating heating and cooling which causes cracks on the die surfaces. For smaller quantities of castings in the lower-melting-point alloys the dies may be made in hardened and tempered plain carbon steel. Cores are usually made from the same material as the die.

Dies are vented by means of shallow grooves cut in the joint faces (maximum depth 0·18 mm). The design of the die is a specialist job, and requires close co-operation between designer of the component and designer of the die. Designs fall into three main classes:—

1. Single impression, giving one component per cycle.
2. Multiple impression, giving many identical component per cycle.
3. Combination Dies, i.e. dies carrying several impressions of different components.

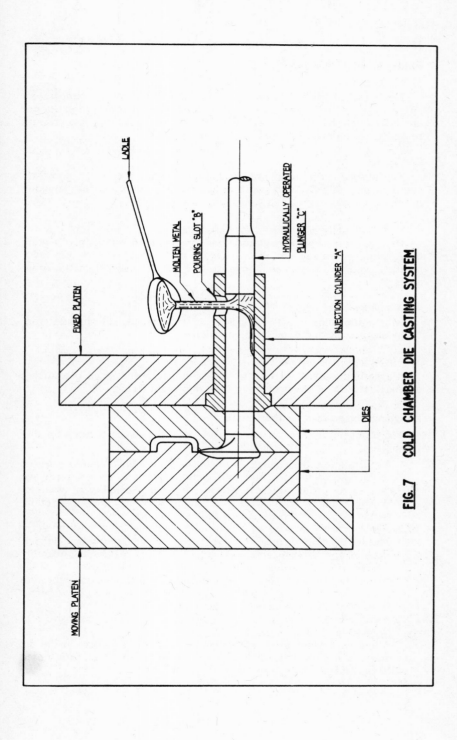

LADLE

MOLTEN METAL

POURING SLOT "B"

HYDRAULICALLY OPERATED
PLUNGER "C"

INJECTION CYLINDER "A"

FIXED PLATEN

DIES

MOVING PLATEN

FIG. 7   COLD CHAMBER DIE CASTING SYSTEM

Materials suitable for Die Casting

1. Lead-base alloys

Lead alloyed with copper, tin, and antimony, melting temperature approximately 330°C. These alloys possess good die casting properties but are heavy and have poor mechanical properties. Used for low-pressure bearings, fire-extinguisher parts, and ornamental metal work.

2. Tin-base alloys

Tin alloyed with antimony, lead, and copper, melting temperature approximately 250°C. Used for bearings, metallic packing rings, milking machines and separators, and surgical apparatus.

3. Zinc-base alloys

High-purity zinc with small additions of aluminium and copper, melting temperature approximately 380°C. Used for motor-car fittings, e.g. door handles, window fittings, radiator grills, and also for many domestic appliances.

4. Aluminium-base alloys

Aluminium alloyed with copper, zinc, magnesium, silicon, and iron. Many engineering and domestic applications.

5. Magnesium-base alloys

Magnesium alloyed with up to 10% aluminium and small percentages of zinc. Used where mass reduction is an important factor.

Designing Components for Die Casting

The following features should be avoided in the design of parts for die-casting:—

1. Avoid appreciable change in thickness of sections; uneven rates of cooling between thick and thin sections produce uneven shrinkage causing distortion, internal stresses, and the possibility of fracture. When variation in thickness is essential, generous fillets or ribbing should be provided between the different sections.
2. Avoid all sharp corners; molten metal has a tendency to burn the sharp edges of the die and cores, and these become ragged, resulting in difficult ejection and distorted castings. Internal sharp corners considerably increase risk of cracking, particularly with shrinkage alloys.
3. Avoid parallel side walls; on cooling the casting shrinks on to the core and difficulty will be experienced in ejection. A minimum draught angle of 5 mm per metre should be provided.
4. Avoid recesses and undercuts; collapsible cores are expensive and slow down production rates.
5. Avoid sunken letters or markings on the castings; letters in the die are far more conveniently stamped or engraved, and then form raised letters on the casting.

CHAPTER TWELVE

PRECISION CASTING

Precision casting, investment casting, and the lost-wax process, are various names given to the process by which small intricate castings can be produced to a high grade of dimensional accuracy and surface finish in materials which prove difficult or impossible to cast and subsequently machine by the more traditional methods, e.g. :—

1. Castings in the heat-resisting nickel alloys as used for gas-turbine components, accurately cast leaving a grinding allowance only for machined surfaces.

2. Components whose shape would prove extremely difficult to produce by normal machining techniques.

The principle of the process is a very old one, and has been in use in the jewellery and dental trades for many years but only adapted to the engineering industry since about 1942 and is under constant development and improvement.

Basically this casting process involves the use of a heat-disposable wax pattern which is invested with refractory material forming a mould (or shell). After the wax pattern has been melted out of the mould, the molten metal for the casting is poured into the pre-heated mould. Upon cooling the mould is broken open, the casting is removed, fettled, and then subjected to rigid inspection procedures.

Main Stages in the Process

Method No. 1. Flask Moulding (using a sand and cement mould) Fig. 1

1. *Make Die for Wax Pattern*

Make a steel or low-melting-point alloy die, having an internal cavity of the same shape as the component required; appropriate contraction allowances must be incorporated in the die dimensions. The cavity surfaces must be smooth and highly polished as the accuracy and finish of the casting is dependant upon this. These dies are usually made in a number of sections in order that they can be quickly and conveniently dismantled to extract the wax pattern without damage.

2. *Make Wax Pattern*

Die cavity is lightly coated with oil, soap solution, or ethyl-silicate to prevent wax sticking; the die is closed and molten wax is injected under pressure forcing it into all parts of the cavity, giving a clean well-defined pattern. Special wax-injection machines are used for this, operating at injection pressures of $0 \cdot 35$ to $0 \cdot 7$ MN/m² ($3 \cdot 5$ to 7 bars) and injection temperatures of 50–90°C according to the type of wax.

3. *Storing Wax Pattern*

Wax pattern is extracted from the metal die and stored in a plaster-of-paris die; this prevents distortion of the wax during subsequent cooling and transportation.

4. *Attach Wax Runner to Pattern*

Runners are made in low-melting-point metal moulds from used wax, i.e. wax run out of previous moulds. The runner is attached to the pattern or patterns by hand, the joining surfaces being softened by means of electrically heated knives. If the component is small several wax patterns may be attached to the same runner, thus saving time and moulding space. The number of patterns in one set-up is governed by size of mould and metal capacity of the casting furnace. The runner is necessary to give a passage for the molten metal and also to provide a head of metal during solidification of the casting.

5. *Attach Metal Base-plate*

A threaded steel insert is moulded into the base of the wax runner; this locates a metal base-plate and an eye-bolt.

6. *Fine Investment*

Wax assembly is now given a smooth highly refractory coating by dipping or spraying with fine liquid refractory material (alumina with sodium silicate, ethyl-silicate, or silica sol as binding agents). This coating is only about $0 \cdot 10$ to $0 \cdot 13$ mm thick. The inside of this coating forms the cavity surface of the mould after wax has been melted out, and thus gives surface finish to casting.

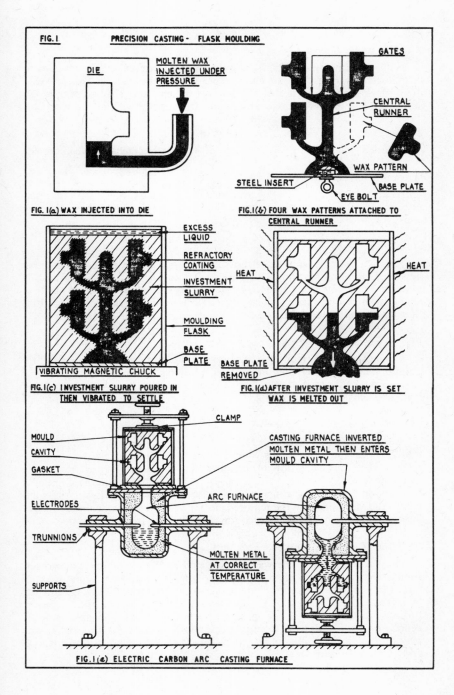

FIG. I   PRECISION CASTING - FLASK MOULDING

DIE

MOLTEN WAX INJECTED UNDER PRESSURE

GATES

CENTRAL RUNNER

WAX PATTERN

STEEL INSERT   BASE PLATE

EYE BOLT

FIG. I(a) WAX INJECTED INTO DIE

FIG. I(b) FOUR WAX PATTERNS ATTACHED TO CENTRAL RUNNER

EXCESS LIQUID

REFRACTORY COATING

INVESTMENT SLURRY

MOULDING FLASK

BASE PLATE

VIBRATING MAGNETIC CHUCK

HEAT   HEAT

BASE PLATE REMOVED

FIG. I(c) INVESTMENT SLURRY POURED IN THEN VIBRATED TO SETTLE

FIG. I(d) AFTER INVESTMENT SLURRY IS SET WAX IS MELTED OUT

CLAMP

MOULD CAVITY

GASKET

ELECTRODES

TRUNNIONS

SUPPORTS

CASTING FURNACE INVERTED MOLTEN METAL THEN ENTERS MOULD CAVITY

ARC FURNACE

MOLTEN METAL AT CORRECT TEMPERATURE

FIG. I(e) ELECTRIC CARBON ARC CASTING FURNACE

7. *Stucco with Coarse Refractory*

While fine investment is still damp, a coarse refractory such as silica sand cr molochite (high aluminium clay) is sprinkled on the surface. This prevents quick drying and cracking of the fine investment and also gives a rough surface to key into the next coating and subsequently with mould material.

8. *Air Dried*

Invested pattern assembly is hung on overhead conveyor and air dried.

9. *Repeat Investment*

After water-proofing the fine investment and stucco processes are repeated to build up a thicker coating. Assembly is air dried again and then taken by conveyor to the mould room.

10. *Make Mould*

Remove eye-bolt from pattern assembly. Locate base plate on magnetic chuck of vibrating machine. Open-ended wax-coated steel moulding flask is placed over the top and sealed to base-plate with molten wax. Mould material in the form of a refractory slurry is poured in until the mould flask is full. Slurry consists of sand and cement with water binder.

11. *Vibrating*

Mould flask is vibrated; this removes trapped air and packs slurry tightly around the wax pattern (equivalent to ramming in sand casting process). Excess liquid rises to the top and when mould has set (approx. 24 hours) this is poured off.

12. *Wax Removal*

After removal of base-plate, the mould is placed in a low-temperature-oven runner end downwards, and heated to approximately 140°C. Wax pattern melts and runs out through the runner channel into a tray. (This wax contaminated with sand, etc. is not suitable for making new patterns but is used for making runners.) Thus there is now a cavity in the solid mould the same shape as the required casting. The wax coating on the mould flask also melts giving a clearance for easy removal from the mould.

13. *High-Temperature Oven*

Only about 85% of the wax is recovered in the low-temperature oven, some being retained on mould surface by surface tension and some soaking into the mould. The mould is now baked and this residual wax is removed by gradually heating to 1000°C. This operation is carried out in a conveyor furnace (gas), the mould taking about $4\frac{1}{2}$ hours to pass through. Rate of heating must be fairly slow as mould is a poor conductor of heat and cracks may appear due to differential expansion. The entry temperature is 250°C and exit temperature 1000°C.

14. *Casting*

The hot mould is removed from the exit end of the conveyor furnace, and is immediately clamped to the casting furnace, the runner channel coinciding with the crucible outlet. The whole arrangement is then inverted so that molten metal runs into the mould. The casting furnace is generally a 12 kVA electric carbon-arc indirect type. $2 \cdot 5$–10 kg capacity. Air pressure of 35–70 kN/m^2 ($0 \cdot 35$–$0 \cdot 7$ bars) is used to force metal throughout cavity. (Inverting process opens air valve to give pressure.) Sufficient metal is melted for one mould only, the quantity being carefully weighed before placing in the furnace. Typical metal charge is in the form of 10 mm diameter bar in 50 mm lengths.

15. *Solidify*

Mould is removed from the casting furnace and placed on foundry floor and is allowed to cool. After solidification, the mould is broken open and the casting extracted. The broken-up mould can be crushed and used again with a percentage of new mould material.

16. *Fettle*

Runners are cut away with the aid of thin elastic grinding wheels, and the casting is sand or shot blast and dressed in the usual way.

17. *Inspection*

The finished castings are subjected to rigid inspection procedure to ensure that they are metallurgically sound, and uniform in quality of surface finish and dimensional accuracy.

Method No. 2. Investment Shell Moulding (using a ceramic-shell mould) Fig. 2

In this method a comparatively thin ceramic shell forms the mould instead of the heavy sand and cement type described in the previous method. The first eight operations apply equally to both methods therefore only the operations subsequent to number eight will be explained:—

1–8. *As Method No. 1*

9. *Repeat Investment*

The fine investment, stucco process, and the air drying are repeated three to six times to give the required thickness of shell. Final thickness is between 3–6 mm depending on type of casting required.

10. *Make Sand Base*

After removal of base-plate, place wax-pattern runner end downwards on a recessed wooden template. Ram core sand around base of pattern to form a flange; blow CO_2 through sand—this hardens it (equivalent to CO_2 method used when core-making in sand foundry).

11. *Wax Removal*

Place invested pattern on conveyor table of a hot-sand-injection machine. Locating from hardened-sand flange, place a mild-steel flask around pattern assembly, and fill flask with hot sand at 300°C. As flask moves along the conveyor, the wax pattern melts due to the heat from the hot sand, and is collected on shallow metal trays. The sand is poured off and hollow moulding shell removed.

12. *High-Temperature Oven*

The hollow moulding shell is heated to 1000°C.

13. *Casting*

Hollow shell is attached to casting furnace and clamped in position, casting unit is inverted, and molten metal runs into shell.

14. *Solidify*

Hollow shell is removed from casting unit and allowed to cool. Break open shell and extract casting.

15. *Fettle*

Fettle casting: runners are cut off with elastic grinding wheel and casting cleaned.

16. *Inspection*

Inspection procedure as in method No. 1.

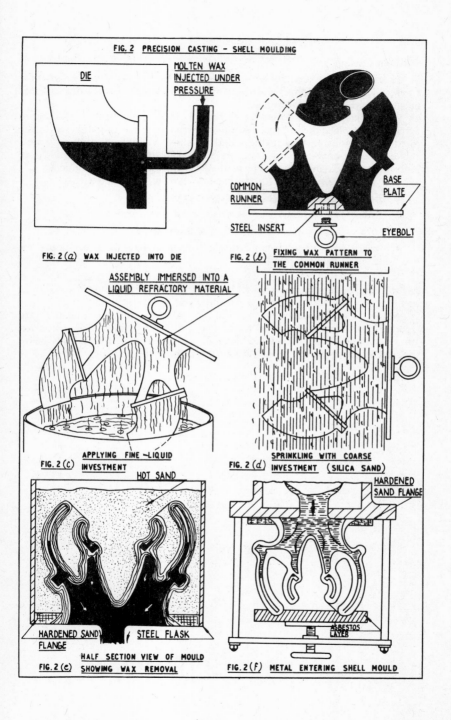

FIG. 2 PRECISION CASTING - SHELL MOULDING

FIG. 2 (a) WAX INJECTED INTO DIE

DIE

MOLTEN WAX INJECTED UNDER PRESSURE

FIG. 2 (b) FIXING WAX PATTERN TO THE COMMON RUNNER

COMMON RUNNER

BASE PLATE

STEEL INSERT

EYEBOLT

FIG. 2 (c) APPLYING FINE ~LIQUID INVESTMENT

ASSEMBLY IMMERSED INTO A LIQUID REFRACTORY MATERIAL

FIG. 2 (d) SPRINKLING WITH COARSE INVESTMENT (SILICA SAND)

FIG. 2 (e) HALF SECTION VIEW OF MOULD SHOWING WAX REMOVAL

HOT SAND

HARDENED SAND FLANGE

STEEL FLASK

FIG. 2 (f) METAL ENTERING SHELL MOULD

HARDENED SAND FLANGE

ASBESTOS LAYER

Vacuum Casting

Precision casting techniques are being developed constantly in an attempt to provide castings of improved mechanical properties, with close dimensional accuracy and good surface finish.

One very important development recently is the introduction of vacuum furnaces to replace the indirect carbon-arc furnaces previously referred to for melting and pouring the casting metal or alloy. Vacuum casting may well prove to be the answer to the designers' request for castings whose strength at high temperature can exceed that of the best-known wrought products.

The advantages claimed for the vacuum-casting technique are:—

1. The formation of oxides and nitrides is minimised.

2. Undesirable impurities are removed by evaporation.

3. More consistent melt composition and properties.

4. New alloys with high-temperature properties have been developed by means of vacuum melting.

Vacuum-casting furnaces vary in both capacity and design. Indirect carbon-arc vacuum furnaces of 12 kg nominal capacity are used, sometimes grouped in pairs with a common pumping station.

Much larger furnaces up to 180 kg capacity, induction-heated, are operated on a semi-continuous basis. The hot flasks or shells are positioned on a turntable which is rotated through a vacuum seal, the moulds being indexed at the appropriate time under the furnace for pouring.

CHAPTER THIRTEEN

FORGING

The forging process is another long-established metal-working technique which can be briefly defined as the art of manipulating metals by means of hammering, squeezing, or bending, after they have been heated to the plastic condition.

All metals exhibit a 'grain-flow' or fibre to a greater or lesser degree. Castings have a crystalline structure due to the progressive solidification by crystal growth from the outside surface of the mould. Rolled bar possesses a grain-flow which follows the direction of rolling. For many engineering applications a casting made in iron or in a non-ferrous alloy is entirely satisfactory; many other components are machined from standard rolled bars or plates, both methods being more economical than forging.

In other cases where the function of a component calls for maximum strength and resistance to shock loading and vibration a forging is essential The forged product is superior in mechanical properties to either the casting or the rolled material, the main difference being the increased toughness and impact strength.

The main effects of forging are threefold:—

1. Welds up shrinkage cavities in the cast ingot.

2. Causes plastic flow resulting in a more uniform homogenous mass of metal.

3. Deformation of the original cast or rolled structure is accompanied by the formation of a new characteristic structure or fibre. This fibre is arranged to give maximum strength in the desired direction; usually it follows the contour of the component.

Note. Large forgings are produced from one or more ingots Small and medium-size forgings are made from hot-rolled blooms, billets, or bars.

Examples illustrating the effect of forging on the grain-flow are given in Figs. 1 to 9.

Fig. 1 Standard rolled bar, grain-flow following direction of rolling.

Fig. 2 Standard rolled bar which has been heated uniformly to the forging temperature; followed by hammering (upsetting operation) the new grain-flow or fibre follows the contour of the component.

Fig. 3 Shows a gear blank machined from a piece of standard rolled bar; grain-flow follows direction of rolling. If teeth are cut on this blank they will all be weak because grain-flow is parallel with the root of the teeth.

Fig. 4 Shows a gear blank machined from a piece of rolled plate; if teeth are cut on this blank some would be strong and others weak (with or against grain).

Fig. 5 Shows a forged gear blank made from an up-ended rolled bar; all teeth cut on this blank would have maximum strength due to the arrangement of the grain-flow.

Fig. 6 Shows a crankshaft machined from a rolled billet; the grain-flow is in direction of rolling and will result in weak webs.

Fig. 7 Shows a component produced by forging a rolled bar (bending), grain-flow following contour of the shaft.

Fig. 8 Shows a lifting hook machined from a rolled billet; planes of weakness due to direction of grain-flow.

Fig. 9 Shows a similar lifting hook produced by bending a rolled bar; maximum strength as grain-flow follows the contour.

Methods of Forging

Three methods of forging are practised, namely:—

1. Hand-Forging

Hand-forging covers the manufacture of small and medium-size components required in small quantities, made by means of hand tools and with the aid of small power hammers.

2. Drop-Forging

Drop-forging was introduced to meet the demands of modern mass production, eliminating much of the manual labour associated with hand-forging. The forging is produced by means of a drop-stamp machine and a pair of drop-forging dies.

3. Machine-Forging

Machine-forging is a process developed to give rapid production of certain types of forgings. Such forgings are produced on a continuous motion machine, designed for a particular type of forging. The action of the machine is one of squeezing rather than hammering.

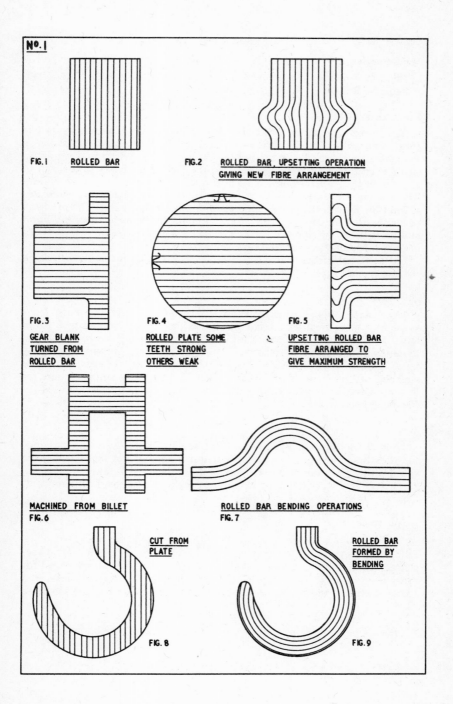

FIG. I   ROLLED BAR

FIG.2   ROLLED BAR, UPSETTING OPERATION
GIVING NEW FIBRE ARRANGEMENT

FIG. 3
GEAR BLANK
TURNED FROM
ROLLED BAR

FIG. 4
ROLLED PLATE SOME
TEETH STRONG
OTHERS WEAK

FIG. 5
UPSETTING ROLLED BAR
FIBRE ARRANGED TO
GIVE MAXIMUM STRENGTH

MACHINED FROM BILLET
FIG. 6

ROLLED BAR BENDING OPERATIONS
FIG. 7

CUT FROM
PLATE

ROLLED BAR
FORMED BY
BENDING

FIG. 8

FIG. 9

Hand-Forging

The main items of equipment and tools essential for hand-forging will include the following:—

Forge Equipment

The forge or hearth in which the smith heats his work is made in various forms and sizes. Fig. 10 shows a typical small-size forge. Combustion is maintained by a supply of air produced by a blower which is driven by a small electric motor. The air is fed into the fuel which burns in the well of the hearth by a water-cooled blast pipe called the 'tuyère' or the 'tue-iron'. The cooling water held in a tank (water bosh) behind the hearth circulates around the nose of the tuyère and prevents it becoming burnt. The products of combustion are led away by natural draught through the overhead hood and on to a flue or chimney stack. The fuel is usually coke breeze, a special coke of a suitable size for the work being forged.

At the front of the hearth a water tank is provided for cooling tools or the workpiece.

The Anvil

A general-purpose single-bick anvil is shown in Fig. 11, made from wrought iron or steel with a hardened steel face, the table and bick being left soft. The anvil is supported on a cast-iron stand as shown, or may be mounted on a massive wooden block let into the floor. Anvils vary in mass up to about 250 kg, but 125–150 kg is a common size; the mass is usually stamped on the front. Two holes are provided in the face, one square for locating tool shanks (hardy hole), and the second circular in shape used for punching operations.

Vice

A steel-leg vice as shown in Fig. 12 is the most useful-type vice for hand-forging work. The leg is usually supported in a floor socket, and much of the shock on the jaws due to heavy hammering or bending is taken by this leg. For lighter type work the smith may use an engineer's vice as shown in Fig. 3, Chapter One.

Swage Block

A swage block is shown in Fig. 13. A rectangular block of cast iron, the four edges carry swage forms or recesses for circular-, hexagonal-, and vee-shaped work, while through the face various-shaped holes are provided for drifting operations. The swage block is mounted on a stand and rests in a recess when flat, and fits into a vertical recess when one of the edges is being used.

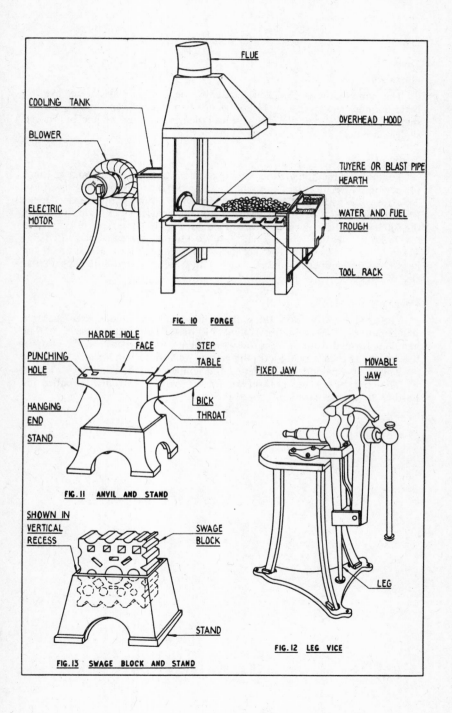

FLUE

COOLING TANK

BLOWER

OVERHEAD HOOD

ELECTRIC
MOTOR

TUYERE OR BLAST PIPE

HEARTH

WATER AND FUEL
TROUGH

TOOL RACK

FIG. 10   FORGE

HARDIE HOLE

FACE

PUNCHING
HOLE

STEP

TABLE

HANGING
END

BICK

STAND

THROAT

FIG. 11   ANVIL AND STAND

FIXED JAW

MOVABLE
JAW

SHOWN IN
VERTICAL
RECESS

SWAGE
BLOCK

LEG

STAND

FIG. 12   LEG VICE

FIG. 13   SWAGE BLOCK AND STAND

Tools:—

Hammers

The hammers most frequently used by the smith or his striker are the hand hammer shown in Fig. 14 and sledge-hammers of various weights and shapes, Fig. 15 shows the double-faced sledge and Fig. 16 the bull-nosed sledge-hammer.

Tongs

To hold and manipulate the hot metal the smith uses a wide range of tongs of varying shapes and sizes. A small selection of these is shown in Figs. 17 to 20. Close Tongs, Fig. 17—the tongs used for holding thin stock. Open-Mouth Tongs, Fig. 18—tongs used for holding heavier stock, gripping along the full length of the jaws. Hollow-Bit Tongs, Fig. 19—the type of tongs used for holding circular-, hexagonal-, and octagonal-shaped stock. Flat-Bar Tongs, Fig. 20—used for holding flat rectangular sections; the lugs on the jaws ensure alignment of stock. Such tongs are made to suit a particular size of bar.

Cold Sets and Hardies Fig. 21

The cold set is a short thick chisel fitted with a handle, used under a sledge-hammer for cutting or nicking cold material in order to sever it. The handle is formed from an iron rod wrapped around a groove in the body of the set, the two ends being left long enough to form a hand-grip.

This tool is made from hardened and tempered carbon steel.

The cold set is often used in conjunction with a bottom tool called the hardie, the shank of which fits into the anvil.

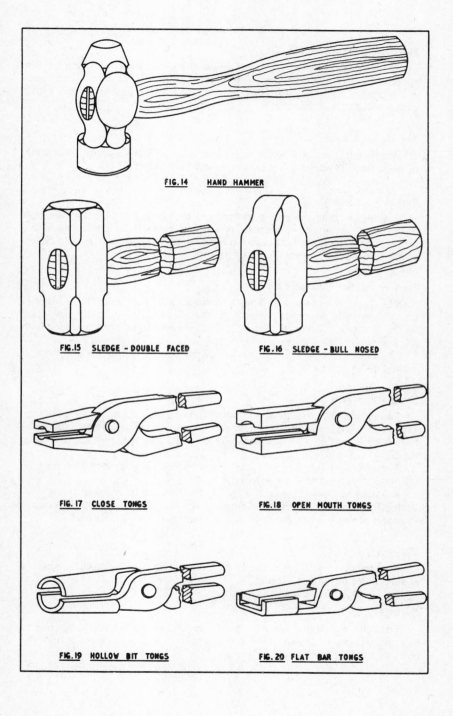

FIG. 14   HAND HAMMER

FIG. 15   SLEDGE - DOUBLE FACED

FIG. 16   SLEDGE - BULL NOSED

FIG. 17   CLOSE TONGS

FIG. 18   OPEN MOUTH TONGS

FIG. 19   HOLLOW BIT TONGS

FIG. 20   FLAT BAR TONGS

Hot Sets and Hardies Fig. 22

The hot set is used for cutting or marking hot material, often used in conjunction with a hardie. Similar in design to the cold set, but not hardened and tempered and having a much smaller angle, it is normally fitted with a wooden shaft like a hammer.

The Gouge Fig. 23

Another form of hot set but possesses a curved cutting edge. A number of these tools of various dimensions would be required.

Fullers Fig. 24

Fullers are made in pairs, the bottom tool fitting into the square hole in the anvil; the top tool has a shaft which is held by the smith. Made in a range of sizes, these tools are used to form shoulders and to reduce thickness of stock as in the drawing-down operation.

Flatters and Set Hammers Fig. 25

The flatter is a tool used to finish or smooth the surface of the work after the approximate shape has been obtained. The work is usually supported on the anvil face, while the flatter resting on top of the work is struck with the sledge-hammer.

The set hammer is a small version of the flatter used to get into corners and confined spaces.

Swages Fig. 26

Swages are used to reduce and finish work to circular or hexagonal form. These tools are made in pairs, the bottom tool supported by the anvil; the top swage is shafted and is normally held by the smith, the striker providing the blow with a sledge-hammer.

The edges of the recesses must be rounded off otherwise fins may be formed resulting in a faulty forging.

A spring swage is shown in Fig. 27, both halves of the tool being connected by a band of spring steel forming the handle. The smith can control this type of swage with one hand and the hammer with the other.

Punches Fig. 28

Punches of various sizes and cross-sections are used to produce roughly shaped holes in the hot forging.

Drifts Fig. 29

The drift is used to finish the roughly punched hole; it has a long taper at one end and a short taper at the other. The drift is driven right through the hole, controlling both size and form.

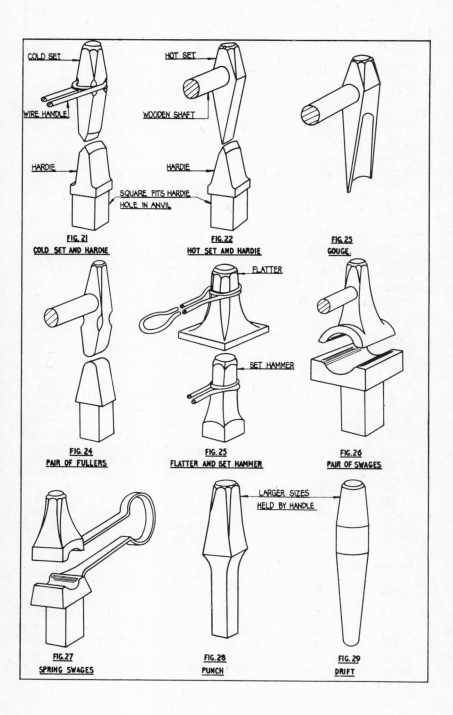

COLD SET

WIRE HANDLE

HARDIE

FIG. 21
COLD SET AND HARDIE

HOT SET

WOODEN SHAFT

HARDIE

SQUARE FITS HARDIE
HOLE IN ANVIL

FIG. 22
HOT SET AND HARDIE

FIG. 23
GOUGE.

FIG. 24
PAIR OF FULLERS

FLATTER

SET HAMMER

FIG. 25
FLATTER AND SET HAMMER

FIG. 26
PAIR OF SWAGES

FIG. 27
SPRING SWAGES

LARGER SIZES
HELD BY HANDLE

FIG. 28
PUNCH

FIG. 29
DRIFT

Hand-Forging Operations

Upsetting

Upsetting, sometimes referred to as jumping up, is a process whereby the hot bar is increased in cross-section while the length is correspondingly decreased. The heated bar may be repeatedly dropped on the anvil, it may be struck with a sledge, or a small bar may be hammered on one end while held in a vice.

The upset may be obtained at any point in the bar. Fig. 30(a) shows the effect when a uniformly heated bar is subjected to heavy blows. Fig. 30(b) indicates the effect when the bar is heated at one end only and is then subjected to end pressure (up-ended). Fig. 30(c) shows the upset obtained when the bar is heated at the centre only.

Drawing Down

Drawing down is a process whereby the hot bar is reduced in width or thickness or both, with a corresponding increase in length. The operation is carried out with the aid of a pair of fullers, followed by using flatters for flat sections, and swages for circular forms. Fig. 31 shows a drawing-down operation; note the reduction is on both sides of the bar.

Setting Down

Setting down is another process which gives a reduction in thickness, but the hot metal is worked from one side only, resulting in a step as shown in Fig. 32.

Bending Fig. 33

Hand-forging frequently involves various types of bending operations. Such bends may be slow or gradual bends, while others are sharp bends. The former type may be made with the aid of special pins located in a suitable plate. Sharp bends may be made in several different ways; over the face or bick of the anvil, over a block held by a shank fitting into the hardie hole, or by holding the metal in a vice. Sometimes special bending fixtures are made in order to produce accurate and uniform types of bends, and pipe bending is often performed in this manner.

Even a simple right-hand bend cannot be obtained by merely hammering the hot metal around the corner of the anvil; the bar will need some preparation before bending. Fig. 34 shows the upsetting operation necessary in order to provide sufficient material to produce a full-section bend.

Punching and Drifting Figs. 28 and 29

Punching is the method used to form holes in hand-forgings. The work is heated to near welding heat, and is supported on a block having a hole slightly larger than that being punched. The appropriate-size tapered punch is driven about two-thirds through the work; this is then turned over and the punch is driven through from the other side. Punching from both sides of the work ensures a fairly parallel hole and prevents undue distortion of the plate.

Having obtained the roughly punched hole, a drift of the desired form is driven through to obtain the final shape and size.

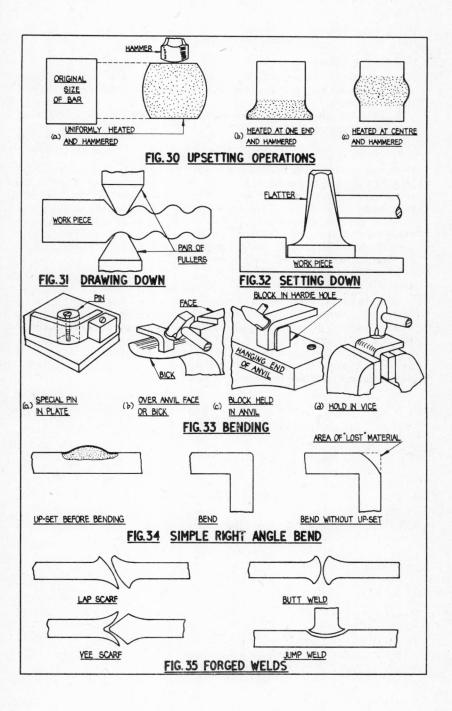

HAMMER

ORIGINAL SIZE OF BAR

(a) UNIFORMLY HEATED AND HAMMERED

(b) HEATED AT ONE END AND HAMMERED

(c) HEATED AT CENTRE AND HAMMERED

FIG.30 UPSETTING OPERATIONS

WORK PIECE

PAIR OF FULLERS

FIG.31 DRAWING DOWN

FLATTER

WORK PIECE

FIG.32 SETTING DOWN

PIN

FACE

BLOCK IN HARDIE HOLE

HANGING END OF ANVIL

BICK

(a) SPECIAL PIN IN PLATE

(b) OVER ANVIL FACE OR BICK

(c) BLOCK HELD IN ANVIL

(d) HOLD IN VICE

FIG.33 BENDING

UP-SET BEFORE BENDING

BEND

AREA OF "LOST" MATERIAL

BEND WITHOUT UP-SET

FIG.34 SIMPLE RIGHT ANGLE BEND

LAP SCARF

BUTT WELD

YEE SCARF

JUMP WELD

FIG.35 FORGED WELDS

Hot-Cutting Fig. 22

Hot-cutting is the process used to remove surplus metal from the forging with the aid of hot chisels or hot sets in conjunction with hand or small power hammers.

Cutting-out, like punching, is usually started from one side of the work and finished from the other.

Forge-Welding

Forge-welding is the operation whereby two separate pieces of metal are united by heating to the plastic condition and hammering them together. In order to obtain a satisfactory weld the joint surfaces must be clean and free from scale. A flux is used to prevent oxide forming on the joint surfaces, and to lower the melting temperature of the scale; the latter can then be more easily expelled from the joint faces during hammering. The most commonly used fluxes include common sand, borax, or borax and sal ammoniac.

Examples of forged welds are shown in Fig. 35.

Example of a Hand-Forging

Fig. 36 shows two methods of hand-forging a tool post key for use on a centre lathe. Method 'A' is used when making the key from flat rolled plate, whereas method 'B' is more suitable if the forging is produced from rolled bar or circular section.

If correctly carried out method 'B' has much to commend it; apart from an obvious saving in material, the upsetting operation gives greater strength to the spanner head due to improved grain-flow.

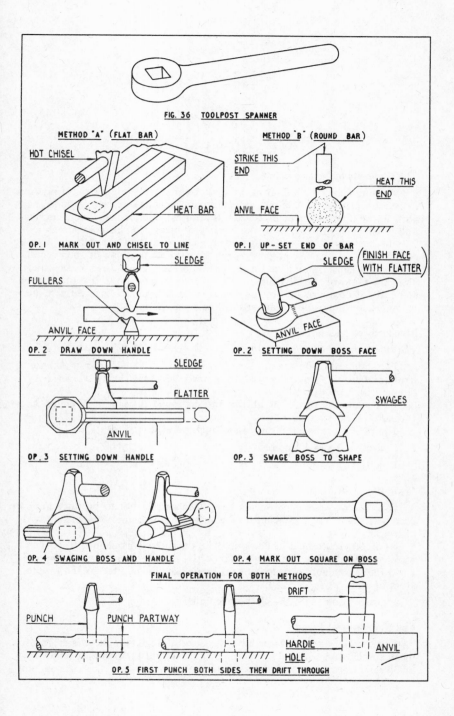

FIG. 36   TOOLPOST SPANNER

METHOD "A" (FLAT BAR)

HOT CHISEL

HEAT BAR

OP. 1   MARK OUT AND CHISEL TO LINE

SLEDGE

FULLERS

ANVIL FACE

OP. 2   DRAW DOWN HANDLE

SLEDGE

FLATTER

ANVIL

OP. 3   SETTING DOWN HANDLE

OP. 4   SWAGING BOSS AND HANDLE

METHOD "B" (ROUND BAR)

STRIKE THIS END

HEAT THIS END

ANVIL FACE

OP. 1   UP-SET END OF BAR

SLEDGE   (FINISH FACE WITH FLATTER)

ANVIL FACE

OP. 2   SETTING DOWN BOSS FACE

SWAGES

OP. 3   SWAGE BOSS TO SHAPE

OP. 4   MARK OUT SQUARE ON BOSS

FINAL OPERATION FOR BOTH METHODS

DRIFT

PUNCH   PUNCH PARTWAY

HARDIE HOLE

ANVIL

OP. 5   FIRST PUNCH BOTH SIDES THEN DRIFT THROUGH

CHAPTER FOURTEEN

MEASUREMENT

The Elements of Measurement

Measurement of components is a vital part of both manufacturing and inspection processes. A large percentage of such measurement is concerned with linear dimensions such as lengths, widths, thicknesses, diameters, etc. and this involves the use of a wide variety of measuring instruments.

The basic principle of linear measurement is that of comparison with a standard of length. The engineer's rule is a simple example of such a comparative measuring standard, the dimension being read by direct observation. The engraving of the divisions on the rule necessitates the use of another standard of comparison, and in turn such standards are indirectly related to the use of an absolute standard of linear measurement.

Standards of Measurement

The International Standard Metre

The standard metre as established by French law consisted of a platinum-irridium bar, the length between two inscribed lines being 1 metre at a temperature of 0°C.

This standard was kept at the International Bureau of Weights and Measures at Sevres near Paris.

The relation between the yard and the metres was:—

1 yard = 0·914 40 metres

1 inch = 25·4 mm

Light Waves as Length Standards

Over recent years experiments have been carried out to produce mono-chromatic light, the wavelengths of which are now being used as standards of length.

At a conference held in Paris in 1960, the metre was defined in terms of wavelengths of light. The legal standard as then stated was 1 metre = 1 650 763·73 vacuum wavelengths of the orange line emitted by the krypton atom of mass 86.

1 yard = 1 509 458·354 712 wavelengths.

End Standards of Length

Commercial line standards have the disadvantage that there is a limit to the accuracy with which they can be produced, and their employment often involves microscopes and other special equipment. For this reason end

276

standards have largely superseded line standards in modern industrial measurements. They are usually in bar or block form having a standard length between the end faces, which are finished accurately flat and parallel to each other. The two most commonly used end standards of length are gauge blocks and end measuring bars, sizes of which are quoted at a standard temperature of 20°C (68°F).

The Micrometer (Fig. 1)

The Micrometer Calliper is an adjustable measuring instrument operated by a very accurate screw which is rotated in a fixed nut, thereby opening or closing the distance between the end face of the fixed anvil and the end face of the adjustable spindle. The workpiece is located between these two faces, and the thimble is turned until the correct contact or "feel" is obtained.

A standard Metric Micrometer possesses a spindle screw of 0·50 mm pitch, thus one complete revolution of the screw will cause the spindle (the unthreaded portion of screw) to move towards or away from the anvil exactly 0·50 mm.

The barrel or sleeve is graduated in millimetres from 0 to 25 mm and each millimetre is sub-divided in 0·50 mm. Therefore it requires two revolutions of the spindle to advance the thimble a distance of 1·0 mm.

The thimble, which is rigidly secured to the spindle, has a bevelled edge graduated in 50 equal divisions, each representing 1/50 of a revolution of the screw which is equal to $1/50 \times 0·50$ mm $= 0·01$ mm.

The method of reading this micrometer is shown in Fig. 2.

The 5 mm graduation is visible on barrel .. .. .. 5·00 mm
One additional 0·50 mm line visible .. .. 0·50 mm
Line "28" on thimble coincides with datum line on barrel:—
    $28 \times 0·01$ mm $= 0·28$ mm .. .. 0·28 mm
                                                    —————
                        Total micrometer reading is .. 5·78 mm
                                                    —————

The metric micrometers have an individual movement of 25·0 mm, and can be obtained in a range of sizes, e.g. 0–25 mm, 25–50 mm, 50–75 mm, 75–100 mm, etc., up to 600 mm.

Inside Micrometer Set

A useful instrument frequently used for measuring holes and other internal dimensions is the inside micrometer. The complete inside micrometer set comprises an adjustable micrometer head, a number of interchangeable extension rods, and a distance piece, as shown in Fig. 3.

The micrometer head has a barrel and thimble graduated in the same manner as the outside micrometer, but its total adjustment is limited to 13 mm. A standard set covers a measuring range of 50–200 mm, the extension rods are arranged in 25 mm increments, the smallest covering 50–63 mm, without the distance pieces; when using the 12 mm distance piece, the same rod covers 63–75 mm range. Five additional extension rods extend the measuring range from 75 mm–200 mm.

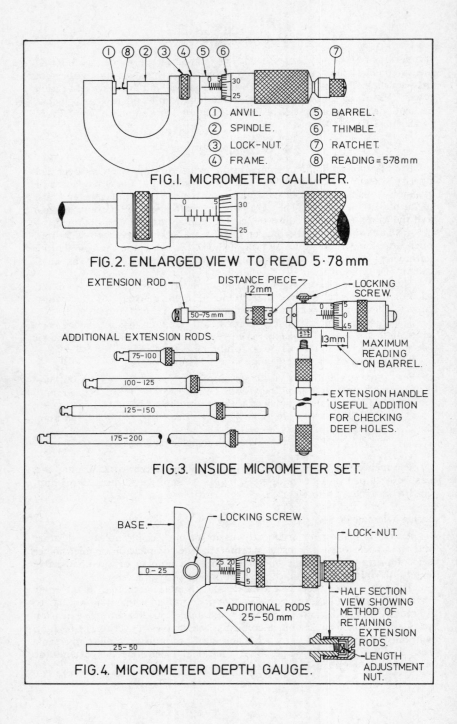

FIG.1. MICROMETER CALLIPER.

① ANVIL.   ⑤ BARREL.
② SPINDLE.   ⑥ THIMBLE.
③ LOCK-NUT.   ⑦ RATCHET.
④ FRAME.   ⑧ READING = 5·78 mm

FIG.2. ENLARGED VIEW TO READ 5·78 mm

EXTENSION ROD

DISTANCE PIECE
12 mm

LOCKING SCREW.

50-75 mm

ADDITIONAL EXTENSION RODS.

75-100
100-125
125-150
175-200

13 mm

MAXIMUM READING ON BARREL.

EXTENSION HANDLE USEFUL ADDITION FOR CHECKING DEEP HOLES.

FIG.3. INSIDE MICROMETER SET.

BASE.

LOCKING SCREW.

LOCK-NUT.

0 - 25

ADDITIONAL RODS 25-50 mm

25-50

HALF SECTION VIEW SHOWING METHOD OF RETAINING EXTENSION RODS.

LENGTH ADJUSTMENT NUT.

FIG.4. MICROMETER DEPTH GAUGE.

Alternative inside micrometer sets are obtainable with an adjustable head giving 25 mm movement, and a sufficient number of extension rods to cover a range of 50 mm–800 mm.

It should be noted that considerable skill and experience is required to use these instruments accurately.

Micrometer Depth Gauge Fig. 4

The micrometer depth gauge consists of a hardened and ground base combined with a micrometer head. The readings are taken exactly as with an outside micrometer except that the barrel graduations·are numbered in the opposite direction. Interchangeable measuring rods, arranged in increments of 25 mm (0–25, 25–50, 50–75 mm range), can be inserted through the micrometer screw and be positively locked by the knurled nut.

The Vernier Scale

The vernier scale was invented by a Frenchman named Pierre Vernier in 1631. It consists of two graduated scales working in conjunction with each other. The main scale is usually fixed, and the vernier scale slides on the main scale.

Various methods of graduating are used, but the two most frequently selected for measuring instruments, e.g. vernier height gauge, vernier calliper, and vernier depth gauge, are the 25-division and 50-division verniers.

25-Division Vernier Scale Fig. 5

The main scale is divided into 1·00 mm and 0·50 mm divisions, each ten whole millimetres is indicated by large figures.

The vernier scale is divided into 25 equal divisions marked 0, 5, 10, 15, 20, 25. These 25 vernier scale divisions occupy the same length as 24·5 mm on the main scale, therefore the value of each division on the vernier scale is equal to $1/25 \times 24·5$ mm $= 49/50$ mm $= 0·98$ mm and the difference between two main scale divisions and one vernier scale division $= 1·0-0·98$ mm $= 0·02$ mm.

To read this instrument, note the reading on the main scale to the left of the zero mark on the vernier scale to the nearest 0·50 mm, then add the number of 1/50 mm (0·02 mm) indicated by the line on the vernier which exactly coincides with a line on the main scale.

Fig. 6 will illustrate the method of reading the 25-division vernier.

(a) Large numbers on main scale	$= 10$ mm	
∴ Number of millimetres shown	$= 3 \times 10$ mm $=$	30·00 mm
(b) Small numbers on main scale	$= 1 \times 7·5$ mm $=$	7·50 mm
(c) Eight divisions on vernier scale	$= 8 \times 0·02$ mm $=$	0·16 mm

Total reading .. 37·66 mm

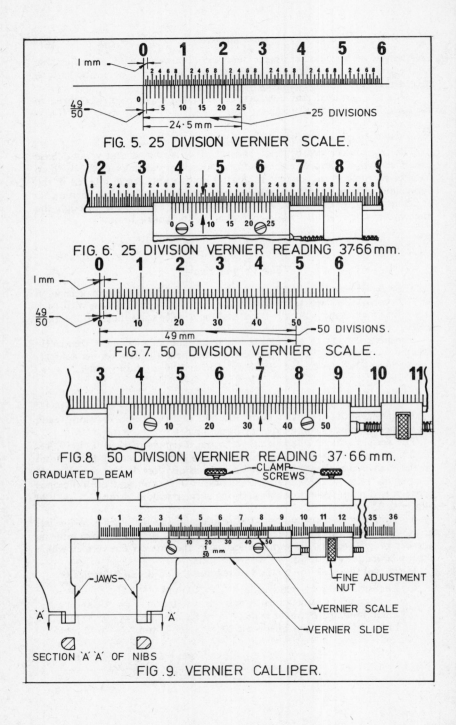

FIG. 5. 25 DIVISION VERNIER SCALE.

FIG. 6. 25 DIVISION VERNIER READING 37·66 mm.

FIG. 7. 50 DIVISION VERNIER SCALE.

FIG.8. 50 DIVISION VERNIER READING 37·66 mm.

FIG. 9. VERNIER CALLIPER.

50-Division Vernier Scale Fig. 7

The main scale is divided into $1 \cdot 0$ mm divisions, each ten millimetres being indicated by large figures.

The vernier scale is divided into 50 equal divisions, occupying the same length as 49 divisions on the main scale, therefore each vernier scale division $= 49/50$ mm $= 0 \cdot 98$ mm, and the difference between one main scale division and a vernier scale division $= 1 \cdot 00 - 0 \cdot 98$ mm $= 0 \cdot 02$ mm.

To read this instrument, note the number of whole millimetres on the main scale to the left of the zero on the vernier scale, then add the number of 1/50 mm ($0 \cdot 02$ mm), indicated by the line on the vernier which exactly coincides with a line on the main scale.

Fig. 8 will illustrate method of reading a 50-division vernier scale

(a) As each large number on main scale $= 10 \cdot 0$ mm

then number shown $= 3 \times 10$ $= 30 \cdot 00$ mm

(b) Additional divisions shown on

main scale $= 7 = 7 \times 1 \cdot 00$ mm $= 7 \cdot 00$ mm

(c) Reading on vernier scale $= 33 = 33 \times 0 \cdot 02$ mm$= 0 \cdot 66$ mm

Total reading .. $37 \cdot 66$ mm

Vernier Calliper Fig. 9

Basically the vernier calliper consists of a stationary member and a movable member. The stationary part is a graduated beam integral with the fixed measuring jaw, hardened, ground, and lapped, made from fine-quality tool steel. The main-scale graduations are engraved on this beam.

The movable part is the vernier-scale assembly, incorporating the movable jaw, the vernier plate with clamping screws, and the fine adjustment nut. The vernier slide is moved as a unit along the beam until both jaws contact the work being measured; the clamp screw over the fine adjusting nut is tightened; the adjusting nut is turned until the jaws engage the work firmly but not too tightly. Clamp screw over the vernier plate is tightened, calliper removed, and reading obtained as previously outlined.

As can be seen from Fig. 9 the inside faces of the two jaws are used to measure outside diameters. The outside edges of the calliper jaws are radiused, and these are used to obtain internal measurements. If the beam carries only one scale then the combined thickness of the two jaws (nibs) must be added to the beam reading when using the instrument for internal dimensions. Often the beam is graduated both sides to provide both outside and inside measurements.

The vernier calliper is a less precise measuring instrument than a micrometer, but it covers a much wider range of measurement, e.g. 0–300 mm.

Vernier Height Gauge Fig. 10

The vernier height gauge like the vernier calliper consists of a stationary and a movable part. The stationary member incorporates a vertical graduated beam securely attached to a substantial base, both beam and base being hardened, ground, and lapped. The beam carries the main scale.

The movable member is a vernier slide assembly which can be raised or lowered to any position along the beam, and is adjusted in hundredths of a millimetre by means of the vernier-plate adjusting nut.

Fig. 10 shows the hardened-steel scriber clamped to the vernier slide, and when the base is located on a machine table or bed, surface plate, or marking-out table, the gauge can be used to mark off vertical distances, locate centre-lines, or check vertical dimensions. By replacing the scriber with other attachments, e.g. dial indicator or depth attachment, the number of applications of the gauge can be considerably increased.

The beam and vernier graduations are usually based on the 50-division vernier scale, giving wider spacing and easier reading than that obtainable with the 25-division system.

Vernier Depth Gauge Fig. 11

The vernier depth gauge differs slightly from the two instruments previously described in that the vernier scale remains fixed while the graduated blade (main scale) is moved to obtain desired measurement in hundredths of a millimetre.

The vernier scale is attached to the hardened and ground base, which is normally held by one hand while the graduated blade is operated by the other. After the blade is brought into contact with the bottom of the slot or recess, the clamp screw adjacent to the fine adjusting nut is locked. The fine adjusting nut is turned to obtain exact measurement and the blade is locked by the vernier-plate clamp screw. The 25-division vernier scale is generally used on this instrument.

Vernier Bevel Protractor Fig. 12

The vernier bevel protractor is a precision instrument for measuring angular surfaces, and is capable of measuring any angle to 1/12 of a degree, i.e. 5 minutes of a degree.

The blade and the graduated protractor dial may be rotated as a unit to any desired position and be locked in place by means of the dial clamp nut. The blade can be moved in either direction lengthwise, and be locked against the dial by tightening the blade clamp nut which operates independently from the dial clamp nut.

The dial is graduated around the entire 360°, reading 0–90; 90–0; 0–90; 90–0°. Each ten degrees is numbered, and each five degrees is indicated by a line longer than those on either side of it.

The vernier plate is graduated in such a way that twelve spaces on the vernier scale occupy the same space as twenty-three divisions on the dial. The vernier plate carries these twelve divisions on each side of the zero line, numbered to read 0–15, –30, –45, –60, each of these four main spaces being again divided into three parts.

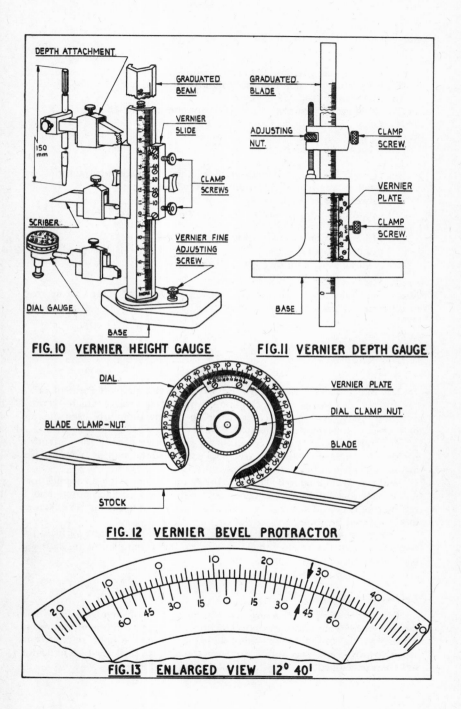

FIG. 10 VERNIER HEIGHT GAUGE

DEPTH ATTACHMENT

GRADUATED BEAM

VERNIER SLIDE

150 mm

CLAMP SCREWS

SCRIBER

VERNIER FINE ADJUSTING SCREW

DIAL GAUGE

BASE

FIG. 11 VERNIER DEPTH GAUGE

GRADUATED BLADE

ADJUSTING NUT.

CLAMP SCREW

VERNIER PLATE

CLAMP SCREW

BASE

FIG. 12 VERNIER BEVEL PROTRACTOR

DIAL

VERNIER PLATE

BLADE CLAMP-NUT

DIAL CLAMP NUT.

BLADE

STOCK

FIG. 13 ENLARGED VIEW 12° 40¹

If vernier divisions equal 23 main-scale division,
Then 1 vernier division equals $\frac{23}{12}$ main-scale divisions $\quad = 1\frac{11}{12}°$
But as each main-scale division $\quad\quad\quad\quad\quad\quad\quad = 1°$
Then difference between one vernier division and two of
the main-scale divisions $\quad\quad\quad\quad\quad\quad\quad\quad = 2 - 1\frac{11}{12} = \frac{1}{12}°$
$\quad\quad\quad\quad\quad\quad\quad\quad\quad\quad\quad\quad\quad\quad\quad\quad\quad\quad\quad = 5'$
Thus each vernier division $\quad\quad\quad\quad\quad\quad\quad\quad\quad = 5'$

Fig. 13 will illustrate the method of reading the vernier protractor.
(a) Reading on main scale number of whole degrees
between zero on main scale and zero on vernier $\quad = 12°$
(b) Counting in same direction the number of spaces
from zero on vernier scale to the line that coincides
with a division on main scale $\quad\quad\quad\quad\quad\quad\quad = 8$
But each space equals 5'
∴ number of minutes to be added $\quad\quad\quad\quad\quad = 8 \times 5' = 40'$
Thus reading shown is equal to $\underline{12° + 40'}$

Note. The multiplication is not necessary, as the actual value can be read
direct from the numbers on vernier scale.

Dial Gauges

The dial indicator, dial gauge, or 'Clock' is the simplest form of com-
parator, which consists of a spring-loaded measuring spindle which operates
a needle pointer above a circular scale. The most commonly used operate
by rack-and-pinion-type mechanism. See Fig. 14.

The train of gears is so designed that a small movement of the measuring
spindle produces a relatively large movement of the needle pointer. The
measuring range varies with different types from 1–50 mm.

Dials are graduated in $0 \cdot 002$ or $0 \cdot 01$ mm units, depending on application.
All gauges are fitted with a detachable ball-tipped contact point, and a
setting ring is provided enabling the dial to be set, and in certain types locked
in any desired position.

The main uses of a dial gauge include the checking of plane surfaces for
parallelism and thickness, end floats or clearances, parallelism of shafts or
bars, and concentricity of holes, etc.

Lever-type Indicators

For applications where a large measuring range is not required and where
the movement would normally be a few hundredths of a millimetre, but where
it was essential to detect very small differences in size, a light, reliable, and
sensitive movement is necessary. For such applications the lever-type indicator
has been developed.

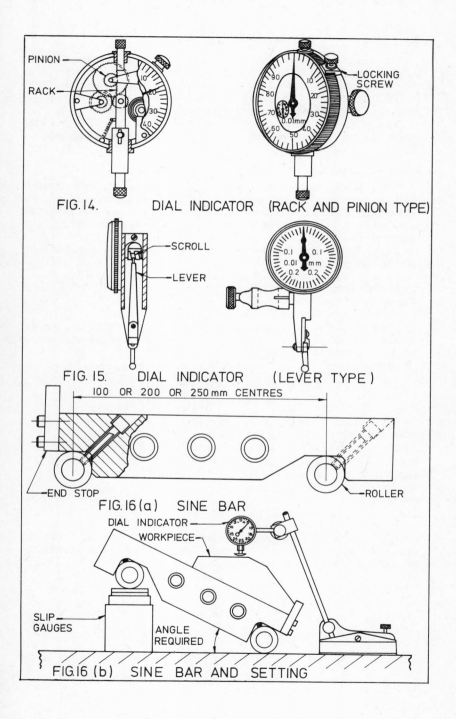

PINION

RACK

FIG.14. DIAL INDICATOR (RACK AND PINION TYPE)

LOCKING SCREW

0.01mm

SCROLL

LEVER

0.1   0.1
0.01 mm
0.2   0.2

FIG. 15. DIAL INDICATOR (LEVER TYPE)

100 OR 200 OR 250mm CENTRES

END STOP

ROLLER

FIG. 16 (a) SINE BAR

DIAL INDICATOR

WORKPIECE

SLIP GAUGES

ANGLE REQUIRED

FIG. 16 (b) SINE BAR AND SETTING

The principle of the lever-type is shown in Fig. 15. The lever operates on a scroll on the spindle to which the indicating arm on the dial is attached, thus the spindle rotates when the lever is depressed. The range of these instuments is only about 1 mm. If the dial is graduated in 0·002 or 0·01 mm it is still possible to take reliable readings to within 0·001 by estimation.

Such an indicator can be used inside quite small bores and other restricted spaces where it would be impossible to use the plunger type of indicator.

Metric Gauge Blocks (Slip Gauges) B.S. 4311: 1968

Gauge Blocks, first introduced by C. E. Johannson, are of rectangular form and are made of high-grade steel, hardened throughout and suitably heat-treated in order to stabilise their dimensions. The measuring faces have a lapped finish and are made flat and parallel to one another with a high degree of accuracy.

In the British Standard for Gauge Blocks (B.S. 4311) five grades of accuracy are specified:—

Three grades for general use are designated Grades 0, I, and II.

Another grade intended essentially for use in measuring other gauge blocks is designated Grade 00.

A further special grade is known as Calibration Grade.

These gauge blocks are obtainable in a variety of selected sets, the size of any required standard being made up by combining the appropriate number of these different size blocks.

One typical set, M.41/1, comprises 41 pieces made up as follows:—

Range mm	Increment (mm)	Number of Pieces
1·00—1·009	0·001	9
1·01—1·09	0·01	9
1·1 —1·9	0·1	9
1·0 —9·0	1·0	9
10, 20, 30	10·0	3
60	—	1
100	—	1

Total 41

With the use of this set, end standards can be built up from 2·001 mm upwards in 0·001 mm steps. For example an end standard of 25·349 mm can be built up with the following gauge blocks:—

1·009
1·040
1·300
2·000
20·000

Sum 25·349 mm

Wringing

Before wringing gauges together, their faces should be wiped free from dust. The gauges should preferably be wrung together by first bringing them into contact at right angles to one another and then turning them through 90°. The gauges are separated in a similar manner.

This wringing action can only be obtained if the contacting faces are clean and very accurately flat and parallel.

When wringing together a number of gauges, the largest pair should be wrung together first, followed by the others in decreasing size down to the thinnest.

The Care and Use of Gauge Blocks

Great care should be exercised in protecting the gauges and their case from dirt and dust.

When not in actual use all gauges should be kept in their case (case kept closed).

Gauges should be wiped clean before use, with a chamois-leather cloth or soft linen cloth.

A very light film of oil is an aid to wringing. Unnecessary handling of the gauges should be avoided. Gauges should not be held above the open case when being wrung together lest one be accidentally dropped.

If during wringing the slightest sign of roughness or scratching is felt, the gauge faces should be examined for burrs or scratches.

Gauges should never be left wrung together for long periods of time. After wiping they should be replaced in their case and only handled with the aid of a cloth.

The Sine Bar (B.S. 3064)

Fig. 16(a) shows a simple type of sine bar, a useful piece of apparatus used for setting or measuring angles. If used in conjunction with a set of gauge blocks the high degree of precision obtainable in linear measurement can also be achieved in the measurement of angles.

The sine bar consists of a hardened and ground-steel bar to which is attached two hardened-steel rollers of identical diameter. The axes of these rollers are mutually parallel, and parallel to the working face (upper face) of the bar. B.S. 3064 provides for three types of sine bar in sizes of 100 mm, 200 mm and 250 mm. These sizes represent the centre distances between the axes of the rollers.

Fig. 16(b) illustrates the method of setting a sine bar. One roller locates on a surface plate, and gauge blocks are placed under the other roller causing the working surface of the bar to lie at an angle relative to the surface plate. When setting the working surface to a specified angle the height of gauge blocks required can be obtained as follows:—

$$\text{Sine of required angle} = \frac{\text{Perpendicular Height}}{\text{Hypotenuse}} = \frac{\text{Height of Gauge Blocks}}{\text{Roller centre distance}}$$

(value obtained from Trig. tables)

∴ Height of Gauge Blocks = Sine of angle × centre distance

Limits and Fits

When designing and manufacturing engineering products a great deal of attention must be given to the mating and assembly of the various components. A high degree of uniformity is essential in any product to be manufactured in large quantities, without it interchangeability would be impossible. No two components can be made exactly alike, therefore limits of permissible error must be laid down for each dimension to allow for variations in both fit and workmanship.

Definitions

Dimension

Dimension is a means of specifying the size of a part, i.e. length, diameter, width, thickness.

Nominal Size

The nominal size of a dimension is the size by which it is referred to as a matter of convenience.

Limits of Size Fig. 17

Limits of size are the extreme dimensions to which it is permissible for the considered size to go. The high limit is the largest size, and the low limit is the smallest size permitted for that dimension.

Tolerance

Tolerance is the difference between the high limit and the low limit of size for a given dimension.

Allowance

Allowance is the prescribed difference in dimension of two mating parts in order to allow for different classes of fit.

Minimum Allowance Fig. 17

Minimum allowance is the difference between the largest permissible shaft and the smallest permissible hole.

Maximum Allowance Fig. 17

Maximum allowance is the difference between the smallest permissible shaft and the largest permissible hole.

(An allowance is positive when there is clearance between the shaft and hole, and negative when there is interference between shaft and hole.)

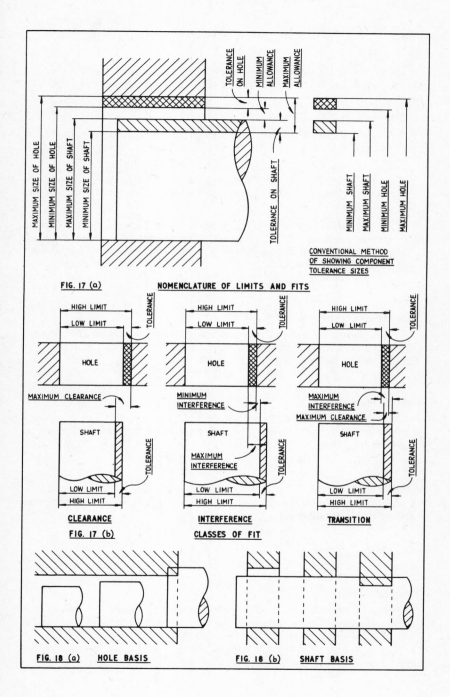

MAXIMUM SIZE OF HOLE
MINIMUM SIZE OF HOLE
MAXIMUM SIZE OF SHAFT
MINIMUM SIZE OF SHAFT

TOLERANCE ON HOLE
MINIMUM ALLOWANCE
MAXIMUM ALLOWANCE

TOLERANCE ON SHAFT

MINIMUM SHAFT
MAXIMUM SHAFT
MINIMUM HOLE
MAXIMUM HOLE

CONVENTIONAL METHOD
OF SHOWING COMPONENT
TOLERANCE SIZES

FIG. 17 (a)   NOMENCLATURE OF LIMITS AND FITS

HIGH LIMIT
LOW LIMIT
TOLERANCE
HOLE

MAXIMUM CLEARANCE

SHAFT
TOLERANCE

LOW LIMIT
HIGH LIMIT

CLEARANCE
FIG. 17 (b)

HIGH LIMIT
LOW LIMIT
TOLERANCE
HOLE

MINIMUM INTERFERENCE

SHAFT
MAXIMUM INTERFERENCE
TOLERANCE

LOW LIMIT
HIGH LIMIT

INTERFERENCE
CLASSES OF FIT

HIGH LIMIT
LOW LIMIT
TOLERANCE
HOLE

MAXIMUM INTERFERENCE
MAXIMUM CLEARANCE

SHAFT
TOLERANCE

LOW LIMIT
HIGH LIMIT

TRANSITION

FIG. 18 (a)   HOLE BASIS

FIG. 18 (b)   SHAFT BASIS

K

Fit

Fit expresses the relationship between two mating parts with respect to the amount of clearance or interference which exists when they are assembled together.

The three classes of fit are:—

1. *Clearance Fit*—where there is a positive allowance between the largest possible shaft and the smallest possible hole (shaft always smaller than hole).

2. *Interference Fit*—where there is a negative allowance between the smallest possible shaft and the largest possible hole (shaft always larger than the hole).

3. *Transition Fit*—covering cases between 1 and 2 where the limits are so disposed that either a clearance or interference fit may be obtained, e.g. when maximum size of hole is greater than minimum size of shaft (clearance fit) or when maximum size of shaft is greater than minimum size hole (interference).

Hole Basis

A limit system is said to be on a hole basis when the hole is the constant member and different types of fits are obtained by varying the size of the shaft as shown in Fig. 18(a).

Shaft Basis

A limit system is said to be on a shaft basis when the shaft is the constant member and different fits are obtained by varying the size of the hole as shown in Fig. 18(b).

Unilateral System

A limit system is said to be unilateral when the permissible tolerance is all positive or all negative, e.g.

$$+0 \cdot 05 \text{ mm} \qquad\qquad -0 \cdot 05 \text{ mm}$$
$$-0 \cdot 00 \text{ mm} \qquad\qquad +0 \cdot 00 \text{ mm}$$
$$50 \cdot 0 \text{ mm} \quad \text{(Hole)} \qquad 50 \cdot 0 \text{ mm} \quad \text{(Shaft)}$$

Bilateral System

A limit system is said to be bilateral when the permissible tolerance is partly positive and partly negative, e.g.

$$+0 \cdot 025 \text{ mm}$$
$$-0 \cdot 025 \text{ mm}$$
$$50 \cdot 0 \text{ mm}$$

Limits and Fits for Engineering B.S. 4500: 1969

The British Standard 4500 is a revision of the former B.S. 1916 intended to bring it into line with the ISO (International Organization for Standardisation) system ISO/R 286, designed to provide a comprehensive range of limits and fits for engineering purposes. It is based on a series of tolerances graded to suit all types of fit and quality of workmanship. This new British Standard is wholly in the metric system.

B.S. 4500 covers a size range from 0 to 3150 mm, in 21 steps, e.g. 0 to 3, over 3 to 6, over 6 to 10, etc. in mm units to a maximum of 3150 mm.

Eighteen grades of tolerance are provided for each size range, and they are designated as IT01, IT0, IT1–IT16 (IT stands for ISO series of tolerances), providing a series of qualities of tolerance to cater for different classes of work, and various grades of accuracy appropriate to different manufacturing processes, e.g. IT1 is suitable for gauge blocks, IT8 is suitable for centre lathe turning, IT16 is suitable for sand-casting and flame-cutting. These standard tolerances are shown in chart 'A'.

It should be noted that Grades IT14–16 do not apply to sizes up to and including 1 mm, and Grades IT01–5 do not exist for sizes above 500 mm.

There are 27 types of fit for holes, designated by the following capital letters:—

A B C CD D E EF F FG G H J K M N P R S T U V X Y Z ZA ZB ZC.

There are also 27 types of fit for shafts, designated by the following small letters:—

a b c cd d e ef f fg g h j k m n p r s t u v x y z za zb zc.

B.S. 4500 allows for the use of a hole or shaft basis system, but for most general applications it is usual to recommend the hole-basis system, where the H hole is selected as the standard hole, and variations in grade of fit are obtained by varying the tolerance on the mating shaft.

The limits for holes are designated by the appropriate capital letter followed by a suffix number denoting grade of tolerance, e.g. H7.

The limits for shafts are designated by a small letter followed by a suffix number denoting grade of tolerance, e.g. g6.

The resultant fit is designated by the hole symbol followed by the shaft symbol, thus: H7/g6.

The three charts B, C, D, which follow, represent only a very small section of the complete range of tables contained in B.S. 4500, and have been included to illustrate the method of converting the hole and shaft symbols specified for a required type of fit into actual limits of size to be stated on the dimensions of the two mating parts.

CHART A. *Standard Tolerances* (B.S. 4500: 1969)

TOLERANCE GRADES (Tolerance Unit 0·001 mm)

Nominal Sizes (mm) Over	To	IT01	IT0	IT1	IT2	IT3	IT4	IT5	IT6	IT7	IT8	IT9	IT10	IT11	IT12	IT13	IT14	IT15	IT16
0	3	0·3	0·5	0·8	1·2	2	3	4	6	10	14	25	40	60	100	140	250	400	600
3	6	0·4	0·6	1	1·5	2·5	4	5	8	12	18	30	48	75	120	180	300	480	750
6	10	0·4	0·6	1	1·5	2·5	4	6	9	15	22	36	58	90	150	220	360	580	900
10	18	0·5	0·8	1·2	2	3	5	8	11	18	27	43	70	110	180	270	430	700	1100
18	30	0·6	1	1·5	2·5	4	6	9	13	21	33	52	84	130	210	330	520	840	1300
30	50	0·6	1	1·5	2·5	4	7	11	16	25	39	62	100	160	250	390	620	1000	1600
50	80	0·8	1·2	2	3	5	8	13	19	30	46	74	120	190	300	460	740	1200	1900
80	120	1	1·5	2·5	4	6	10	15	22	35	54	87	140	220	350	540	870	1400	2200
120	180	1·2	2	3·5	5	8	12	18	25	40	63	100	160	250	400	630	1000	1600	2500
180	250	2	3	4·5	7	10	14	20	29	46	72	115	185	290	460	720	1150	1850	2900
250	315	2·5	4	6	8	12	16	23	32	52	81	130	210	320	520	810	1300	2100	3200
315	400	3	5	7	9	13	18	25	36	57	89	140	230	360	570	890	1400	2300	3600
400	500	4	6	8	10	15	20	27	40	63	97	155	250	400	630	970	1550	2500	4000
500	630	—	—	—	—	—	—	—	44	70	110	175	280	440	700	1100	1750	2800	4400
630	800	—	—	—	—	—	—	—	50	80	125	200	320	500	800	1250	2000	3200	5000
800	1000	—	—	—	—	—	—	—	56	90	140	230	360	560	900	1400	2300	3600	5600
1000	1250	—	—	—	—	—	—	—	66	105	165	260	420	660	1050	1650	2600	4200	6600
1250	1600	—	—	—	—	—	—	—	78	125	195	310	500	780	1250	1950	3100	5000	7800
1600	2000	—	—	—	—	—	—	—	92	150	230	370	600	920	1500	2300	3700	6000	9200
2000	2500	—	—	—	—	—	—	—	110	175	280	440	700	1100	1750	2800	4400	7000	11000
2500	3150	—	—	—	—	—	—	—	135	210	330	540	860	1350	2100	3300	5400	8600	13500

CHART B. *Standard Tolerances for Holes* (B.S. 4500)

Nominal Sizes (mm)		Symbols and Tolerances (0·001 mm units)											
		H6		H7		H8		H9		H10		H11	
Over	To	High	Low	High	Low	High	Low	High	Low	High	Low	High	Low
0	3	+6	0	+10	0	+14	0	+25	0	+40	0	+60	0
3	6	+8	0	+12	0	+18	0	+30	0	+48	0	+75	0
6	10	+9	0	+15	0	+22	0	+36	0	+58	0	+90	0
10	18	+11	0	+18	0	+27	0	+43	0	+70	0	+110	0
18	30	+13	0	+21	0	+33	0	+52	0	+84	0	+130	0
30	50	+16	0	+25	0	+39	0	+62	0	+100	0	+160	0
50	80	+19	0	+30	0	+46	0	+74	0	+120	0	+190	0
80	120	+22	0	+35	0	+54	0	+87	0	+140	0	+220	0
120	180	+25	0	+40	0	+63	0	+100	0	+160	0	+250	0
180	250	+29	0	+46	0	+72	0	+115	0	+185	0	+290	0
250	315	+32	0	+52	0	+81	0	+130	0	+210	0	+320	0
315	400	+36	0	+57	0	+89	0	+140	0	+230	0	+360	0
400	500	+40	0	+63	0	+97	0	+155	0	+250	0	+400	0

CHART C. *Standard Tolerances for Shafts* (B.S. 4500)

Nominal Sizes (mm)		Symbols and Tolerances (0·001 mm units)									
		j6		m6		p6		r6		s6	
Over	To	High	Low	High	Low	High	Low	High	Low	High	Low
0	3	+4	−2	+8	+2	+12	+6	+16	+10	+20	+14
3	6	+6	−2	+12	+4	+20	+12	+23	+15	+27	+19
6	10	+7	−2	+15	+6	+24	+15	+28	+19	+32	+23
10	18	+8	−3	+18	+7	+29	+18	+34	+23	+39	+28
18	30	+9	−4	+21	+8	+35	+22	+41	+28	+48	+35
30	50	+11	−5	+25	+9	+42	+26	+50	+34	+59	+43
50	65	+12	−7	+30	+11	+51	+32	+60	+41	+72	+53
65	80							+62	+43	+78	+59
80	100	+13	−9	+35	+13	+59	+37	+73	+51	+93	+71
100	120							+76	+54	+101	+79
120	140	+14	−11	+40	+15	+68	+43	+88	+63	+117	+92
140	160							+90	+65	+125	+100
160	180							+93	+68	+133	+108
180	200	+16	−13	+46	+17	+79	+50	+106	+77	+151	+122
200	225							+109	+80	+159	+130
225	250							+113	+84	+169	+140
250	280	+16	−16	+52	+20	+88	+56	+126	+94	+190	+158
280	315							+130	+98	+202	+170
315	355	+18	−18	+57	+21	+98	+62	+144	+108	+226	+190
355	400							+150	+114	+244	+208
400	450	+20	−20	+63	+23	+108	+68	+166	+126	+272	+232
450	500							+172	+132	+292	+252

CHART D. *Standard Tolerances for Shafts* (B.S. 4500)

Nominal Sizes (mm)		Symbols and Tolerances (0·001 mm)					
		f7		g6		h7	
Over	To	High	Low	High	Low	High	Low
0	3	−6	−16	−2	−8	0	−10
3	6	−10	−22	−4	−12	0	−12
6	10	−13	−28	−5	−14	0	−15
10	18	−16	−34	−6	−17	0	−18
18	30	−20	−41	−7	−20	0	−21
30 40	40 50	−25	−50	−9	−25	0	−25
50 65	65 80	−30	−60	−10	−29	0	−30
80 100	100 120	−36	−71	−12	−34	0	−35
120 140 160	140 160 180	−43	−83	−14	−39	0	−40
180 200 225	200 225 250	−50	−96	−15	−44	0	−46
250 280	280 315	−56	−108	−17	−49	0	−52
315 355	355 400	−62	−119	−18	−54	0	−57
400 450	450 500	−68	−131	−20	−60	0	−63

Example 1. Consider interference fit H7/p6, 25·00 mm nominal diameter.

Hole Size
H7 from Chart B   High Limit = + 0·021
                         Low Limit =   0·000
∴ Hole dimensions   = $\dfrac{25·000}{25·021}$

Shaft Size
p6 from Chart C   High Limit = + 0·035
                         Low Limit = + 0·022
∴ Shaft dimensions   = $\dfrac{25·035}{25·022}$

∴ Maximum Metal Condition   = Smallest Hole—Largest Shaft
                                 = $\overline{25·000-25·035}$

Minimum Metal Condition   = $\overline{25·021-25·022}$

Example 2. Consider transition fit H7/j6, 13·000 mm nominal diameter.

Hole Size
H7 from Chart B   High Limit = + 0·018
                         Low Limit =   0·000
∴ Hole dimensions   = $\dfrac{13·000}{13·018}$

Shaft Size
j6 from Chart C   High Limit = + 0·008
                         Low Limit = − 0·003
∴ Shaft dimensions   = $\dfrac{13·008}{12·997}$

∴ Maximum Metal Condition   = $\overline{13·000\text{Hole}-13·008\text{Shaft}}$

Minimum Metal Condition   = $\overline{13·018\text{Hole}-12·997\text{Shaft}}$

Example 3. Consider clearance fit H7/g6, 9·500 mm nominal diameter.

Hole Size

H7 from Chart B	High Limit $= + 0\cdot015$
	Low Limit $=\ \ \ 0\cdot000$
∴ Hole dimensions	$= \dfrac{9\cdot500}{9\cdot515}$

Shaft Size

g6 from Chart D	High Limit $= - 0\cdot005$
	Low Limit $= - 0\cdot014$
∴ Shaft dimensions	$= \dfrac{9\cdot495}{9\cdot486}$

∴ Maximum Metal Condition $=$ 9·500 Hole − 9·495 Shaft

∴ Minimum Metal Condition $=$ 9·515 Hole − 9·486 Shaft

Limit Gauges

Limit-gauging systems have played an essential part in the development of the technique of quantity production where interchangeability of parts is essential. With the increased precision called for in modern production many types of limit-gauges are being superseded by direct measuring apparatus, i.e. indicating gauges and comparators which give direct readings not dependent on sense of touch. Despite the previous remark, limit-gauges will continue to be extensively used for many types of production work, due to their simplicity, speed of operation, and low initial cost.

Design of Limit-Gauges

Limit-gauges are frequently used by semi-skilled operators, therefore it is essential that such gauges be of simple design, enabling them to be used without special knowledge or skill. Gauges should be of such proportions as to facilitate convenient handling and must be foolproof in operation.

Such gauges can be broadly divided into two main groups: 1. Fixed-size gauges, e.g. Plug, Snap, Ring, and Pin gauges. 2. Adjustable-size gauges, e.g. External Snap or Calliper gauges, and Adjustable Thread gauges.

Fixed-Size Gauges (Suitable for plain cylindrical work)
1. *Double-ended Limit Plug Gauges* Fig. 19

The most common of all plug gauges, consisting of two hardened-steel cylinders joined by a common handle. The longer cylinder and smaller in outside diameter is the 'Go' end, and the shorter and larger diameter cylinder is the 'Not-Go' end. The difference in size between the two ends is determined by the tolerance of the hole which the gauge will be used to check. The 'Go' end will be of such a size that it will enter the hole in the workpiece when the hole is no smaller than the lower limit. The 'Not-Go' end is of such a size that it will not enter the hole when the hole is up to the highest limit.

2. *Single-ended Plug Gauges* Fig. 20

Plug gauges of larger diameters may be made single ended, that is a 'Go' gauge mounted on its handle, and a separate 'Not-Go' gauge; both are necessary to check that the hole is within limit of size specified. The gauging members may be recessed to reduce the weight.

3. *Single-ended Limit Plug Gauge* Fig. 21

Consisting of a cylinder of hardened steel having two slightly different diameters, the smaller of which, the 'Go' portion, is at the front or entering end of the gauge, the larger diameter, the 'Not-Go' portion, being at the back. Such gauges are limited in application, only suitable for 'Through' holes where the 'Go' end passes out at the back of the hole, allowing for the 'Not-Go' portion to engage the hole. If the hole is of the correct size the 'Not-Go' diameter arrests further progress of the gauge into the hole, showing that the hole is within the tolerance. Gauges of this type cannot be used on 'Blind' holes.

4. *External Calliper or Snap Gauges*

The types of snap gauges shown in Figs. 22(a) and (b) are usually produced from low-carbon-steel forgings with hardened and ground jaws.

Type (a) is a double-ended gauge, one pair of jaws forming the 'Go' gauge, and a separate pair of jaws forming the 'Not-Go' gauge.

Type (b) is a single-ended gauge; the jaws are so ground that the front portion forms the 'Go' and the rear portion the 'Not-Go' gauge.

Type (c) shows the 'Horse-shoe' plate calliper gauge made from gauge plate, hardened, tempered, and ground to the correct size. Such gauges may also be made double-ended.

When using snap gauges for checking external diameters the component should be gauged in a number of positions along and around its surface, otherwise possible taper or ovality outside the limits of size may be overlooked. This type of gauge can also be applied when components are mounted between centres on the machine.

5. *Taper Gauges*

Figs. 23(a) and (b) show a taper plug and ring gauge suitable for checking the accuracy of the standard tapers used in engineering, e.g. Morse, Brown and Sharpe, or Jarno, etc.

These gauges are usually made to the exact length of the taper required, and the largest and smallest diameters are ground to close limits of accuracy. Such gauges can be obtained as standard products from a variety of different gauge manufacturers.

Non-standard or special taper plug and ring gauges are frequently made in the toolroom of a specific company to meet their own particular requirements. Figs. 24(a) and (b) show one type of taper plug and ring limit-gauge, the high and low limits being indicated in each case by a step ground at the appropriate end of the gauge.

When using the plug gauge to check the accuracy of a tapered hole the gauge is lightly smeared with engineer's marking blue, is inserted into the

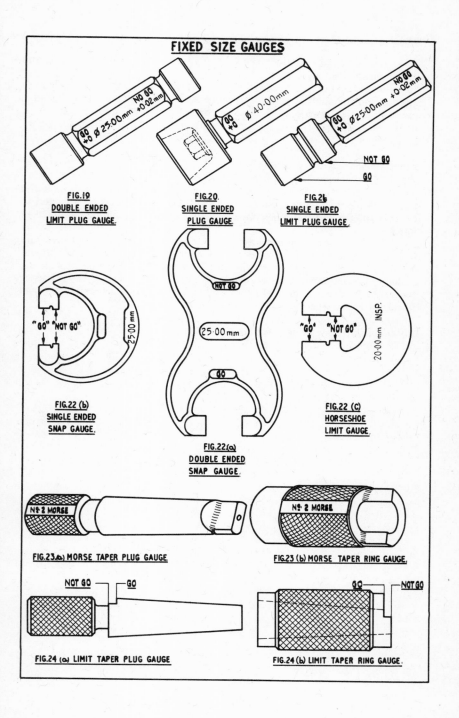

FIXED SIZE GAUGES

FIG.19
DOUBLE ENDED
LIMIT PLUG GAUGE.

FIG.20.
SINGLE ENDED
PLUG GAUGE.

FIG.21
SINGLE ENDED
LIMIT PLUG GAUGE.

FIG.22 (b)
SINGLE ENDED
SNAP GAUGE.

FIG.22 (C)
HORSESHOE
LIMIT GAUGE.

FIG.22.(a)
DOUBLE ENDED
SNAP GAUGE.

FIG.23.(a) MORSE TAPER PLUG GAUGE

FIG.23 (b) MORSE TAPER RING GAUGE.

FIG.24 (a) LIMIT TAPER PLUG GAUGE

FIG.24 (b) LIMIT TAPER RING GAUGE.

hole, and is partially rotated. The area of contact will be clearly visible, and will indicate accuracy of fit.

When checking the accuracy of a tapered shaft the marking blue is smeared on the shaft and the ring gauge is assembled with the shaft and is partially rotated; as before the area of contact will indicate the quality of fit, while the position of the gauge on the shaft will be a check on the actual diameter of the taper.

Adjustable-Size Gauges (Suitable for plain cylindrical work)

Adjustable External-Limit Gauges Fig. 25

For larger sizes it is often advisable to have 'Go' and 'Not-Go' point on the same gauge as shown in Fig. 25. These can be readily adjusted to compensate for wear, and be conveniently re-set to cover a range of different limits.

The frame is made of hard cast iron, or as a steel forging. The anvils are a sliding fit in holes which are bored and lapped in the frame. The adjustment of the anvils is carried out by fine-pitch screws, which can be locked and sealed to prevent unauthorised alteration. The setting is obtained by reference to precision gauge blocks. The 'Go' or high-limit size is represented by the front anvils, and the 'Not-Go' by those at the rear.

Adjustable Calliper Gauges for Screw Threads. See Figs. 26 and 27, notes on screw-thread measurement, p. 305.

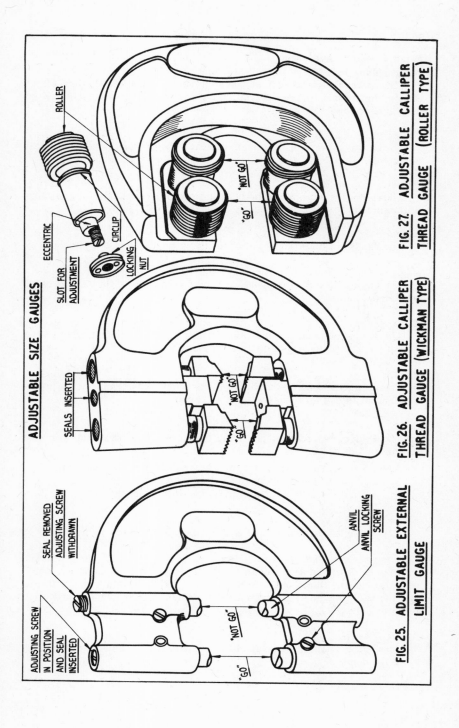

ADJUSTABLE SIZE GAUGES

ROLLER

ECCENTRIC

CIRCLIP

SLOT FOR
ADJUSTMENT

LOCKING
NUT

"NOT GO"

"GO"

FIG. 27. ADJUSTABLE CALLIPER
THREAD GAUGE (ROLLER TYPE)

SEALS INSERTED

"NOT GO"

"GO"

FIG. 26. ADJUSTABLE CALLIPER
THREAD GAUGE (WICKMAN TYPE)

SEAL REMOVED
ADJUSTING SCREW
WITHDRAWN

ADJUSTING SCREW
IN POSITION
AND SEAL
INSERTED

ANVIL
ANVIL LOCKING
SCREW

"NOT GO"

"GO"

FIG. 25. ADJUSTABLE EXTERNAL
LIMIT GAUGE

Screw-Thread Measurement

Nomenclature Fig. 28

The successful inspection of screw threads entails the verification of certain dimensions, or elements of the threads. These elements may be defined as follows:—

Crest

The crest is the prominent part of a thread, whether the thread be external or internal.

Root

The root is the bottom portion of the groove between the flanking surfaces of the thread.

Flanks

The flanks are the straight sides which connect the crest and root.

Angle of Thread (Included angle)

The angle of a thread is the angle between the sides of flanks, measured on an axial plane.

Flank Angles

The angles between the individual flanks and the perpendicular to the axis of the thread, measured on an axial plane.

Pitch

The distance measured parallel to the axis between corresponding points on adjacent thread forms in the same axial plane.

Lead

The lead of a screw thread is the distance it advances axially in one revolution.

> *Note:* On a single-start thread the lead and the pitch are identical.
> On a double-start thread the lead is twice the pitch.
> On a three-start thread the lead is three times the pitch.

Major Diameter

This is the largest diameter of a screw thread on a screw or nut.

Effective or Pitch Diameter

May be described as the diameter of an imaginary cylinder which would pass through the threads at such points as to make the width of the thread and the width of the spaces between the threads at these points equal, each being half the pitch.

Minor Diameter

This is the smallest diameter of the screw or nut (major diameter minus twice the depth of thread).

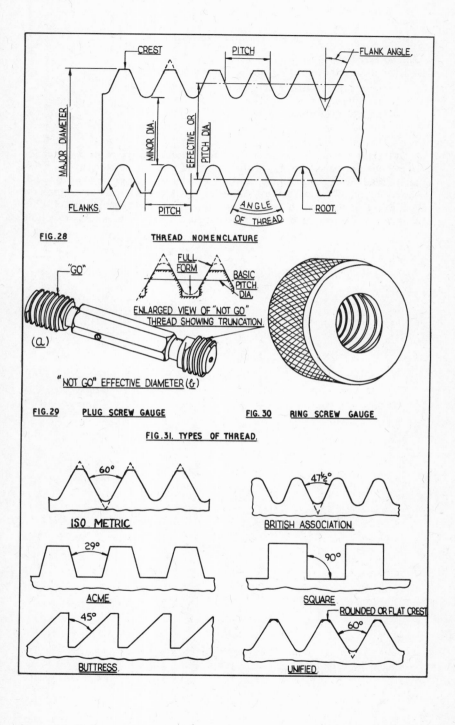

CREST   PITCH   FLANK ANGLE

MAJOR DIAMETER

MINOR DIA.

EFFECTIVE OR PITCH DIA.

FLANKS   PITCH   ANGLE OF THREAD   ROOT

FIG.28   THREAD NOMENCLATURE

"GO"

FULL FORM   BASIC PITCH DIA.

ENLARGED VIEW OF "NOT GO" THREAD SHOWING TRUNCATION.

(a)

"NOT GO" EFFECTIVE DIAMETER (b)

FIG.29   PLUG SCREW GAUGE   FIG.30   RING SCREW GAUGE

FIG.31. TYPES OF THREAD.

60°
ISO METRIC

47½°
BRITISH ASSOCIATION

29°
ACME

90°
SQUARE

45°
BUTTRESS

ROUNDED OR FLAT CREST
60°
UNIFIED

Thread Elements

The most important elements of a screw thread are:—

1. The major or outside diameter.
2. The minor or root diameter.
3. The effective or pitch diameter.
4. The pitch.
5. The angle of thread.

All these features must be checked for accuracy in the routine inspection of production parts. Errors on the major or minor diameters would cause interference with the mating thread, or alternatively cause weakness due to the reduction of thread sections. The effective diameter largely determines the quality of fit between the two mating threads, and any errors on effective diameter will either cause interference or slackness and weakness of section.

Screw-Thread Gauges

The simplest method of checking threads in the production shop is by means of screw-thread limit gauges. These gauges possess the same thread form as the mating thread, and are assembled with the thread being checked.

Plug Screw Gauges

When gauging nuts or internal threads a full-form 'Go' plug gauge is used as shown in Fig. 29(a). The 'Go' gauge is accurately made to the minimum dimensions of the required thread, therefore if it will assemble with the component it will ensure that the major, minor, and effective diameters are not below the minimum dimensions; it will also ensure that any errors in pitch, angle, and thread form are insufficient to reduce the effective diameter below its minimum dimension.

Fig. 29(b) shows the 'Not-Go' effective gauge, whose effective diameter is made to maximum tolerance, and also having its threads truncated at both crest and root, ensuring that this gauge only makes contact with the flanks of the thread.

Ring Screw Gauges Fig. 30

For the gauging of bolts or external threads the equivalent mating gauges are known as ring screw gauges. As in the case of plug screw gauges a limit system can be provided by a full-form 'Go' and a 'Not-Go' effective ring gauge. All the factors involved are exact counterparts of the gauging of internal threads. The 'Go' ring gauge has a full-form thread, and the 'Not-Go' gauge is truncated on the minor diameter, and cleared on the major diameter at the root of the thread.

Adjustable-Calliper Gauges for Screw Threads

In principle, these gauges are the equivalent of the normal gap gauges, but having thread forms on the anvils.

Fig. 26 shows a Wickman type of adjustable-calliper thread gauge. The frame is of hard cast-iron, designed for lightness and rigidity. The hardened-steel anvils are a sliding fit in the holes in the frame, and a flat which locates on the frame prevents the anvils from turning or tilting. Each pair of anvils may be adjusted to within 0·0025 mm to a setting piece (usually a screwed plug gauge), the adjusting arrangements being similar to those employed in the calliper gauges used for plain work.

The front anvils are a complete-form 'Go' gauge of suitable length. No element of the screw which passes these anvils can be too large. The rear anvils form a 'Not-Go' effective-diameter gauge, the threads being cleared away at the crest and root. No effects of pitch error in the screw being gauged are taken into account.

(If the pitch error is too great and the screw is to pass the 'Go' anvils, the effective diameter must be reduced to such an extent that it will also pass through the 'Not-Go' gauge and therefore be rejected.)

To compensate for wear the anvils can be re-ground on the front face and re-set.

Adjustable Screw-Thread Gauges with Roller-Type Anvils Fig. 27

Similar in general principle to the above, but having roller-type anvils. At the front is a pair of full-form 'Go' rollers, at the back a pair of 'Not-Go' rollers whose threads are truncated at both crest and root so that contact is made only on the flank of the thread. The rollers are of annular thread form corrected to compensate for helix angle interference. They are mounted on eccentric studs locked in position to the frame, a circlip retaining them on the studs without preventing their free rotation. The initial setting is determined by special double-ended setting plugs. The rollers are secured by tightening the locknut with the special adjusting key. Interference with the setting is prevented by the use of lead seals.

QUESTIONS

1. Explain with the aid of a diagram, the construction and principle of operation of a quick-grip fitter's vice.
2. (a) Sketch a flat file, name each part, indicate which part is left soft.
   (b) Write brief notes on the following terms:—Single-cut; double-cut; standard grades; safe-edge.
3. (a) Sketch three types of file, and state their main applications.
   (b) Explain the differences between "cross-filing" and "draw-filing".
4. (a) Sketch an adjustable hacksaw frame, indicate method of holding and tightening the blade.
   (b) State the factors which govern the selection and use of hacksaw blades.
5. (a) Sketch two types of hand hammers suitable for bench work.
   (b) When is a rawhide hammer used in preference to a standard hammer?
6. (a) Sketch three types of hand chisels and give an example of the use of each.
   (b) Indicate on a simple diagram, the point, rake, and clearance angles suitable for a flat chisel when cutting mild steel.
7. (a) Explain the purpose of a flat scraper, and method of checking the flatness of the scraped face.
   (b) Describe the method of scraping a half bearing to suit its mating shaft.
8. Explain how both internal and external threads can be produced with the aid of hand tools.
9. Explain the purpose of the marking-out operation, illustrate your answer with three typical examples indicating equipment required.

CHAPTER TWO

1. (a) Sketch three types of hand shears, state the main purpose of each.
   (b) Sketch and describe a bench shears.
2. Sketch a treadle guillotine, explain the principle of operation. State the main danger points and minimum safety requirements.
3. Illustrate with diagrams, one operation carried out with the aid of each of the following:—hatchet stake; half moon stake; tinsmen's mandrel; creasing iron.
4. Make neat sketches of the wheels you would select when using a universal jenny machine for:—closing metal around wire; turning up edges on circular blanks; making a paned down joint.
5. (a) Describe two folded joints used in sheet metal work.
   (b) Explain the sequence of operations when wiring the edge of a flat sheet.
6. (a) What are the basic stages in making a good soft soldered joint?
   (b) Write brief notes on the common types of flux, state their applications.
7. (a) Sketch a general purpose soldering bit, explain how it is prepared for use.
   (b) "Liquid solder displaces the flux." Show by means of a diagram how this displacement takes place.
8. Draw the development of a cone frustum clearly indicating the true and slant heights.
9. Explain the stages in laying out a pattern for an obliquely cut cylindrical pipe.

CHAPTER THREE
1. Explain, with the aid of a diagram, the method of assembling ready for use high pressure oxy-acetylene equipment; stress all safety precautions.
2. Write concise notes on each of the following:—(a) Selection of blowpipe nozzle; (b) Adjustment of blowpipe flame; (c) Backfire and Flashback.
3. (a) Describe the rightward method of oxy-acetylene welding.
   (b) Sketch and describe single operator vertical welding.
4. (a) Illustrate with diagrams the four principal joints used in oxy-acetylene welding, make reference to edge preparation where applicable.
   (b) Write brief notes on the common defects found in gas welds.
5. Briefly describe the oxy-acetylene flame cutting process, outline the factors which govern its success.
6. Explain the basic principles of metallic arc welding.
7. State the main advantages and disadvantages of metallic arc welding when compared with oxy-acetylene welding.
8. (a) Discuss all the important factors which govern successful metallic arc welding.
   (b) Sketch four types of butt joint used in the metallic arc process, indicate metal thickness and relevant edge preparation.
9. Give two examples of typical metallic arc welds in each of the following positions: (a) Horizontal; (b) Vertical; (c) Overhead.

CHAPTER FOUR
1. (a) Briefly define machine tools, and state their basic functions.
   (b) State some of the primary requirements of machine tools.
2. Discuss three methods of machine tool classification.
3. (a) Explain, and give an example of (i) generated surface; (ii) formed surface.
   (b) Give an example of a surface produced by a combination of the generating and forming principles.
4. Draw simple line diagrams to show the relative work and tool movements for:—
   (a) Two methods of generating a flat surface.
   (b) Two methods of generating a cylindrical surface.
5. (a) What are the main physical properties of workpiece material which influence machinability.
   (b) Define "tool life", and discuss some of the factors which influence it.
6. Write concise notes on three cutting tool materials, and state their main applications.
7. Calculate the cutting speed in m/min, and the volume of metal removed in cm³ per minute, when a lathe tool is cutting a 100 mm diameter bar at 110 rev/min, depth of cut is 5 mm, feed 0·4 mm/rev.
8. A mild steel bar 50 mm diameter is machined at 150 rev/min. At what rev/min should a brass bar 40 mm diameter be machined if the cutting speed for brass is to be 2¼ times that of mild steel.
9. Calculate a suitable rev/min for a 40 mm diameter drill when drilling grey cast-iron. If the drill is ground with a standard point angle calculate time necessary to drill through a 50 mm thick block. Assume cutting speed 24 m/min and feed rate 200 cuts/25 mm.

CHAPTER FIVE

1. (a) State the basic operations performed on a standard centre lathe.
   (b) Explain the method used to designate lathe sizes.
2. (a) Show with a line diagram the main parts of a centre lathe.
   (b) Sketch and describe one type of lathe spindle nose.
   (b) Sketch and describe one type of lathe spindle nose.
3. Write notes on lathe bed design, and sketch two types in current use.
4. Describe a sliding gear type headstock suitable for a centre lathe.
5. Write brief notes on each of the following:—(a) Solid tools; (b) tipped tools; (c) tool bits.
6. Make neat sketches of a knife tool indicating:—(a) front and side clearance; (b) front and side rake. State the purpose of these angles, and discuss factors which affect their magnitude.
7. (a) Explain how tool setting can affect both rake and clearance angles.
   (b) Sketch two methods of taper turning on a centre lathe, and state their limitations.
8. (a) Explain the principle of single point screw cutting.
   (b) Calculate suitable change wheels for cutting the following threads:
   (i) 1·75 mm pitch, (ii) 5 mm pitch, (iii) 12 mm pitch × 2 start.
   Assume the lathe has 6 mm pitch leadscrew, gears 20–100 in steps of 5.
9. (a) How does a capstan differ in design from a centre-lathe.
   (b) Sketch two types of box tools used on a capstan.
   (c) Describe one method of holding the work on a capstan lathe.

CHAPTER SIX

1. Describe the main features of a column and knee milling machine, and clearly state its advantages and disadvantages.
2. Sketch a standard milling arbor, indicate two methods of supporting the outer end.
3. What are the principle uses of the following milling cutters? (a) Side and face; (b) Standard end-mill; (c) Face-mill.
4. Sketch the form of tooth used on (a) Prolific type cutters; (b) Form relieved cutters; show the principle features and indicate where the teeth are re-sharpened.
5. Discuss the main methods of work holding used on milling machines, and explain the precautions necessary to eliminate distortion in the finished workpiece.
6. Using the index plates supplied on a Cincinnati dividing head (Chap. 6, p. 172) calculate the index crank settings for the following equally spaced divisions: (a) 27; (b) 56; (c) 52; (d) 18°–40′.
7. When is differential indexing necessary? Determine the indexing and gearing suitable for (a) 119; (b) 77 equal divisions. (Assume Victoria Head. Chap. 6, p. 176.)
8. Calculate the gear ratio and table setting required to cut a helical groove of 320 mm lead and 6 mm deep on a 50 mm diameter shaft. (Use Victoria Head Chap. 6, p. 176.)
9. With the aid of sketches explain the following terms:—(a) Up-cut milling; (b) Straddle milling; (c) Gang milling.

CHAPTER SEVEN

1. What are the principal abrasives used in the manufacture of grinding wheels? Discuss the applications of each.

2. (a) Clearly explain the standard marking system for abrasive grinding wheels.
   (b) Give the marking you would expect to find on a wheel used for (i) Grinding case-hardened steel; (ii) Fettling aluminium castings.

3. (a) Why is wheel balancing so important on precision grinding machines?
   (b) Explain in detail how wheel balancing is carried out.

4. With the aid of neat sketches indicate wheel and work movements on the following types of grinding machines:—(a) Plain external; (b) Plain internal; (c) Horizontal spindle surface grinder with reciprocating table.

5. Describe the procedure to be adopted when truing a grinding wheel, and sketch the relative positions of wheel and diamond truing tool.

6. (a) Explain with the aid of a diagram the principle of centreless grinding.
   (b) Indicate two methods of feeding the work on a centreless machine.

7. External and internal tapers can be ground on a Universal grinding machine. Explain how these operations can be performed.

8. Briefly describe two types of surface grinding machines and state the type of work for which each is best suited.

9. Discuss alternative methods of locating the workpiece on a grinding machine. State the advantages or disadvantages associated with these methods.

CHAPTER EIGHT

1. (a) Sketch one type of quick return mechanism used on a shaping machine, clearly showing the cutting and return strokes.
   (b) Explain how the length and position of the stroke are adjusted.

2. What is the function of the clapper box? Sketch the relative positions of tool and clapper box when shaping (a) a vertical face; (b) an angular face.

3. Clearly describe how a vee-block of the type shown on p. 37 would be produced on a shaping machine.

4. What are the advantages and disadvantages of a shaping machine as compared to a milling machine.

CHAPTER NINE

1. Write notes on the following machines clearly explaining their construction and uses; (a) Pillar drill; (b) Radial drilling machine.

2. (a) With the aid of a diagram explain the important features of a standard twist drill.
   (b) What are the important points to be observed when grinding the drill point to ensure that it will cut efficiently and correct size?

3. What is the function of a reamer? Sketch (a) a machine reamer; (b) a hand reamer, clearly indicate where cutting takes place.

4. (a) Explain the method used to locate and remove (i) Taper shank drills; (ii) Straight shank drills.
   (b) What is the function of a centre drill?

CHAPTER TEN

1. Describe the basic stages in the production of a sand casting.
2. Write concise notes on each of the following:—
   (a) wood patterns; (b) contraction allowance; (c) machining allowance; (d) core print; (e) loose piece.
3. With the aid of diagrams describe the various stages in the making of a two-part mould for a small solid sand casting.
4. Describe the core making process, and indicate the method of locating the core in the mould.
5. Discuss the common casting defects and state their cause.

CHAPTER ELEVEN

1. Briefly describe the gravity die casting process, indicating how it differs from sand casting.
2. (a) State the main advantages of the gravity die casting process.
   (b) Explain the circumstances which make a collapsible core essential.
3. Sketch and describe one hot chamber system of pressure die casting, indicate the type of work for which it is suitable.
4. Contrast the cold chamber system of pressure die casting with the hot chamber system, clearly indicating its advantages.
5. (a) Write short notes on the main die casting alloys.
   (b) Outline the features to be avoided when designing a component for die casting.

CHAPTER TWELVE

1. State the main reasons for the introduction of precision casting in the engineering industry.
2. Describe the basic stages in the making of a precision casting by the flask moulding method.
3. Explain the ceramic shell moulding method of making a precision casting.
4. Sketch and briefly describe a typical carbon arc electric furnace used for precision casting.
5. Contrast the relative merits of sand, die, and precision castings making reference to accuracy, finish, production rates, cost, and physical properties.

CHAPTER THIRTEEN

1. Define the forging process, and write concise notes on the three basic methods of forging.
2. "Forging enables the grain flow to be arranged in the most suitable direction." Discuss this statement and give examples.
3. Contrast the structure of a casting with that of a forged product.
4. Sketch and describe (a) a typical small size forge; (b) anvil and stand.
5. Describe the following forging operations and indicate equipment required; (a) up-setting; (b) drawing-down; (c) setting down; (d) swaging; (e) hot-cutting.
6. With the aid of diagrams describe three methods of bending material by the hand forging process.
7. Clearly explain the technique of producing holes by hand forging methods.

CHAPTER FOURTEEN

1. (a) "Line standards of length are now largely superseded by end standards." Discuss this statement.

   (b) Sketch and describe a standard metric micrometer calliper, indicate clearly how it is graduated.

2. (a) Explain the system used in order to obtain a wide measuring range with an inside micrometer set.

   (b) How does a micrometer depth gauge differ from a micrometer calliper.

3. Using clear line diagrams explain the principle of a 25-division vernier scale.

4. A vernier bevel protractor is capable of measuring an angle to 1/12 of a degree. Explain how this is achieved.

5. (a) Briefly explain the principle and application of: (i) Dial gauges; (ii) Gauge blocks.

   (b) How can the gauges mentioned in (a) be used in conjunction with a sine bar?

6. With the aid of diagrams explain the following terms:—

   (a) Tolerance on hole and shaft; (b) Maximum and minimum allowance; (c) Clearance fit; (d) Interference fit.

7. (a) Using the charts from B.S. 4500 (pp. 293–5) establish maximum and minimum metal conditions for each of the following types of fit for nominal size of 30 mm diameter: (i) H7/s6; (ii) H7/m6; (iii) H7/h7.

   (b) Sketch the limit gauges you would select in order to check a standard 50 mm diameter hole and its mating shaft.

8. (a) Describe with the aid of a diagram all the important elements of a screw thread.

   (b) Sketch and describe the gauges used to check the accuracy of both external and internal screw threads.

INDEX